WELCOME to the Racing Post's latest guide to the Flat which not only looks at the new season but gives you a helping hand with entering the Totepool/Racing Post Ten to Follow.

Inside these pages we have an in-depth look at the firepower from eight British trainers, while our experts look at the scene in Britain, Ireland and France. We have analysis from the Racing Post's betting and bloodstock desks, and James Pyman leaves no stone unturned as he pinpoints original angles to help find winners.

In addition we have pen portraits of the 250 horses in this season's Ten to Follow, guidance on names to consider for your entries and some strategies to think about, which should prove invaluable in selecting your squad.

I hope you find the information in these pages useful and that it will help you find some winners throughout the season.

David Dew
Editor

Contributors

Scott Burton
David Carr
Dave Edwards
Nicholas Godfrey
Dylan Hill
James Hill
Bruce Jackson
Paul Kealy
Jon Lees
Kevin Morley
Tom Pennington
Stuart Riley
Colin Russell
Peter Scargill
Simon Turner
Johnny Ward
Nicholas Watts

Published in 2014 by Racing Post Books
Raceform, High Street, Compton, Newbury, Berkshire, RG20 6NL

Copyright © Raceform Ltd 2014

The Racing Post specifies that post-press changes may occur to any information given in this publication.

A catalogue record for this book is available from the British Library.

ISBN: 978-1909471467

Edited and designed by David Dew
Printed by Buxton Press, Palace Road, Buxton, Derbyshire, SK17 6AE

LOWDOWN FROM THE TRAINERS

RACING POST EXPERTS

TEN TO FOLLOW

STATISTICS

Hoping Thistle Bird can fly and prove flagbearer with top-flight success

ROGER CHARLTON: THIS SEASON'S BRIGHTEST HOPES

I N previous seasons there have been the likes of Cityscape, Bated Breath, Definightly and Genki. For the last two years Roger Charlton had Group 1 campaigns to plan for Al Kazeem, Thistle Bird, Mince and Dundonnell. Now, with Lady Rothschild having reversed the decision taken at the end of last season to retire her, Thistle Bird is all that remains.

"She's now the only confirmed Group horse in the yard," says Charlton. "The past few years we've had several but this year she's the only one. So we're really looking forward to trying to win a Group race with her, and maybe even a Group 1.

"She's become a very tough and consistent mare. There's always a question when keeping older mares in training because it might not work and she's six now. Maybe the Nassau was run to suit her, maybe they went to fast, but she ran a great race to finish second and she was also beaten only a neck when third in the Prix de l'Opera on her final start last season, so she doesn't have to improve much to win at the top level.

"She's not really bred to stay that far and I had my doubts, but on those two runs it's clearly worth continuing at a mile and a quarter. The target is to win a Group 2, if not a Group 1, and I'm more confident about

travelling her now. The Middleton Stakes at York in mid-May is where we're likely to start her."

While new recruit *Seolan* may not yet be a proven Group performer, she certainly has the potential. A Listed scorer, beating two subsequent Group 3 winners, on the second of her two unbeaten runs in Ireland as a two-year-old, she was then sold to America where she ran only twice, disappointing both times. Charlton has been charged with reviving a once promising career.

"She was a good two-year-old filly on soft ground in Ireland, she didn't show much in America but probably wasn't suited by the fast conditions out there as her form in Ireland was on heavy ground. We need to build her back up but she's run only four times so there's a chance we can turn her career around.

"It's nice to have a filly like her who is a bit of a challenge as it makes it more interesting. She's related to Grey Lilas and Golden Lilac, both of whom were very decent in France, and we'll be trying to get her back to her best but we don't really know what to expect, or how good she might be."

Despite a lack of proven Group performers, Charlton has a plethora of lightly raced, improving sorts, like Seolan, with whom to target the season's biggest handicaps, and it is easy to see one or two progressing through to Group company.

Captain Cat is another example. The Lincoln is his more likely starting point and he could be in Listed company before long. "He had a setback last spring and made a

Thistle Bird will be aimed at winning a Group 2 contest, or even scoring in Group 1 company

DID YOU KNOW

Roger Charlton won the Derby in 1990 with Quest For Fame. The son of Rainbow Quest was owned by Khalid Abdullah and was later trained in the US by Robert Frankel, who was one of the most successful trainers in American history, but sadly died in 2009. Abdullah decided to name a Galileo colt after him, and he turned out to be rather good . . .

belated debut at Goodwood in July. We then tried blinkers at Newmarket but he went off too fast and it wasn't until we switched him to the all-weather that he became far more consistent.

"He's in the Lincoln but I wouldn't want to run him if the ground was soft. He's rated 99 and is getting close to being able to run in Listed races. He's been a bit backward and is lightly raced, so I hope he'll continue to progress. I think a mile and a quarter is his ideal trip."

We have seen what can happen when sprinters get on a roll, with the trainer's now retired Mince a perfect example. She progressed from a mark of 70 to 113 and landed a Group 3. *Secondo* improved by 10lb in his last three runs and now sits on 93.

While not sure if he is Group-class yet, Charlton definitely feels there is more to come. "He was a bit in and out last year and I think he might need a little time between his races. He won at Haydock very easily and I took a chance running him at Newmarket with a penalty eight days later and he disappointed. Then after a nice break he was beaten only just by a progressive horse at York. He's been raised to a mark of 93, but I think he'll cope with that, and he'll be aimed at the good six-furlong handicaps."

Charlton is known for his success with older horses and it is partly down to the big, backward types he acquires, and partly due to his patient approach through their formative years. *So Beloved* might become the latest example of one who blossoms for this softly-softly approach.

"He's a very big, tall horse, he's 16.3hh, and is a very good mover. He is a bit quirky and can get on his toes on occasions. He's

been gelded and because of his size I felt it was worth giving him another go as he might have needed to grow into himself. He didn't have a bad season last year, but if it all comes right there is the potential for him to be better than his current mark of 90."

The Queen's *Border Legend* is described as "a very big, rangy and late-maturing type," and he is one for the better handicaps between a mile and a quarter and a mile and a half. "When he won at Nottingham it appeared he would stay further, so we stepped him up to a mile and a half for the November Handicap but it was horrible ground and we knew we were in trouble before the start.

"Whether he gets the trip remains open to question, but I would imagine he'll start this season over a mile and a quarter but we may try him over further. He's rated 89 so he may not always get in, but we'll target some of the better 0-95 or 0-100 handicaps."

Rated slightly higher and due to be tackling slightly further is *Clowance Estate*. "He was very consistent last year and stays very well. That said, he doesn't quite stay the distance of the Cesarewitch in which he finished mid-field on his final start.

"He's rated 95 but is lightly raced so I hope he'll improve. He could start at a mile and a half, but really he wants to be running in the good staying handicaps over a mile and three-quarters or two miles, probably on fast ground."

While one or two may progress to Group company, Charlton thinks it is unlikely any of them can join Thistle Bird in contesting Group 1s. "I'm not sure if we have anything that can progress to that level this year, I'd say probably not. But in the three-year-old

department a lot of them are rated in the 80s or 90s and are unknown quantities."

Laugharne fits into that category, but last year he also became Charlton's first two-year-old runner in a Group 1 since 2008, so the fact he was taken to France for the Criterium de Saint-Cloud highlights the regard in which he is held.

"He won really well at Goodwood on very soft ground and then we took a chance and ran him in a Group 1 race, which was a step too far. He's a nice, staying handicapper and hopefully he doesn't need soft ground. I've earmarked him for the good staying handicaps over a mile and a half and further."

Be My Gal is still a maiden but according to her trainer is another with the potential to earn black type. "She ran a race full of promise on her only start at Kempton and I think it was quite a decent race. She has a lot of five- and six-furlong speed on her dam's side, but the way she ran and the way she behaved I'd like to think she'll get a mile and a quarter.

"As with any Galileo filly it's always nice to harbour plans of getting some black type. We'll start her off in a maiden over a mile or a mile and a quarter, but then hopefully we'll be looking at Listed races. She's certainly above average."

Another who looks above average is *Sea Defence*. "He's always shown promise, he's a good mover and travels well. He was immature last year but has size and scope, so should progress. The handicapper has given him a chance off 82 and he should have no trouble staying a mile."

Hiking is another Charlton feels the handicapper has been kind to. "She's related to Bated Breath and had a good season,

winning two of her three races and was a little unlucky not to win all three as she was beaten a short head in a nursery on her final start. I think a mile on fast ground will suit her and we'll start her in handicaps as I think she's reasonably treated on a mark of 83."

When asked to pick out one three-year-old definitely capable of winning Charlton does not opt for Sea Defence or Hiking, but for *Hooded*. "He is a big, laid-back horse and a good mover. First time out he didn't show much and then made all at Lingfield in a fair race. He has the pedigree, size and strength to progress. He could stay a mile and a half and if I had to pick one horse as a definite winner it would be him."

Highlighting a few darker horses with potential who might go under the radar on a reading of form alone, the trainer mentions *Amber Isle*. "She's a sister to Dundonnell and I thought she ran well at Newbury on her debut, but unfortunately she came back with a split pastern and didn't make it back to the racetrack. We'll find a maiden for her and I expect her to progress as a three-year-old. She should stay a mile."

The well-bred but as yet unraced *Catadupa* is also exciting the trainer. "She's a sister to Cubanita, who had a good time last year, clearly stays well and likes soft ground. This filly is probably very similar with regards to ground and distance. She did very little last year as she was too backward so she's an unknown quantity, but she's got size and scope and is by Selkirk, who has been kind to me." *[Stuart Riley]*

Clowance Estate (left): consistent and his trainer is hopeful of improvement this season

CHARLTON: ASSESSING THE STATS

2013 was a good year for Roger Charlton as he reached a significant milestone in his training career. Last season's tally of 43 winners was steady although nothing out of the ordinary, but it was his prize-money amassed that caught the eye, busting the £1 million barrier for the first time. More than half of that was earned by Al Kazeem, who notched three Group 1 wins, *writes Kevin Morley*.

Al Kazeem improved as a five-year-old and Charlton is often pigeon-holed as a trainer who likes to take his time with his horses. The layers seem to be aware of this and price his runners accordingly. However, it means they often underestimate his ability to train juveniles. Consequently, they have returned a level-stakes profit over the last five seasons and did so last term. In fact, Charlton has sent out more two-year-old winners than four-year-old-plus winners since 2010.

Group winners come via obvious and fancied horses which means following his runners in this area results in a long-term loss, so handicaps are the area to concentrate on. Although three-year-olds provide the majority of his winners in this sphere, they don't return the best results in terms of strike-rate and profit, making youngsters in nurseries and older horses a better bet.

The Beckhampton handler is a master trainer of sprinters but bookmakers are aware of this. Narrowing down Charlton's runners to those between 7f and 1m2f is therefore the way to go.

Not known to start the season fast, April is rarely a good month for Charlton but his stable clicks into gear during May and holds its form well during the summer.

Since being retained by Khalid Abdullah, a big supporter of Charlton's, James Doyle has been entrusted with the job of steering most of the stable's winners and has made a good job of it. George Baker comes in for most of the spare rides, but a selective approach is required with both jockeys in order to secure a profit. Those ridden by Steve Drowne have rewarded punters handsomely over the years but he has had more than his fair share of injuries of late.

Charlton's strike-rate on the all-weather isn't outstanding and he tends to concentrate on the turf. He has a solid record at all types of tracks from switchback courses like Epsom and Goodwood to those of a more galloping nature like Newmarket and Newbury.

On the gallops at Beckhampton, from where Roger Charlton sent out 43 winners last season and amassed over £1 million in prize-money

Afsare leads the way as Bedford House team look to maintain momentum

WITH 69 winners last year Luca Cumani enjoyed his best season for over 20 years. What was even more remarkable was that he sent out only 333 runners in Britain and was therefore operating at strike-rate of 21 per cent – his best since 2003.

It wasn't just a successful season numerically because Cumani won prize-money of more than £1m in Britain, a figure he hadn't achieved since 2004, and that total was boosted by more than 40 per cent when winnings abroad being were added to the mix. This came through Danadana, who landed a valuable Group 2 event in Turkey in September and Mount Athos, who improved on his fifth place in 2012 by finishing third to Fiorente and Red Cadeaux in the Melbourne Cup at Flemington in November.

A former assistant to Sir Henry Cecil, Cumani bought Bedford House stables in Newmarket 1976 and although the Derby wins of Kahyasi in 1988 and High-Rise in 1998 have been the highlights of his career in Britain, he has also enjoyed notable international success with smart performers like Falbrav, Starcraft, Alkaased and the miler Barathea.

In more recent years the Melbourne Cup, which in 2013 carried a first prize of £2.5 million, has been high on his list of races to win, and although he has yet to achieve his goal, both Bauer (2008) and Purple Moon (2009) finished second, bringing back plenty of Australian dollars to Newmarket.

Mount Athos, though, will not be going back to Melbourne for a third bid under Cumani's tutelage as the seven-year-old is no longer at Bedford House. However, the trainer's other flagship performer of 2013, *Afsare,* remains in training at seven. He has been a star performer over the years, winning six of his 18 races, including the Hampton Court Stakes at Royal Ascot as a three-year-old and finishing a fine second in the Arlington Million two years later.

Last season Afsare ran just four times, winning the Group 3 Sovereign Stakes at Salisbury followed by the Celebration Mile at Goodwood.

His trainer says: "We'll give him a similar campaign to last year. His owner is very keen for him to go to Royal Ascot so we'll give him one run before and have him in full flight for that. He needs the fast ground."

Danadana won the 2012 Zetland Gold Cup at Redcar but has since proved much better than a handicapper. Last season he won the Group 3 Huxley Stakes before landing that valuable race in Turkey in the autumn.

Cumani says: "He's very consistent, winning two Group races last year. He's a mile-and-a-quarter horse and we'll run him in similar races to last season. He needs good or fast ground."

The four-year-old *Ajman Bridge* is another worth following. A son of Dubawi, he has run only four times in his career but

Danadana (left): should continue to do well at Group level over middle distances

has won twice, landing a Kempton maiden on his only outing as a two-year-old and then a Pontefract handicap first time out in 2013 before being placed in two similar events.

His trainer says: "He'll be campaigned in handicaps. He showed progressive form as a three-year-old and as he's not had much racing he should continue to improve. He's a mile-and-a-quarter, perhaps a mile-and-a-half horse, and likes good, fast ground."

The four-year-old *Elhaame* is another lightly raced sort who remains in training and is likely to improve with racing. It took him a while to get off the mark but he progressed particularly well when stepped up to middle distances last autumn, winning a couple of mile-and-a-quarter handicaps in the midlands before finishing an excellent second in a valuable Ascot handicap over a mile and a half in September.

"He was another who was progressive last year and ran really well in the Ascot race. He's a mile-and-a-quarter, mile-and-a-half horse, he's not bred to stay any further. He's best on fast ground."

Cumani's Ebor horse this year could be *Havana Cooler*, who has run only five times but is going the right way as he showed

when finishing third in the competitive Melrose Handicap at York in August.

"He was progressive last year. He's bred to stay and could be an Ebor horse, although he'll have to go up a bit first. We'll start him off at a mile and a half and see where we go," says his trainer.

Another very interesting four-year-old is *Seussical*, who was formerly with David Wachman in Ireland and won a handicap at York which earned him a Racing Post Rating of 116 on his only outing for Cumani, who says: "He was impressive at York but he's been raised to a mark of 111 which is above the level for handicaps so we'll have to aim him at Group races at a mile and a quarter or perhaps a mile and a half. We'll probably start him off at Sandown in either the Gordon Richard or the Brigadier Gerard Stakes."

Cumani has always brought on his horses gradually and in most years his strength is his team of three-year-olds. Last season, for example, 44 of his 69 winners were in that division.

For 2014 he picks out seven he considers should win their share of races. The first is *Lawyer*, a colt by Acclamation who improved towards the end of last season by winning

over six and seven furlongs at Wolverhampton. Cumani says: "I hope he can carry on where he left off. He's not harshly handicapped and I think a mile will be his trip and he should win some more races."

Mount Logan, a colt by New Approach, ran below par when stepped up in grade on his final start in the autumn, but his trainer reckons he is better than he showed that day.

"He won his maiden well but disappointed in a Group race at Newmarket next time. He's better than he showed that day and he should do well as a three-year-old this year. I think he'll be a mile-and-a-quarter horse."

Another three-year-old Cumani holds in high regard is *Postponed*, who is a colt by Dubawi. He won a Yarmouth maiden on his second start but stepped up on that effort when running on strongly to finish runner-up to Oklahoma City in the £500,000 Tattersalls Millions Two Year Old Trophy at Newmarket in October.

"I like him a lot. He finished well in that valuable race and seven furlongs was too short. He needs at least a mile, he'll certainly get a mile and a quarter but I'm not sure he'll get beyond that."

The home-bred *Second Step* shaped

ONE TO FOLLOW

Havana Cooler Backward as a youngster, his second-season timeline mirrored his progressive profile and further improvement is anticipated. A winner at ten and 12 furlongs, he was a beaten favourite when third in the Melrose at York in August but Luca Cumani's four-year-old will have strengthened up and looks a smart stayer in the making. *[Dave Edwards, Topspeed]*

Ajman Bridge (black spots) has won two of his four races and should prove worth following in middle-distance handicaps

Seussical: won at York on his first outing for Luca Cumani and will be aimed at Group races over a mile

really well when runner-up in a backend maiden at Yarmouth on his racecourse debut.

Cumani says: "He ran a good race even though he was a bit green. He's progressive and is going to be a mile-and-a-half horse."

One of the Cumani trademarks over the years has been his success with fillies, and he has several three-year-olds he hopes could be Listed or Group-class this year.

Jordan Princess, who is by Cape Cross, ran only twice last season but won on the second occasion.

"She won her maiden at Newcastle despite hating the soft ground. She's going to be a mile-and-a-half filly and I'm hoping that she'll be Group class."

The Invincible Spirit filly *Joys Of Spring* is another lightly raced three-year-old and, like Jordan Princess, had just two runs as a juvenile. Although she shaped well on quick ground when fourth at Leicester first time out, she failed to go on from there.

Cumani says: "She was disappointing on the soft ground at Doncaster but she's much better than that. She's certainly up to winning races and hopefully will be a black-type filly at seven furlongs or a mile."

The third of the three-year-old fillies he nominates is *Volume*, who won two of her three races last season. She shaped with promise first time out at Newmarket and confirmed that with wins in a maiden at Newcastle and a decent nursery at Nottingham.

Cumani says: "She's a filly I like. She did well last year and I was particularly pleased with the way she won at Nottingham. She's bred to stay a mile and a half and ought to get some black type this year." *[Colin Russell]*

DID YOU KNOW

Luca Cumani has won races all around the world. Australia is his one glaring omission, but how close he has been to winning the Melbourne Cup. Twice he has finished second – with Purple Moon in 2007, beaten half a length, and a year later when Bauer was beaten a nose. Given his superb international record, his time in the race must come soon.

CUMANI: ASSESSING THE STATS

In terms of volume, Luca Cumani enjoyed his best season for many a year in 2013. Last term's tally of 69 was his best since the 72 winners he sent out in 1991 while he also managed to nudge past the £1 million marker in prize-money, thanks mainly to some placed efforts in valuable contests, *writes Kevin Morley*.

Group 1 glory eluded Cumani last term but he struck six times in pattern races and would have returned a level-stakes profit for any punter backing him blind in this area. A loss was incurred for followers of his handicappers in 2013, but his runners are usually profitable to side with in this sphere.

Known as one of the more patient handlers in the game, juveniles account for the least success in his yard so it is unsurprising to learn that the Classic generation and older horses provide the majority of the victories.

Cumani has earned the respect of bookmakers over the years and there aren't many distances at which punters can gain an edge. If there's one area where he is slightly underestimated, however, it is with stayers. Those running over 1m5f and beyond have returned a plus figure over the past five seasons, and that was also the case with his runners competing between 1m3f and 1m4f.

Kieren Fallon and Kirsty Milczarek ride the majority of the yard's winners but a better weapon for punters regarding riding arrangements is Adam Kirby. His record for Cumani last year was staggering as he won on half of his 18 rides for the stable. It is also worth keeping an eye out for those horses ridden by Andrea Atzeni. William Buick, although used sparingly, is also a positive booking.

Cumani's runners seem to handle undulating tracks well with solid strike-rates at Brighton, Epsom, Goodwood, Pontefract and Ripon but most winners these days on the turf come at Nottingham and Yarmouth, where last season and during the previous five years they secured a level-stakes profit.

Cumani has a fair record on the all-weather but there is no doubting what his favourite sand venue is as Kempton accounts for around three-quarters of his winners on synthetic surfaces.

A busy scene in the office at Bedford House Stables in Newmarket

Exciting times with Classic hopefuls among team going from strength to strength

I**T IS an exciting time for Richard Fahey, who is based at Musley Bank on the southern edge of Malton in north Yorkshire, where there is team of horses brimming with quality.**

Fahey has three for the Guineas, last season's Mill Reef Stakes winner Supplicant, the Group-placed Parbold and the smart filly Sandiva – and if you add to them last season's Yorkshire Cup winner Glen's Diamond, Group winner Garswood, Mill Reef runner-up Rufford and a host of useful handicappers, the new season promises to be truly memorable.

Fahey is enthusiastic about his squad, and of his top three-year-old colts he says: "*Supplicant* did well last season with his win in the Mill Reef being the highlight. He is rated 110, so he'll go for the top races and his first aim will be the 2,000 Guineas. We'll see how he gets on there before mapping out the rest of his season.

"I'm delighted with *Parbold*. He's a big, strong, fine-looking horse and I don't think I've ever had one who's done so well. He'll start in one of the trial races, possibly the Free Handicap, and then go for the Guineas."

Sandiva was the yard's star juvenile filly last season. She ran five times, won on three occasions, including a Listed event at Naas and a Group 3 at Deauville and ended the campaign by finishing seventh on very soft ground in the Prix Marcel Boussac at Longchamp.

Fahey says: "She's done very well, I'm pleased with her and she'll be aimed at the 1,000 Guineas although I wouldn't want to run her again on ground as soft as it was at Longchamp as she wouldn't get home on it. She has a lot of speed but she should stay a mile so we'll start her off that way and can always bring her back if she doesn't stay."

Another high-class juvenile from last year is *Rufford*, whose best run was when second to stablemate Supplicant in the Mill Reef.

Fahey says: "He's rated 105 and we may start him off in the Free Handicap."

At this stage last year *Garswood* was being prepared for a tilt at the 2,000 Guineas. All seemed set fair for a big run after his convincing win in the Free Handicap but little went right for him in the Newmarket Classic and he finished only seventh behind Dawn Approach.

He ran some decent races in top company after that, winning the Lennox Stakes at Goodwood and rounding off his season with a good third to Moonlight Cloud in the Prix de la Foret.

"He's done very well over the winter. He's a big, strong horse and could have a really good year. He's far too highly rated for handicaps so he'll be running in all the best races. We'll start him in the Sandown Mile and if he does well there we'll go for the Lockinge. We thought we'd try him back over a mile again and if it doesn't work out he can always go back to seven furlongs – I'd even run him at six again if the ground was soft."

Glen's Diamond is another Group-class performer. His finest hour last season came

Garswood: has done well over the winter and will be aimed at the big races over a mile. He could even drop back to seven furlongs

when he landed the Yorkshire Cup in May. He didn't fare so well after that, but as Fahey says: "I've got it wrong with him as all his life. I thought he'd be a Melbourne Cup horse, but finally I found out he doesn't stay two miles. He'll be going back to York again. There seemed to be an excuse for him every time he ran after he won there last season, but he wasn't really getting home.

"I'm certainly not worried about dropping him back to a mile and a half, and he might start off in something like the John Porter."

Gabrial is another smart performer. He won a Listed race at Doncaster last spring and performed with plenty of credit in Group and Listed races. He made a bright start to the year by winning a valuable handicap at Meydan in January and made the money in

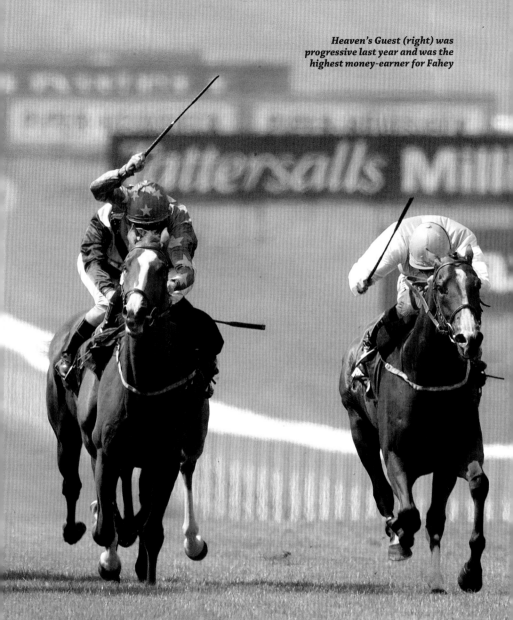

Heaven's Guest (right) was progressive last year and was the highest money-earner for Fahey

Dubai several other times as well.

"He'll be campaigned in Group 2 or Group 3 races. He's more than paid his way over the years and seems to be just as good over a mile and a quarter as he is at a mile, but his win in Dubai was at nine furlongs."

Don't give up on ***Romantic Settings***, who ran the race of her life to finish runner-up in the Musidora last May, but failed to progress.

DID YOU KNOW

Richard Fahey's first Group 1 winner did not come in Britain. In 2010 Fahey went to Paris for the Arc meeting with Wootton Bassett and landed the Prix Jean Luc Lagardere. His first Group 1 on home soil came in the July Cup two years later with mudlover Mayson.

Fahey says: "I don't think we've got to the bottom of her. She's a decent filly I can assure you of that, but every time she ran after the York race there was a genuine excuse for her. We'll probably end up running her in Group races, but she's rated only 92 and she's better than that so we might try to find a decent handicap for her first."

The stable's highest money-earner last year was *Heaven's Guest*, who won four races and more than £177,000 in prize-money. He started his winning spree by scoring off a mark of 79 at Hamilton in May and finished it by taking the £93,000 first prize off a mark of a 100 in a seven-furlong heritage handicap a Ascot in October.

"He had a fantastic three-year-old season but I expect he'll be rated out of handicaps this time so we'll have to go for Listed or Group races with him. He's tough, and hopefully will continue to progress."

Hi There is another Fahey improver. His first win for the trainer two years ago came off a mark of 62 and after three wins last term he is now rated 98.

"It's not going to be easy for him now as he had such a fantastic time last year, but he's a tough, genuine sort so it wouldn't surprise me at all if he carried on improving and won a few more," his trainer says.

Majestic Moon won three handicaps in the middle of last season and despite the inevitable rise up the ratings he continued to run well in some better-class events.

"He had great time of it last season and should go on and win some more races. He loves fast ground and is best at six or seven furlongs."

In contrast, *Majestic Myles* failed to score last term. He won a Listed event at Chester in the summer of 2012 and was rated 111 at his peak, but he's dropped in the ratings and that, according to his trainer, makes him a very interesting prospect this season.

Fahey says: "He had a blank season in 2013, I don't know why, but he's back in now and is in great form. He looks fantastic. He's dropped down the weights and I can see him doing plenty of damage off his mark of 94."

The William Hill Lincoln is the target for *Gabrial's Kaka*, who progressed well last season, winning a decent Pontefract mile handicap in August and ending his campaign with a good run when second at York.

"He's going to Doncaster first. He's a decent horse and he should pick up a useful prize this season."

Top sprint handicaps are on the agenda for the versatile *Alben Star*, who seems equally at home on grass or the all-weather. After running some good races in defeat during the winter, he finally bagged a decent prize at Wolverhampton in January.

Fahey says: "He's now rated 100 on the all-weather and 97 on turf, and if we can keep him right he'll go for all the decent six-furlong handicaps. We've always thought there was a decent race in him."

Another to note for sprint handicaps is *Polski Max*, who won his first two races last season before his form tailed off.

"He had a good enough season, but rather lost his way towards the end of the year. He's come down a bit in the weights and should find some races."

Also worth noting is *Roachdale House*, a home-bred three-year-old by Mastercraftsman, who won two of his four races last season. "He won a decent seven-furlong nursery at Doncaster in the autumn on his last run. We tried him over a mile at Ayr before that and he looked like trotting up but didn't get home. He's stronger this season, he'll get a mile, and there's a decent race at Musselburgh for him to start with and we'll work away from there."

Another three-year-old, *Eastern Impact*, ran only twice last time, but showed useful form by winning on his debut and finishing third in the National Stakes at Sandown.

"He was owned by David Barker, who sadly died in February. He was a great guy and we'll all miss him greatly. Eastern Impact had a setback last season after showing decent form early on and he'll be going for all the top three-year-old sprint handicaps, five or six furlongs, and he might even get seven."

After winning his first two races as a juvenile, the four-year-old *Flyman* failed to win last season but Fahey has not lost faith in him.

He says: "It's not uncommon for good two-year-olds like him not to show their true form at three. He had a relatively light campaign last season but he could come good this year. He'll be aimed at the decent sprint handicaps but might stay seven furlongs."

Time And Place is an interesting four-year-old. He won on his reappearance at Yarmouth last season, but failed to add to that tally in three further runs.

"He's had little niggly problems all his life but we think he's a very good horse. If I can get a clear run with him he'll win some races as he's better than his rating of 79."

One of the longest-serving residents at Musley Bank is six-year-old *Sir Reginald*, and his trainer is very bullish about his prospects for this year, saying: "He's had issues with his feet, but they're perfect at the moment and I wouldn't be at all surprised if he were to win a decent handicap this time." *[Colin Russell]*

ONE TO FOLLOW

Secret Keeper Hails from a late-maturing family her trainer Sir Mark Prescott knows well. Should prosper in handicaps after failing to do much in three quick backend runs at two. *[Simon Turner, Racing Post Ratings]*

Polski Max (left) has an attractive handicap mark and is expected to progress this season

FAHEY: ASSESSING THE STATS

Last year could be deemed a success for Richard Fahey as he sent out 164 winners during 2013, a total surpassed only by Richard Hannon and Mark Johnston. Fahey achieved higher tallies in 2010 (181) and 2009 (165) but the prize-money earned last term was a personal best, totalling just under £2.5 million, *writes Kevin Morley*.

Handicaps make up the bulk of the yard's success and Fahey frequently lands some of the more valuable contests, but backing his runners blind would lead to heavy losses given the sheer amount of runners he has.

Fahey has a fairly even split in his yard with a slight balance leaning towards the older horses above two- and three-year-olds. Finding an area in which he is profitable is difficult given the volume of runners in all types of races but those competing in nurseries seem to oblige at rewarding odds. Fahey also likes to aim his youngsters at the valuable sales contests and landed Newbury's Super Sprint last term with Peniaphobia.

As far as the distance of races to concentrate on goes, the best place to back Fahey is again with juveniles over the sprint trips. On a far smaller scale, he is an underrated trainer of stayers and his three-year-olds return a profit when asked to distances in excess of 1m4f.

One of the advantages of having a large string is you can pretty much keep the scoreboard ticking over all year round and his runners often have a fitness advantage in the early exchanges of the turf season, where the opposition need a run or two.

Despite taking the position of retainer to Hamdan Al Maktoum in 2012, Paul Hanagan still rides regularly for the yard although the majority of the rides now go to Tony Hamilton. Both return a level-stakes loss and punters are advised to watch out for when Ryan Moore, Graham Lee or Jamie Spencer is booked, with the latter often riding those in the silks of Marwan Koukash.

On the all-weather, Fahey has far more winners at Southwell and Wolverhampton than he does at Kempton or Lingfield. On turf, his runners are best followed at Pontefract and Musselburgh, while his raids south are most effective at Windsor and Yarmouth.

Exercising on the gallops at Fahey's Musley Bank stables

Classic success could be on the cards from quality team packed with talent

GODOLPHIN **might have won the 2,000 Guineas last year with Dawn Approach, but it was not until the St Leger that either Charlie Appleby or Saeed Bin Suroor were represented in another Classic. Their big-race hand looks far stronger in 2014, with Breeders' Cup Juvenile Turf winner Outstrip, the exciting Be Ready and UAE Oaks winner Ihtimal all prominent in ante-post markets for the season's first four Classics.**

Bin Suroor is responsible for both *Ihtimal* and Be Ready, and on the filly who is contesting favouritism for the Oaks and is prominent in most 1,0000 Guineas lists, he says: "Ihtimal won the UAE Guineas and then came home ten lengths clear in the UAE Oaks. She's been working extremely well in Dubai and we could look at the 1,000 Guineas for her first run back in Britain."

Unlike Ihtimal, *Be Ready* has not been kept busy this winter. Consequently he will not go straight to the Guineas and instead will take in a trial. Twice raced, he won the Listed Flying Scotsman on his final start last season and

Bin Suroor says: "He's a Listed winner and has had a break this winter. He's in good form He could have a prep race, but the 2,000 Guineas will be his aim."

It is a race in which the operation could be double-handed. Already a Group 1 winner, Outstrip has already earned his place in the 2,000 Guineas line-up, although his participation is dependant on the ground, a lesson learned from his Dewhurst third on good to soft. "His target is the 2,000 Guineas, provided we get a sound surface as that is crucial for him. He'll probably go straight there," says Appleby.

Tattersalls Millions 2YO Fillies' Trophy winner **Wedding Ring** could target another sales race at Newmarket or take in one of the 1,000 Guineas trials, although the main event is not on her radar after she found a mile too far in the UAE 1,000 Guineas,

finishing fourth behind Ihtimal.

"She won the UAE Guineas trial and ran well in the Guineas," says Appleby. "Her aim will either be the sales race at Newmarket over six furlongs or one of the guineas trials over seven, but I think a mile is too far for her at this stage."

It is not just the Guineas trials Godolphin are looking to target, the Derby and Oaks equivalents have been pinpointed for several of their middle-distance prospects with Racing Post Trophy flop **Pinzolo** top of the list.

Appleby still has faith in the winner of two of his three starts, and says: "He's held in high regard but he didn't deliver in the Racing Post Trophy. He's training well and we're very happy with him. He was thought of as a potential Derby horse last year and we'll tiptoe down that route. There are no

firm plans, but he'll probably start in one of the Derby trials."

A similar route could be taken with *Sudden Wonder*, although he has the option of starting his season in a sales race. "I was pleased with his last run and he is another potential Derby horse," says Appleby. "We'll either start him off in one of the 1m2f sales races or a trial and see where he fits in."

While Ihtimal is second favourite for the Oaks, Appleby is hoping *Sound Reflection* can join her and take prominence among the three-year-old middle-distance fillies. "She's wintered in Britain and has done well. She's held in high regard and ran creditably in the Fillies' Mile. We'll decide if we start her at a

mile or over ten furlongs in one of the Oaks trials. We've not pressed on with her yet but I think she'll be a good middle-distance filly."

It is not solely in the three-year-old department that Godolphin look strong this year. Despite the retirement of Lockinge and Champion Stakes winner Farhh they look to have a crack squad of older horses too.

Encke, who denied Camelot a place in history as the first triple crown winner since 1970 when winning the 2012 St Leger, has spent the winter in Dubai and is being aimed at a Royal Ascot return with the Hardwicke his potential target.

"He wintered in Dubai, although it was not on his radar to run," says Appleby. "He's done well and will be aimed at Royal Ascot, possibly at the Hardwicke, and the middle-distance races in late summer and autumn will be his aim. He would prefer a bit of cut in the ground."

Leger winner Encke (left) has Royal Ascot's Hardwicke Stakes as an early target

Stablemate *Certify* won the Group 1 Fillies' Mile at two by four and a half lengths and headed the ante-post betting for last year's 1,000 Guineas before she was ruled out. She made a successful return to action in Dubai, winning the Group 2 Cape Verdi before suffering a first career defeat in the Group 2 Balanchine. "She's come out of her last run fine and we'll look to bring her back at Royal Ascot for something like the Windsor Forest," says Appleby.

The newest member of Godolphin's

training ranks acquired last year's Derby runner-up *Libertarian* midway through last season and is looking forward to getting him out again this year after his first winter in Dubai. "He wintered in Dubai but we had no intention of running him. He's one for the second half of the season, once all the good middle-distance races start, and he'll be out around Royal Ascot," he says.

Appleby has also picked up two useful recruits from 24-time French champion trainer Andre Fabre. The prospect of trying to improve a horse who was in Fabre's care must be daunting, but any trainer would welcome one who was good enough to finish fifth behind Treve in last year's Arc, and that is exactly what *Penglai Pavilion* achieved on his final start for Fabre.

A winner of four of his eight races, he excites Appleby, who says: "I like him. We ran him on Super Saturday as we needed to find out about him, and middle distances with some cut seem to suit him."

It is a similar story with *Vancouverite*, who won four of his six starts for Fabre, including the Group 2 Prix Guillaume D'Ornano. "He's another to have come from Andre Fabre, where he won a Group 2. We started him over 1m2f on Super Saturday, but that was about getting our bearings with him."

It is not just Appleby who has inherited a high-class performer from Fabre. *Tasaday* made two starts for Bin Suroor in Dubai after finishing second by a nose in the Group 1 Prix de l'Opera. A first Group 1 win will no doubt be the aim for her and Suroor says: "She won her last start in Listed company and I think she's a mile-and-a-half filly. There's no set plan for her at the moment but she's in great form."

Suroor has always done well with staying types and *Cavalryman* has had another good winter in Dubai, winning a Group 3 over a mile and three-quarters, although his turn of foot has prompted his trainer to consider a drop rather than a step up in trip. "He's working well and appears at his best over a mile and a half or a mile and three-quarters. He could have a similar campaign to recent years."

Ahzeemah is another stayer, although he may want slightly further than Cavalryman. "He's a nice one for the future and we will target the staying races," says Bin Suroor, who also has the progressive *Royal Empire* for such races. "He won the Geoffrey Freer last season and went out to Flemington in Australia for the Melbourne Cup, where he finished 14th. I think he'll be at his best over a mile and three-quarters-plus." *[Stuart Riley]*

Cavalryman: wintered well in Dubai.
Might be dropped in trip this year

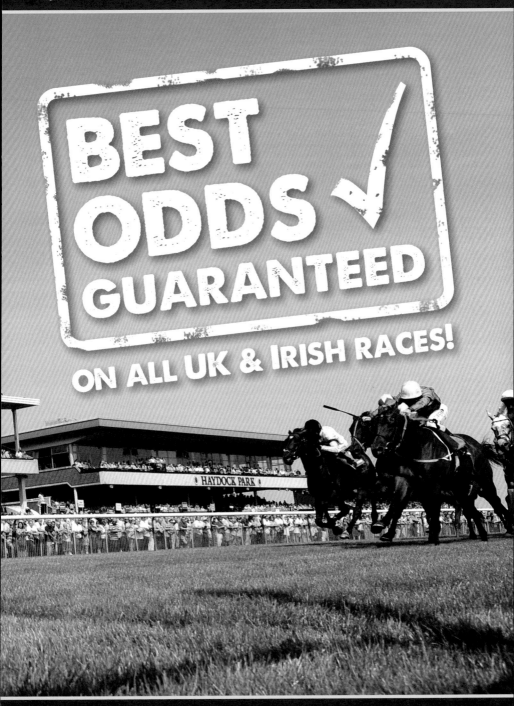

GODOLPHIN: ASSESSING THE STATS

Considering Godolphin had to overcome the Mahmood Al Zarooni scandal last year, the operation enjoyed a good season under difficult circumstances. Charlie Appleby *(right)* was able to step into the void in July, meaning that a two-tier training operation could remain in place, *writes Kevin Morley*.

Saeed Bin Suroor kept plugging away throughout the controversy and rewarded his employers with 106 winners, amassing more than £2.6 million in prize-money, which included victories in the Lockinge and Champion Stakes courtesy of Farhh. His exploits were matched by Appleby, who nearly reached the £1 million barrier with 60 winners from just a half season. He also justified Godolphin's decision as Al Zarooni's replacement by rewarding them with success in the Breeders' Cup Juvenile Turf with Outstrip.

It is clear from looking at a breakdown of each trainer's respective figures, that Bin Suroor has the ability of handling the pick of the older horses while Appleby gets to train most of the juveniles.

Bookmakers act with caution when it comes to pricing up horses from Sheikh Mohammed's operation but it seems Appleby's three-year-old handicappers were underestimated last season, particularly over distances in excess of a mile, judging by the positive figure in the level-stakes column.

It is notable how Godolphin tend to finish the season strongly. This has long been a habit with Bin Suroor but the trait was also apparent with Appleby in his debut season and it is something punters can cash in on at a time when plenty of other horses are over the top having done enough for the year.

Silvestre de Sousa and Mickael Barzalona have the majority rides split between them with Bin Suroor slightly favouring De Sousa and Appleby using Barzalona more frequently. Outside those two, it is worth watching out for Harry Bentley's mounts for Bin Suroor, while Martin Lane had a good record for Appleby last term.

Godolphin-trained runners seem highly effective on all-weather surfaces and both handlers return a level-stakes profit with a high strike-rate. On turf, Bin Suroor excels at Windsor and his figures at Ascot are also impressive considering the competitive nature of racing. Appleby performed well at the Berkshire venue last season while his runners on Newmarket's Rowley Mile and July course are worthy of the utmost respect.

Saeed Bin Suroor overseeing work in Dubai

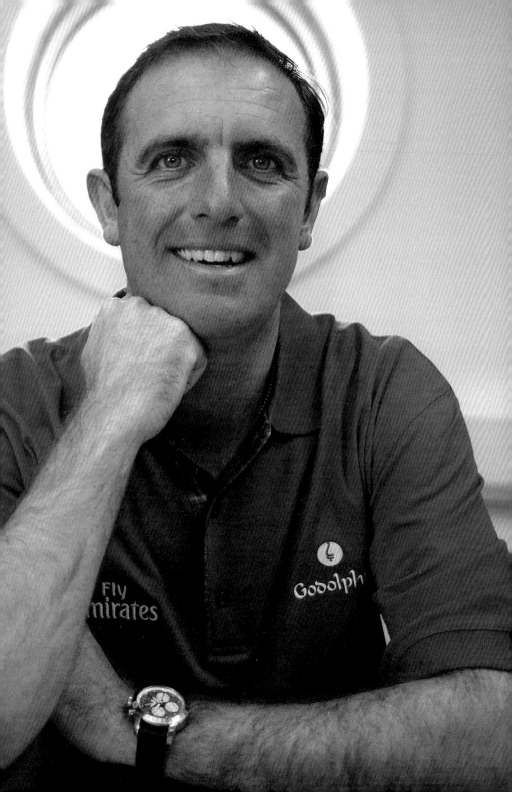

Exciting Kingman out to give Gosden a first success in the 2,000 Guineas

I**T HAS been the nature of the type of horses John Gosden tends to train that he is more prolific in the second half of a Flat campaign than the first.**

Of his 60-plus Group or Grade 1 scorers only three have been Guineas winners and all of them fillies, Lahan providing his only success in the 1,000 Guineas and Valentine Waltz and Zenda landing the Poule d'Essai des Pouliches.

That record might be set to change this year as Gosden, who has trained the winner of a Derby and four winners of the St Leger, has *Kingman* among his team – one of the ante-post favourites for the Qipco 2,000 Guineas, although it is a prominence Gosden believes the Khalid Abdullah-owned colt has earned more through bookmaker hype than performance.

An impressive six-length victory in a Newmarket maiden last June was sufficient to get the colt to the front of the Classic betting market and, while a minor setback prevented Kingman contesting the Prix Jean Luc Lagardere after a follow-up win in the Group 3 Solario Stakes, he has remained a fixture near the front of ante-post lists ever since.

Kingman underwent surgery to have a chip removed from a joint in October and is now being readied for a Guineas campaign, the time when the colt can show whether the excitement surrounding the horse was justified or misplaced.

"Kingman is cantering on Warren Hill," says Gosden. "He's entered in the 2,000 Guineas, the French Guineas and Irish 2,000 Guineas. We're happy with him at this stage. He underwent surgery in the autumn and I'm pleased with him.

"You know my views on the hype of maiden winners. I thought it was all silly. He won a Solario but unfortunately that was the end of his season. I think he might have won a Grand Criterium [Lagardere] but you need to be there on the day to prove those points."

Gosden has saddled just nine runners in the 2,000 Guineas and only three this century. His first, Anshan, who was third in 1990, remains his highest-placed finisher. "I haven't won the 2,000 Guineas and haven't had a lot of runners. Down the years I have trained a lot of owner-breeder horses, staying types and a lot of fillies as owner-breeders sell their colts, so we've never had much in the way of candidates."

Kingman could be an exception and his development this spring will shape the Gosden campaign through the early part of the season although before that *The Fugue*, the only Group 1-winning survivor of the trainer's 2012 Flat championship winning team, has a date at the Dubai World Cup meeting.

The five-year-old mare kept up her big-race contribution last term in winning the Yorkshire Oaks and Irish Champion Stakes but two others went begging. In the Breeders' Cup Turf she was headed on the line by Magician and was an unlucky loser in the Hong Kong Vase at Sha Tin in December,

defeats there may be an appetite to avenge later this year.

"She was unlucky in Hong Kong and got caught late by a horse with a superb finishing kick at Santa Anita at the Breeders' Cup. She got boxed in and pushed back when a horse stopped in front of her and she had nowhere to go."

Elusive Kate and Winsili have been retired while Hollywood Derby winner Seek Again has joined Bill Mott in the United States, leaving Gosden with 18 older horses and 150 three-year-olds and unraced juveniles.

Hype or the real deal? Kingman will get a chance to answer the big question in the first Classic of the season

"Gregorian [winner of the Hungerford Stakes] is still here," says Gosden. "The targets for him are all later on. Seven furlongs is his optimum trip as he proved in the Hungerford, but there is no programme for him early so I'm being patient."

Candidates for the Derby and Oaks trials will no doubt emerge throughout the campaign, and among his new intake of juveniles is a son of Sea The Stars out of Global World who fetched 460,000gns at the Tattersalls October Sale, a rare auction purchase by Abdullah.

"I don't have a lot of obvious big-race contenders at this stage, unexposed horses maybe, one-time maiden winners, that sort of thing but not horses with obvious Group form on them." Gosden says: "It's all early days for the Derby. There are horses who might have won a maiden or run well in maidens at two but no obvious black-type performing two-year-olds."

Gosden appreciated capturing a first trainers' title two years ago but could not match the firepower of Richard Hannon Snr last year and finished 2013 in sixth place. It is an opportunity he accepts may not come his way again, at least this year, with Hannon's son Richard inheriting another vast string, Aidan O'Brien again targeting the major races plus the Godolphin operation to compete against.

"Richard Hannon has a great outfit with a superb group of horses and then you have Aidan O'Brien who comes in for the elite events with probably the group of best bred horses in the world," Gosden says.

"Everybody is up against it. I think you only have to look at the betting for who is going to be champion trainer to see that one is odds-on, the other is even money and I think I'm 12-1 which probably says it all.

"We had a good year last year, a great year the year before but you're like a football manager. You're as good as your horses as long as you get them to play right at the right time. All a trainer can go is realise a horse's true potential."

And that will be Gosden's goal with Kingman. *[Jon Lees]*

Patient approach: Hungerford winner Gregorian is unlikely to have early targets

DID YOU KNOW

John Gosden was assistant trainer to both Vincent O'Brien and Noel Murless – not a bad apprenticeship. He was assistant to O'Brien in 1976/77 and was part of the team that won the Derby with The Minstrel. Two years after leaving Ballydoyle, Gosden moved to California and took out a licence. He eventually moved back to train in Britain and won the Derby under his own name with Benny The Dip.

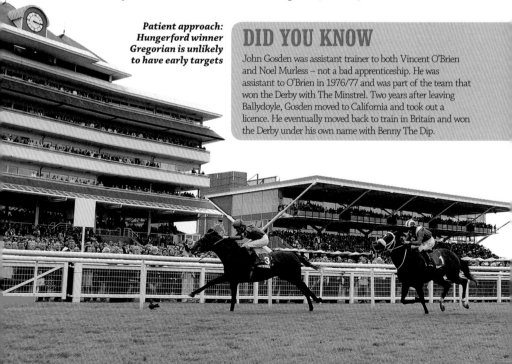

TOTEPOOL
live information

Get up to the minute pool sizes, results and payouts with our new live information app!

GOSDEN: ASSESSING THE STATS

He didn't quite match his record-breaking 2012 exploits but last year was still a solid one for John Gosden, who notched his third century in the last four seasons with 108 winners (sent out 99 winners in 2011) and accrued over £2 million in prize-money, *writes Kevin Morley*.

Despite having slightly less ammunition at his disposal in 2013 compared to the previous season, the Newmarket handler still managed to notch up his fair share of big-race success. Group 1 victories came courtesy of Elusive Kate in the Falmouth, Winsili, who gave Gosden his second successive Nassau Stakes, and The Fugue, who landed the Yorkshire Oaks and Irish Champion Stakes. It's great to see The Fugue remains in training and she looks sure to add to her impressive Pattern-race haul.

Gosden failed to secure Classic success last year but the St Leger is a race in which he has performed well recently, winning it three times since 2007. As far as punting goes, the trainer's three-year-olds are best followed blind at Group level and that age group secured a level-stakes profit in Pattern races in 2013.

One race missing from his Classic cv is the 2,000 Guineas but Gosden has a fine chance of rectifying that situation with Kingman in his ranks.

Group races aside, it is the older horses who are generally best followed at a lower level. Four-year-old and older runners account for a lower portion of his winners but the rewards are far greater for punters, particularly in handicaps.

Stable jockey William Buick rides the most winners to a healthy strike-rate but to a slight level-stakes loss. Rab Havlin comes in for plenty of spare rides and those who oblige tend to do so at generous prices. Ryan Moore is called upon far less but the hint is worth taking when he is.

Gosden has a fair strike-rate at most courses but seems best followed at those of a galloping nature. He has been profitable to back at Doncaster, Newbury and Newmarket's July course over the last five seasons and returned a plus figure at those three venues last term.

With his background in American racing, it is no surprise to see Gosden's string performs well on the all-weather, generally with healthy strike-rates posted at all four sand tracks with Kempton providing the most winners but Lingfield providing the most profit.

John Gosden in his office and among his squad at Clarehaven Stables

High hopes Mukhadram can make breakthrough to score at the top level

THIS SEASON'S BRIGHTEST HOPES

THE scoreboard clicked up a first 100 winners in 2014 for William Haggas and with those 107 successes came record prize-money for the Derby- and Oaks-winning trainer. Yet the cricket-loving Yorkshireman, who topped £1m for the sixth consecutive season, did not hit enough Group-race boundaries for his liking and failed to clear the ropes for another Group 1 winner.

"We had some big handicap winners with Danchai in the John Smith's Cup [along with runner-up Stencive] and Rex Imperator in the Stewards' Cup but Group races are what we want and we didn't have enough of them last year," he says.

It was not for the want of trying by bold front-runner *Mukhadram*, who had ended his three-year-old days in 2012 struggling with his rise into a three-figure rating when

fifth in the Cambridgeshire. Sheikh Hamdan Al Maktoum's colt was a different proposition last year, leading the way for the stable after announcing his improvement in winning the Group 3 Brigadier Gerard at the end of May.

The Shamardal five-year-old then twice locked horns with Al Kazeem, literally in the Coral-Eclipse as the winner barged him into the rails costing him a clear second.

Mukhadram deservedly took a top-30 position in the Longines World Rankings with a rating of 122, only 2lb behind Al Kazeem.

When Sheikh Hamdam keeps horses, especially stallion prospects, in training at this age he is usually rewarded – remember the likes of Muhtarram and Mubtaker.

Haggas has his sights set on going further in the quest for top honours in Britain this year. "I still have to talk to Sheikh Hamdam but I really want to step him up in trip this year for a midsummer target.

"I'd love to go for the King George – I think it's his race – a mile and a half on fast ground and he loves Ascot. He showed in the Champion there that he can't quicken on slow ground."

reaches maturity? Haggas hopes so and says: "He looks terrific and looks to have matured. Everything is going well."

Talking of maturity naturally leads to the family pipeline with the trainer's father Brian having enjoyed great success with broodmare Frog, who sadly died last year.

Harris Tweed is back at the age of seven, trying to add to his career earnings of over £350,000 gained from rare consistency that has seen him finish out of the frame just twice in the last three seasons and winning seven races in all.

Only the inspired Johnny Murtagh on Royal Diamond denied Harris Tweed ending last year on a high in the Group 3 Champion Long Distance Cup at Ascot.

"He ran such a marvellous race at Ascot and is such a thoroughly genuine tough horse and will bash away at all those races tailormade for him – he likes cut in the ground and a trip. I think he's better going right-handed."

His little half-sister **Tweed** has a way to go to match him but has more than upheld family tradition with two wins from two starts on turf, the last by seven lengths at Newmarket in November resulting in a hike in his rating to 87.

"The family gets better with age and the main target is to get her black type this year," says Haggas. "She's done well over the winter but is difficult to assess as she's useless at home. Again she clearly stays well and likes cut so the trick will be keeping the pair apart."

The Newmarket trainer has high hopes of his Stewards' Cup winner **Rex Imperator**, who could not follow up his impressive Goodwood win off his revised mark of 110, although it was only by a neck he failed at Listed level on unfavourably easier ground at York next time before his season was cut short.

"He had a flake of bone removed from his knee but is back with us now," explains Haggas. "He's a huge talent and top of the ground suits him – he was deeply impressive in the Stewards' Cup.

"I don't know what level he'll reach but hopefully it will be onwards and upwards. He wants a fast, flat track and York would suit him well."

Another speed machine at Somerville Lodge stables is **Heeraat**, who finished a place behind Rex Imperator when the pair finished down the field in the Group 1 Betfred Sprint Cup at Haydock.

Heeraat, who blazed away for four of the six furlongs before being eased, was compromised by unfavourably soft ground on that occasion. He had earlier chased home subsequent Nunthorpe heroine Jwala in the City Walls, a Listed sprint at York while twice unable to contain Sole Power in the top midsummer sprints.

The five-year-old is back for another top sprint campaign and Haggas says: "He's very useful and hopefully will go on again. He definitely wants a flat track – he's a Newbury, York and Doncaster horse, is very genuine and will do well again this year."

Graphic was transferred by the Ascot Racing Club to the care of Haggas last summer. Four wins and a fourth in the Cambridgeshire followed.

"He improved 28lb apparently in two

Harris Tweed (2): tough, consistent and can add to his haul of seven successes

DID YOU KNOW

William Haggas's career is on the rise looking at his tally of winners year on year. In 1988 he finished the season with 12 winners. In 1998 it stood at 24. By 2008 it was 86 and last year Haggas recorded his first century of winners in a calendar year. You get the feeling he could become champion trainer one day.

months last year according to the handicapper and is now rated 110," says the trainer. "He was a breath of fresh air for us last year and is one to enjoy this time. We're aiming at better races, starting with the Winter Derby at Lingfield. Whether he's going to improve again at the age of five I don't know. Hopefully we can find a nice race or two at Ascot with his owners, not just for the royal meeting."

A filly who has crept under the radar is the Oppenheimer's home-bred *Our Obsession*, who has raced twice in each of her first two seasons, winning both last year's runs culminating in a Listed win at York where she beat Aidan O'Brien's Say, who went on to win a Group 3 and finish a close third in the Group 1 Matron Stakes.

"It looks like she'll improve physically and the plan is to get some more black type with her this year."

The stable's three-year-olds failed to contribute to the Group-race score last season but Haggas hopes it will be different this year.

First up is likely to be *Seagull Star*, who holds the English and Irish Derby entries and is penciled in to start in the Listed Feilden Stakes, won last year by subsequent Group 1 performer Intello.

"He has the pedigree to be good. He's not very big but has obviously got the ability. He surprised when winning at Newmarket and he won that maiden comfortably so we're going to aim to start in the Feilden probably – that mile and a furlong ought to be a minimum for him. He's by Sea The Stars and was coming home strongly at Newmarket. His dam was second in the Yorkshire Oaks and won a Listed race."

One who has a Classic entry is *Queen Of Ice*, another winner on her only start last year. The Cheveley Park Stud's home-bred has been entered in the Prix de Diane (French Oaks).

"She's difficult to assess but is another well-bred filly – I couldn't believe she won at Newmarket. I don't think it was much of a race but she's done well over the winter and could be one who comes alive on the track. She'll start off in an Oaks trial."

Our Obsession will be going for more black type after her Listed win at York last season

Ertijaal has something to live up to having run last season's top domestic two-year-old Toormore – unbeaten in three climaxing with the Group 1 National Stakes – to a neck on their debuts at Leicester last May. Sheikh Hamdan's home-bred Oasis Dream colt then bolted up in his maiden by six lengths at Yarmouth a month later.

"He showed promise last year – I think he might be more of an Ascot type. While Toormore progressed through the season, what I liked about that first run was the pair of them finished a long way clear of the rest."

The trainer volunteers one of the three-year-old maidens who should not remain without a win for long judged on his sole start last backend.

Latest of the family's home-breds *Mange All* was beaten inches when third to two Derby entries Godolphin's Moontime and the John Gosden-trained favourite Munjaz.

"He's a big, fine horse and was running on very well and would have won in another beat. We'll win his maiden and then see."

Saayerr had bragging rights among last year's two-year-olds being the one Group winner in the pack when beating subsequent Dewhurst runner-up Cable Bay in the Richmond Stakes at Glorious Goodwood. He got stuck in the mud behind Astaire in the

Gimcrack on his only subsequent start and trends suggest this Acclamation colt faces an uphill task this year if he develops into a sprinter.

"He's got a Group 2 penalty to shoulder this year so he's likely to start in the Free Handicap at Newmarket [rated 108]. He's not a certain stayer for seven furlongs and might end up a sprinter."

Starting from a much lower level is *Token Of Love*, who can pay her way this year. "She's a nice filly. She won an ordinary race at Leicester – she's rated 77 so will start off in a handicap," is the trainer's synopsis of this Oppenheimer home-bred.

The winners look set to keep flowing for the Newmarket trainer, who burst his Somerville Lodge yard at the seams and took on Flint Cottage Stables a year ago to cater for his three-figure team. This year there looks to be more big Group-race hitters padded up in the pavilion. *[Bruce Jackson]*

Richmond Stakes winner Saayerr (9) could remain over sprint distances this season

HAGGAS: ASSESSING THE STATS

The only thing missing from William Haggas's list of achievements last year was a Group 1 victory as 2013 was a success from every other angle. He surpassed the century barrier for the first time in his training career and accrued a record £1.8 million in prize-money, *writes Kevion Morley*.

Despite not being able to notch a success at the very top level, Haggas still managed to pick up a few Pattern races but it is in handicaps where his abilities come to the fore. The Newmarket handler is one of the best in the business in this area and was at it again last term picking up some of the major races like the Stewards' Cup, John Smith's Cup and November Handicap.

His exploits are well known to the odds compilers but that didn't prevent his handicappers returning a level-stakes profit during 2013. Most of his handicap wins come via the Classic generation but it was the older horses who did more damage to the layers.

Handicap success aside, Haggas had 30 juvenile winners last season, a personal best. His youngsters returned a level-stakes profit which bodes well for his stable for the coming season.

In terms of distance, it seems the best results are returned from backing those running between seven furlongs and a mile, although the few stayers he has also return positive results.

Although Haggas seems to provide a steady stream of winners throughout the year, he always makes sure he leaves something in reserve for the closing months of the turf season and his strike-rates from September to November are reliable.

Haggas uses a wide range of riders and often acquires the services of the best around. Ryan Moore and Richard Hughes have high strike-rates but looking outside the obvious, Adam Beschizza's rides for the stable over the past five years have returned a solid profit while those ridden by Seb Sanders obliged at an impressive rate in 2013.

Haggas has a high win ratio at most tracks although his strike-rate at Ascot is bizarrely low. His figures at some of the flat, galloping tracks are impressive with Newbury and Haydock catching the eye while many trainers would envy his record on the Knavesmire at York.

William Haggas's string at work on Warren Hill in Newmarket

The steady approach that keeps producing winners at highest level

I**T WAS one of those great moments that seem to happen only in horseracing, a moment when all calmness was discarded in the sheer excitement and thrill of a pulsating three-horse battle to the finish.**

What made this show of untempered joy special was that it happened to be the Queen and it happened to be as her filly *Estimate* thrust her way to the front in the Gold Cup at Royal Ascot.

"It was very special that day and you could see her absolute joy," trainer Sir Michael Stoute says. "And the crowd were delighted to see that too."

Things did not go to plan after Royal Ascot for Estimate, who picked up a small injury when being prepared for the Lonsdale Cup at York before soft ground scuppered her chances in the Long Distance Cup on Champions Day.

Back from a break at Sandringham, Estimate is being prepared to defend her Gold Cup title and is likely to start off in the Sagaro Stakes at Ascot in May.

"I would say it's odds-on she'll go to the Sagaro and the plan is the Gold Cup. We're not looking beyond that at the moment," says Stoute. "She's only lightly raced and I hope we can run her a little more this year. We won't be trying her on soft ground again."

Assessing his team for the season ahead, Stoute says he is looking forward to running his older horses. Top of the list is dual Grade 1-winner *Dank*, who took the US by storm with wins in the Beverly D Stakes and Breeders' Cup Filly & Mare Turf. Both successes came on firm ground with the mare running on Lasix, and Stoute says: "She certainly goes on fast ground and she was impressive in Ireland as well before going to America. As for Lasix, I don't think she needs it but it was a case of 'when in Rome'.

"She's in work and we'll be looking at big races for her this year. We know she travels so well and has a great temperament, so we can look overseas for her too."

The ability to be patient with horses is often cited as something that marks out the top trainers from the rest and Stoute's early patience with some backward fillies has left him with some exciting prospects.

He says: "*Integral* did fantastically well last season and finished off being placed in the Sun Chariot. We always liked her but she was very immature and had little niggles so we're very hopeful there is more to come.

"She'll start off in the Dahlia Stakes over nine furlongs at Newmarket in May and we'll then see what direction we go trip-wise. She's bred to get further but Ryan [Moore] said she'll go seven furlongs."

Moving on to *Waila*, Stoute says: "We hope the soft ground was against her when she was down the field in the mares' race on Champions Day. She's a top-of-the-ground filly.

"She had been very badly struck into when winning at Newmarket in the summer and needed a lot of stitches in her hind legs so that's why she was off for so long. I ran her in a hood that day as she was a little spooky but I think she's growing up and there is more to come."

And of Mango Diva and Astonishing, the trainer says: "*Mango Diva* is a progressive filly who got messed around when a beaten favourite in the Sandringham at Royal Ascot. She was very classy afterwards and will start off in the Middleton at York.

"*Astonishing* surprised us by winning a Listed race easily by seven lengths at Newmarket in the autumn. It's important to get her switched off in her races, which is what we did that day, and we'll look to Group contests with her now."

Of *Pavlosk* Stoute says: "She was a good winner of her first two starts and had excuses on her next two runs – it was too much too soon for her in a Group 1 at Royal Ascot and at Goodwood she slipped on the bend before flying home – but ran two very moderate races at the end.

"We had a long debate about keeping her in training and decided she could have won a Group race last year so we'll carry on. That's the plan this year, to win a Group race."

Few horses generated more talk in 2013 than *Telescope*, who was heavily touted for the Epsom Derby. Stoute feels some of the obsession with the horse was "a bit ridiculous" but hopes there is more to come now he has matured over the winter.

Integral wins at Sandown. She is pencilled in to start her campaign in Newmarket's Dahlia Stakes in May

"I'm happy with him. Horses tend to do well over the winter as they have six months off hard exercise, but he's done particularly well," the trainer says. "Given he's not had much racing and that he's progressed physically I hope he can go on this year. We'll have to see. He'll start in the John Porter at Newbury or the Gordon Richards at Sandown."

Along with Telescope, *Hillstar* will fly the flag for the males following a win in the King Edward VII Stakes at Royal Ascot backed up by an excellent third in the King George VI & Queen Elizabeth Stakes on his next start.

Dropped back in trip to ten furlongs, Hillstar was unplaced in his next two starts but Stoute says: "I don't think ten or 12 [furlongs] are a problem for him. He's just a Group 2 horse at the moment. We always thought highly of him at home which is why he ran at Royal Ascot and things hadn't gone right in handicaps before that."

Others looking to follow Hillstar out of the handicap ranks into Group races this season are Bold Sniper and Gospel Choir, and Stoute is in no doubt the duo have the capability to make the step up in grade.

"*Bold Sniper* had run well at Ascot in the summer but hung at Goodwood on his last start and we could never find out why so we decided to end the season for him and start again," says Stoute.

"The Queen likes to have runners at Royal Ascot so we'll see what races there are for him there but it's early days. We'll look for better races with him this year.

"*Gospel Choir* is capable of winning Group races. The soft ground was against him in the Cumberland Lodge. He's had very little racing for his age and is a really lovely, decent, honest horse."

Moving on to the three-year-olds and the fillies have an early advantage over the colts based on their form as juveniles.

Hillstar: gets the better of Battle Of Marengo to land the King Edward VII Stakes at Royal Ascot

Stoute has twice saddled the winner of the 1,000 Guineas and has two potential candidates for the Classic in his yard in Radiator and Along Again. However, how the fillies train this spring and their performances in any trials will determine if they make the race in early May.

Radiator looked to have a huge future when scorching to a 15-length win in a Lingfield maiden in September in a time that left clockwatchers thoroughly impressed.

It came as a disappointment to all that the daughter of Dansili could not follow up when favourite for the Listed Oh So Sharp Stakes on her next start and Stoute says: "Radiator was disappointing on her last run in the Oh So Sharp. We were not happy with her when she came back after the race. It's a dangerous time of year for fillies and she may

have picked up something. She was beaten a long way from home and was never travelling in the race the way she had before. We've always liked Radiator and hope to have her back in the right direction and she'll go for a trial in the spring."

Along Again's season was cut short after a close third in the Princess Margaret Stakes at Ascot in the summer and is likely to join Radiator in running in a trial this spring.

"All Along progressed nicely with racing last year and found six furlongs too short in the Princess Margaret. If I'd have run her again she'd have gone over further but she had to have a bone chip

DID YOU KNOW

Sir Michael Stoute was knighted in 1998. The reason being was for services in tourisim to Barbados. Stoute's father was chief of police in the Caribbean haven and the Newmarket handler lived there until he was 19 when he moved to Britain to start a legendary training career. He remains true to his roots in being a cricket fanatic.

taken out of one of her fetlocks," Stoute says.

"She's a progressive filly and does nothing at home as she saves it all for the course. I love horses like that. We'll know what to do with her as the spring progresses."

Stoute also has a pair of potential contenders for the Oaks at Epsom although he freely admits that Asyad and Surcingle have plenty to find in the spring to make the final field.

Of Yarmouth maiden winner *Asyad*, the trainer says: "She has a long to go but she did well to win on ground that didn't suit her at Yarmouth. She's a fast-ground filly and it was soft that day. She's in the Oaks and we'll look for a trial with her and see if she's good enough.

"*Surcingle* is also in the Oaks although she ran moderately on her last start. The ground was terrible that day and it was late in the year so we'll look to run in an Oaks trial and take it from there."

Stoute talks about the early part of the year being an exciting time for the three-year-olds as their work is upped and they are given the opportunity to progress on the promise they showed at two.

Leading the sophomore colts is *Snow Sky*, who left his trainer scratching his head after a laboured effort in the Racing Post Trophy. Previously, the Khalid Abdullah-owned runner had taken apart a maiden at Salisbury, winning by 11 lengths and prompting

connections to supplement him for Doncaster.

"It didn't turn out the best supplementary entry we've ever made," Stoute says. "He had annihilated them at Salisbury but was first off the bridle at Doncaster – I thought he was going to be tailed off!

"There is such a range of 'soft' ground in Britain and I think it was easier to get through at Salisbury compared to Doncaster. He's in the Derby and we'll see how he's working this spring. He should stay the trip."

The multiple champion trainer also saves a good word for three other colts who are worth keeping an eye on.

"I hope we have a lot of fun with *Top Tug*," Stoute says. "He's owned by a very long-standing owner of mine and he should be capable of winning more races for her.

"*Gothic* was a good winner of not a very strong maiden at Leicester at the backend of last year. He's a big, scopey horse who has got a bit of presence to him and can hopefully go on.

"And then there is *Munaaser*. We do like this horse. We thought he would win first time out at Yarmouth and he came back with sore shins after being beaten into third.

"He's done really well over the winter and I have a lot of time for him. I've left him in the Derby although I have some doubts about the trip, but I have no doubt he is a Group horse."

[Peter Scargill]

Highly regarded: Radiator impressed with a runaway win in a Lingfield maiden

STOUTE: ASSESSING THE STATS

Sir Michael Stoute's numbers were up last term with 87 winners and over £1.6 million an improvement on the previous year, *writes Kevin Morley*.

Stoute had endured disappointing campaigns in 2011 and 2012 but he was in resurgent form last term, with Estimate's victory in Ascot's Gold Cup the highlight – and hopes must be high for the coming season that he can reach the 100-winner mark for the first time since 2007.

Although the stable's standards have not been as high as is usually the case in recent seasons, the bookmakers haven't dropped their guard when assessing his runners. Despite possessing solid strike-rates in races of all types with horse of all ages, Stoute returned a level-stakes loss in nearly all areas which shows the regard in which he is held by layers and punters alike. The most effective way to profit from backing his string would have been to side with those running over further than a mile, up to and including 12 furlongs.

Stoute rarely hits the ground running for the beginning of the turf season and his runners often need a run in April, but his yard tends to kick on from May and the stable often excels in the summer.

Ryan Moore rides the majority of the yard's winners to a healthy strike-rate but the odds compilers understandably keep his mounts onside. Khalid Abdullah sends decent horses to Stoute, something which enabled James Doyle to have good record for the stable last term with punters in the black for a level-stake on his rides for the yard. However, the most eyecatching booking is Richard Hughes. The occasions are few and far between but his strike-rate is better than one in four over the last five seasons, while he struck with three winners from nine rides last term.

Stoute generally has a high calibre of horse in his yard so it is not surprising to see he has a good record on the all-weather. He rarely has a runner at Southwell and his string is much better suited to Polytrack. His figures at Wolverhampton and Kempton are no more than fair but his record at Lingfield is impressive.

On turf it is noteworthy when Stoute sends runners to a northern track. His strike-rates at Beverley, Carlisle, Newcastle and Thirsk are phenomenal.

Sir Michael Stoute supervises work on Warren Hill

Quality and quantity should help ensure successful campaign

ROGER VARIAN has more horses in his care this year than any other trainer in Newmarket, according to Horses In Training, and there is undeniable quality to go with the obvious quantity.

An increased sense of anticipation around the yard is down to the fact that one of those 174 listed inmates of Kremlin House Stables is a prime Classic candidate.

Kingston Hill tops most shortlists for the Qipco 2,000 Guineas and the Investec Derby thanks to a memorable sequence of three wins in five weeks last autumn.

Having defied greenness to score first time out at Newbury, he readily followed up in the Autumn Stakes at Newmarket then sluiced in by four and a half lengths in the Racing Post Trophy at Doncaster – a Group 1 race that has been won by three subsequent Derby winners in the past ten years.

The colt's fine cruising speed and turn of foot suggest he ought to have the pace for a Guineas, while the way he races and the stamina pointers in his pedigree both suggest he will get the Derby trip.

"He's done well through the winter, he's grown a little and looks stronger," Varian says. "We've had a clear run with him and I'm pleased with where he's at.

"We'd certainly be looking at the Guineas and if we were happy he could go straight there. He's always travelled comfortably in his races and shown a good turn of foot and is quite a versatile, straightforward sort. He relaxes very well and that gives every chance he'll get a bit further.

"He looked good last year and if he carries that form into this year he's going to be really exciting."

But this is no one-horse yard, and the Classics also beckon for *Princess Noor*. Although she was a 25-1 chance when landing the Princess Margaret Stakes at Ascot last summer there was no fluke about that Group 3 victory and she proved the point with an excellent second in the Cheveley Park Stakes at Newmarket two months later.

But neither the speed she showed at both tracks nor the evidence from her breeding suggests she is certain to stay the extra quarter-mile of the Qipco 1,000 Guineas.

Varian says: "We would be unsure of her trip. She showed a lot of speed last year and we'd probably train her for the Guineas and I think we'd go straight there. If she doesn't stay we can always come back to shorter trips but Johnny Murtagh got off after the Cheveley Park and said she had a chance to get a mile."

There is plenty of speed in the pedigree of the unbeaten *Mushir*, by top sprinter Oasis Dream out of Moyglare Stud Stakes runner-up Shimah, and he looks to have inherited a good deal of his parents' ability.

Having got up in the final stride on his debut at Kempton, he overcame trouble in running to follow up in the Listed Rockingham Stakes at York and it is anybody's guess how good he might be.

"We quite liked him through the year but he had a setback which was why he didn't run earlier," Varian says. "He could start off in the Free Handicap. We would have our stamina doubts and it might be that sprinting will ultimately be his game but we might ask him a question over seven furlongs and that could dictate where we go through the season."

Baarez is another unknown quantity, having run just twice at two and confirmed the promise of a Newmarket debut second by comfortably landing a backend maiden at Haydock.

"He's big and was a bit raw and unfurnished last year so he did well to run twice and show ability both starts," Varian says. "His work will determine where we start, whether we go for a handicap or the trial route, but I quite like him."

DID YOU KNOW

Kingston Hill was Roger Varian's first Group 1 winner in Britain. His early victories at Newbury and Newmarket mirrored fellow Racing Post Trophy winners Motivator and Authorized, who both scored at those tracks at the start of their careers. Both went on to win the Dante and the Derby.

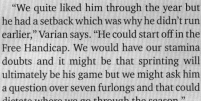

Kingston Hill: has done well throughout the winter and could go straight to Newmarket for the 2,000 Guineas

The classiest new recruit among the three-year-olds is *Ambiance*, who was bought for 75,000gns out of Mick Channon's stable after showing himself a smart juvenile in 2013, notably winning the Listed Dragon Stakes at Sandown and finishing third in the Molecomb at Goodwood.

"He looks fast and it might be that he's a five-furlong horse," Varian says. "There is a nice conditions race for three-year-olds at York in the middle of May which might be a good starting point."

One dark horse Varian picks out is *Idder*, a Derby entry who won a Newmarket maiden last November.

"He's one to look forward to and he'll probably stay ten furlongs," the trainer says.

A high-class band of returning older horses is headed by *Aljamaaheer*, who has already proved himself up to tackling top company, finishing third in the Lockinge at Newbury and then finding only Declaration of War too strong in the Queen Anne Stakes at Royal Ascot before making short work of Group 2 opposition in the Summer Mile at Ascot last July.

But a different campaign is planned in 2014 as Varian says: "We're keen to give him a go at sprint distances as he's very fast. It might be that to win his Group 1 he needs to come back in trip."

Ektihaam is worth another chance having failed to do himself justice on his final appearance, trailing in well beaten in the King George VI And Queen Elizabeth Stakes at Ascot.

That effort is easily forgiven as he was clearly harbouring bad memories of the frightening incident when he slipped up on the bend in the Hardwicke Stakes at the Royal Ascot, and he was given the rest of the year off.

It is to be hoped he can get back on track as he had looked an improved performer, particularly when routing his rivals from the front in a Listed race at Ascot in May.

"He looks very well and we've given him a bit of time to forget about slipping up," Varian says. "I think when he won at Ascot he

showed really good staying ability. The way he stayed he might get a mile and six, and the Yorkshire Cup might be a race for him. On his day he's good and he'll win a good race."

Mutashaded is another on the comeback trail, having packed an awful lot into a career that has comprised just three races.

The winner of a Yarmouth maiden at two and a Sandown handicap last spring, he defied his inexperience by finishing third on a steep step up in class for the Group 2 King Edward Stakes at Royal Ascot.

Frustratingly, that was it in 2013 but he should not be hard to place this season, proven at 1m4f and penalty-free even in Listed races.

"He's been delicate but his third at Royal Ascot was a good run for such an inexperienced horse and we hope he'll make a middle-distance performer who will compete in Group races," Varian says.

Middle distances will also be on the agenda for *Elkaayed*, who won twice over 1m2f in good company last spring, although he did not run after finishing sixth in the Gordon Stakes at Goodwood.

"He's really nice and I'd be disappointed if he couldn't make his mark in Group races this year," Varian says. "He ran very well in a very good race at Royal Ascot last year. You can put a line through Goodwood as it was a mess of a race on bad ground. I think he'll be best at a mile and a quarter."

Others likely to be campaigned at similar trips include *Cameron Highland*, who has won the last two runnings of the Listed August Stakes at Windsor, and Sound Hearts, a mare who might have been retired to the paddocks after making her breakthrough at Listed level last autumn but will be back this season.

"Cameron Higland is a delicate, late-summer/autumn sort who has pretty good ability on his day," Varian said. "He might eke out a little more improvement as a five-year-old.

"*Sound Hearts* would need to improve 4lb or 5lb to win a Group race but she might do."

Ektihaam: good on his day and could be aimed at the Yorkshire Cup

Princess Loulou also stays in training, and Varian says: "She's a progressive filly. She was fourth in a Listed race on the last day of the season and didn't quite stay ten furlongs. She could be a nice filly to go to war with, she has only run five times and there could be a bit of improvement in her."

Varian proved most profitable to follow in races at up to 1m in 2013 and he has plenty of ammunition for sprints this season.

Justineo improved so much last term that he ended up tackling Europe's best in the Prix de l'Abbaye at Longchamp and was beaten only four lengths at the line.

Other than when outstayed over a testing six furlongs at Newcastle, his recent record has been one of solid progress and the decisive way he took the Listed Scarbrough Stakes at Doncaster from the front suggests he will be competitive in Group races.

"Since we dropped him to five furlongs he has been a revelation and it was a good run from a bad draw in the Abbaye," Varian said. "I think we will hold his own at Pattern level this year."

Morawij should also continue to give a good account in 5f Group races, having won in Listed company last year and been beaten only a length into third place in the Group 3 Sapphire Stakes at the Curragh.

"He was third to Slade Power in Ireland and time has shown that was pretty good form for a three-year-old against the older horses," Varian says. "He ought to be a Group-level sprinter, and five furlongs would be his best trip."

Steps (blue and white): will continue to be a player in big handicaps and Pattern races

Steps and Rocky Ground appear ripe for promotion to that level. Steps has improved every season and, after being beaten narrowly in the Portland Handicap at Doncaster, he got the best of a tight finish to a Listed race at Ascot last October.

The lightly raced *Rocky Ground* improved significantly when dropped back to five furlongs last autumn and the way he squeezed though a narrow gap to prevail at Beverley augured very well for the future.

"*Steps* is one of those versatile horses to flip-flop between the big handicaps and pattern races," Varian says. "He wants a fast-run five furlongs and to get his toe in the ground.

"It was a good note for Rocky Ground to finish on when he won at Beverley from seasoned sprinters and if we have a clear run he could be pattern class."

Of all the huge number of horses in his care, *Eton Forever* may be the one Varian has the softest spot for as he gave the trainer both his first victory, in the Spring Mile at Doncaster in 2011, and his first Royal Ascot success, in the Buckingham Palace Stakes the following year.

And the stalwart campaigner ran well last season, when a Listed triumph at Haydock made it three wins in his last six starts. "He's getting a little bit delicate with age but he looks as good as ever," Varian says. "Seven furlongs when he can just get his toe in appear to be his best conditions and he could race in top handicaps and pattern races." *[David Carr]*

VARIAN: ASSESSING THE STATS

Since taking over at Kremlin House from the late Michael Jarvis in 2011, Roger Varian has maintained similar training patterns with the juveniles and older horses providing a steady stream of victories while the Classic generation remain the backbone of the stable's success, *writes Kevin Morley*.

What Varian has managed to do is increase the amount of success in his three seasons as a trainer, with 53 winners in his debut year in 2011, rising to 72 in 2012 and then up to 89 last term when he also succeeded in breaking the £1 million barrier in prize-money for the first time and did so comfortably.

Varian has increasingly impressed on the numbers front but what was more eyecatching about his exploits last term was the amount of Group-race success he had. With just two winners at that level throughout 2011 and 2012 combined, the Newmarket handler sent out five in 2013, earning his first British Group 1 victory in the process, via Kingston Hill in the Racing Post Trophy.

That was also of benefit to punters who would have cashed in a level-stakes profit on his Group-race runners last term. However, even greater rewards can be reaped by backing his three-year-olds in handicaps who have given a healthy over the past three seasons.

It is worth noting that his runners are best followed over certain distances. His sprinters (5f-6f) can be backed with confidence but it's over 7f to 1m where his inmates excel. There is still some mileage in siding with his string up to 1m2f but beyond that the profits tend to dwindle.

In past years Neil Callan had been the jockey entrusted with most of the yards rides and he has enjoyed his fair of share of success, but that role has since been passed on to Andrea Atzeni, who had an excellent strike-rate on Varian's string last term, returning a level-stakes profit. Last year's figures suggest it's worth watching for those ridden by Dane O'Neill and also on the rare occasions when Jamie Spencer and Ryan Moore are booked.

Varian has a record on the all-weather which compares favourably with most trainers, and has decent strike-rates at all four sand venues. On the turf, Haydock is his most successful course followed by Doncaster which are both flat, galloping left-handed tracks.

Roger Varian watching and organising work on the gallops

Host of Classic hopefuls should ensure another stellar year for O'Brien

T**HE more things change, the more they stay the same. The saying perfectly depicts the state of Irish Flat racing as it emerges from its winter snooze with yet another Ballydoyle beauty sitting pretty at the top of the Epsom Derby market, but subtle changes are sure to add intrigue to the 2014 campaign.**

Australia, on whom Aidan O'Brien heaped extraordinary plaudits after he won a Group 3 on his third start, is well clear of the remainder in the Epsom betting despite, on the face of it, having a good deal to prove.

Ballydoyle, with stud allies Coolmore holding the undisputed stallion ace in Galileo, are as ever heavily armed with potential Derby winners in a bid to follow up Rule The World's success last summer. There are, however, other trainers with some promising three-year-olds this season.

Perhaps the story that prompted most discussion in Irish Flat racing circles in 2013 was the Aga Khan effectively chopping quarter-century-old ties with John Oxx, when he was told that no yearlings would be Currabeg-bound last year. Oxx's loss, seemingly, is principally Dermot Weld's gain, with the impressive Mick Halford also training for the Aga Khan this year.

Weld will have felt a little unease given his longstanding friendship with Oxx but he will have whiled away many winter hours speculating about just how smart *Balansiya*, his first runner for the Aga Khan, might be at three after she routed her Leopardstown maiden rivals in a backend maiden.

The manner of that victory suggested the Shamardal filly might even upstage *Free Eagle*, whose own Leopardstown debut rout had him promoted to Derby favourite at one stage. Free Eagle then floundered when he countered Australia, but Weld's regard for the colt has wavered little if at all.

Australia, being by Galileo out of Ouija Board, has Derby written all over him. If hype is to hold all weight, he has little to fear from stablemates *Geoffrey Chaucer* and *Johann Strauss*, yet both are intriguing middle-distance candidates for the stable too this term.

Geoffrey Chaucer impressed in winning the Beresford, a race won in recent times by Sea The Stars and St Nicholas Abbey, and gives the impression he will find more than enough for the whip too.

The pick of Ballydoyle's milers is likely to be the hardy *War Command*, whose Coventry Stakes romp at Royal Ascot was breathtaking. He disappointed on his next start but ended the campaign with a gutsy success in the Dewhurst, impressing with how he coped with soft terrain for which he is certainly not bred. Otherwise, the Irish challenge for the 2,000 Guineas appears weak with *Tapestry* appearing to be the best of the Irish fillies on juvenile form – also trained by Aidan O'Brien.

Tapestry, another Galileo-bred, was beaten just a head in the Moyglare Stakes by Rizeena, a grand yardstick for top juvenile form in 2013. The jury is undecided about what her optimum trip might be, with two other classy fillies in the same boat.

One of them is the aforementioned Balansiya. The other is *My Titania*, trained by Oxx. What a story should one beat the other in some Classic or other this term.

My Titania, the smartest offspring yet of Sea The Stars, seemed a speedy type at two, scoring readily in a Group 3 in September, but her dam is out of a winner over 1m5f and she may well stay the Oaks distance.

David Wachman also has a stylish prospect on his hands in Elnadim filly *Come To Heel*.

Of all the positive changes in Irish racing in the past handful of years, our unexpected and somewhat inexplicable progression in

Moyglare Stakes runner-up Tapestry is near the head of the betting for the 1,000 Guineas

the sprinting division is something the game needed to a degree, giving Eddie Lynam, Tom Hogan and Maarek's various trainers some days in the sun and a chance to win Group 1 races in which Coolmore tend to be poorly represented.

Sole Power, *Maarek*, *Gordon Lord Byron* and *Slade Power* coming along all around the same time seems nothing more than a fluke but a welcome one at that. With Ireland, incredibly, not having a single sprint race above Group 3 level (juvenile races excepted), that we have genuinely top-class horses for racing over the minimum trip adds variety to the programme.

Moreover, sprinters tend to hang around, and they are gaining in supporters in Ireland despite Flat racing remaining the poor relation of the jumps in the popularity stakes.

There are not a great deal of older horses staying around in 2014 and perhaps *Leading Light* can lead the way, with all roads pointing to Royal Ascot and the Gold Cup on the evidence of his Leger win. At some stage he can expect to duel with the likes of *Royal Diamond*, the 2012 Irish Leger winner and now in the hands of Johnny Murtagh.

Murtagh's announcement close to Cheltenham that his riding days were over contradicted the superb impression he made in 2013 as a veteran rider when, to eyes trained and untrained, he was clearly as good as ever. Concentrating on training, with a growing yard at the Curragh, Murtagh looks nailed on to make waves.

Jim Bolger had another spectacular season in 2013, Dawn Approach and Trading Leather bringing him Classic glory. It is incredible to think Dawn Approach is now a stallion: it seems like only a year or two since his father New Approach, who has made a sensational start to his career at stud, was strutting his stuff.

Trading Leather, at least, stays in action on the track and can mop up middle-distance heats in 2014.

Irish Flat racing is at the peak of its powers right now with the health of Coolmore ensuring the best-bred horses are trained in Ireland. Our results at the Duabi Carnival

were exceptional and the success of Dundalk's all-weather – which is to embrace sectional timing this year – is to be cherished, catering for all level of thoroughbred talent with a surface widely hailed. The inaugural Champions Weekend, boasting prize-money of €3.73 million, will illuminate the campaign, Leopardstown and the Curragh sharing two days of unquestionably world-class Flat racing in September.

Messers Prendergast, Bolger, Weld and Oxx are all veteran trainers now to some degree or other but – while they are doing what they do – Ballydoyle will face stern opposition in 2014. Racing fans want competition and in Ireland they have competition among the greatest horses and horsemen. Bring it on.

Aidan O'Brien has another wealth of talent to go to war with this season

War commands an early interest for the Guineas at generous 8-1

1,000 GUINEAS

Tapestry has a superb pedigree, being by Galileo out of Rumplestiltskin, who won the Marcel Boussac as a two-year-old for Coolmore. She more than lived up to her illustrious breeding last season too, winning two of her three starts and being unluckily defeated in the other.

Aidan O'Brien's filly's best performance came on her second start when easily landing the Group 2 Debutante Stakes from stablemate Perhaps. She seemed to benefit there from the strong pace set by her stablemate and came through under Joseph O'Brien inside the final furlong to win going away.

That success primed her for a challenge in the Group 1 Moyglare Stud Stakes at the Curragh on her final start but nothing went right for her in what was a messy race. First of all she got hemmed in by the wayward Kiyoshi when looking to improve and then she lost out again when Rizeena made her winning run. Considering she was beaten less than a length and finished on the bridle, there has to be every chance she would have won had every horse held a true line.

Although she was promoted to second after the demotion of Kiyoshi, she lost her unbeaten record – but her chances of 1,000 Guineas glory are still good.

The extra furlong at Newmarket will help her enormously as she is a strong stayer at a mile who may even get an Oaks trip in time.

The fact that Ladbrokes only go 5-1 about her when 9-1 is available elsewhere is also illuminating. They are shortest price, have been all winter, and rarely get it wrong with horses from Ballydoyle.

2,000 GUINEAS

The colts division is harder to work out. Kingman is near the top of the market but perhaps doesn't deserve to be there judged on what he has actually done. *War Command* has achieved more. He was beaten only once last season, in the Phoenix Stakes, and that was put down to trainer error by Aidan O'Brien. Other than that he looked awesome, winning the Coventry Stakes at Royal Ascot in a canter before annexing the Futurity Stakes and Dewhurst later in the campaign.

Although Australia is quoted just behind him in the betting and represents the same connections, War Command would appear to be the logical 2,000 Guineas Ballydoyle representative based on breeding. As he has already been to Britain and won, he ought to be a major player at Newmarket and could easily start shorter than the 8-1 available.

EPSOM DERBY

The Derby betting at this stage is dominated by Ballydoyle horses and the difficulty is trying to gauge which one of their beautifully bred two-year-olds of last season will have blossomed over the winter and will state their case in the trials.

Australia is the obvious one, but at juicier odds it might be worth following *Geoffrey Chaucer*. He was only workmanlike in a couple of wins last season, but he won the Beresford Stakes on his last start and that has traditionally been a rich source of Classic talent.

The way he did it was hardly jaw-dropping, but the second horse, Oklahoma City, had much more experience going into the race and also had form with Kingston Hill, giving O'Brien a great line on the Derby form.

Geoffrey Chaucer is a half-brother to the great Shamardal and should come into his own over middle distances so the 16-1 looks good value.

EPSOM OAKS

While Tapestry could be an Oaks player, Dermot Weld's *Tarfasha* definitely should be based on her stout pedigree. She is closely related to Galileo Rock and Saddler's Rock and showed abundant promise on her three two-year-old starts.

She was a close second behind Geoffrey Chaucer on her debut at Leopardstown, won next time at Galway, and then finished third

in a Group 3 on her final outing behind My Titania. Although well beaten in that race it is probable she didn't run to her best, and seven furlongs, even as a two-year-old, wasn't far enough for her.

She can be backed at 33-1 for Oaks glory, a price that could prove huge as she could be a big improver over a trip.

Geoffrey Chaucer looks worth supporting at 16-1 for the Derby

ROYAL ASCOT

Weld won the Ascot Gold Cup a few years ago with Rite Of Passage and has another interesting candidate for this year's renewal in the mare **Pale Mimosa**.

She easily won the Saval Beg Stakes on her first outing last term but was below par in two subsequent starts. Only seventh in the Irish Leger, she did improve on that to finish fourth at Ascot on her final start behind Royal Diamond in the Long Distance Cup on Champions Day.

The soft ground may well have hindered her on that occasion as she is better on faster, but she was beaten only a length and three-quarters and it was an effort that suggested she may be up to Group 1 staying standard when she gets her ground.

As a previous winner of the Galtres Stakes at York she certainly appears to enjoy her forays to Britain and, as Weld has already indicated the Gold Cup may be an objective, the 33-1 price has plenty of scope to contract, particularly if she can win the Saval Beg again.

Among the sprinters, Jim Goldie's **Jack Dexter** shouldn't be dismissed in his bid to land a precious Group 1 sprint. He came close on a couple of occasions last season, notably when fourth in the King's Stand at Royal Ascot, beaten less than two lengths.

That was a praiseworthy effort that came on ground too fast for him. He held his form, finishing second in the Champions Sprint before winning a Listed race at Doncaster in November.

It will be a surprise if Jack Dexter doesn't get his ideal testing conditions at some stage

Pale Mimosa (yellow cap) seems likely to have the Ascot Gold Cup on her agenda and can be backed at 33-1

during the season. When he does, he is a highly effective performer.

Alan King is primarily known for his jumping exploits, but he loves to keep his hand in over the summer and he has the exciting *Tiger Cliff* to go to war with. He'll be fresh and well for the start of the Flat season as a jumping career has been temporarily shelved.

Last year with Lady Jane Cecil, Tiger Cliff proved most progressive and landed the Ebor in August after a late thrust from Tom Queally got him home. He is quite high in the handicap, but it would be no surprise if he proves up to Group class, and a race like the Sagaro Stakes early in the season may suit him. He is definitely one to have on your side.

Finally, *York Glory* is a handicapper to follow in sprints. He won a big one last season

ONE TO FOLLOW

Moviesta Had plenty to find on ratings when hot-footing to victory in the King George Stakes at Goodwood in August when his final three splits were superior to every other runner. The wheels came off when last in the Nunthorpe at York but Bryan Smart's sprinter can get back on track.
[Dave Edwards, Topspeed]

when hosing up in the Wokingham and although he didn't win again he probably should have done so at Beverley in the 'Bullet' when Jamie Spencer gave him an awful lot to do and he was only just denied. He is quite high in the handicap now but has plenty of class and if he turned up off topweight somewhere you wouldn't rule him out as he thrives off a fast pace and has a good finishing kick.

From start to finish – dissecting the season to find profitable angles

JAMES PYMAN: HOW TO MAKE A PROFIT THIS SEASON

BEFORE JUNE

The start of the British Flat turf season can be a culture shock for some racing enthusiasts with the traditional curtain-raising Lincoln meeting at Doncaster sandwiched between the Cheltenham Festival and the Grand National.

When it comes to picking the winner of the Lincoln itself, lightly raced four-year-olds are the logical starting place. This century, four-year-olds who had raced fewer than seven times previously are punching well above their weight in valuable British turf 4yo+ handicaps run before June. They are accounting for 8.4 per cent of the winners of such races with a first-prize of at least £20,000, from just 5.1 per cent of the runners.

Six of the last 11 Lincolns have gone to this age group and three of those winners had no more than six previous starts on the clock.

Why unexposed four-year-olds are proving successful stems from them running off handicaps marks reflecting performances as three-year-olds when many of these runners had not reached full maturity. Those who then strengthen over the winter prove to be well handicapped in the spring.

The Brocklesby run over five furlongs is a test of pure speed for precocious juveniles so always ensures the first day of the meeting is an explosive one and typifies two-year-old racing at this time of year.

There are trainers who routinely exploit the fact that variation in physical maturity between the two-year-old population in the earlier months is significant, affording naturally speedy, precious types a brief window of opportunity.

This is something Bill Turner recognises and he has won five of the last 12 runnings of the Brocklesby with his runners showing a £1 level-stake profit of £22 in the race since 2002. You can expect Turner's early two-year-old runners to be fitter and straighter than many of their rivals, and blindly backing his juveniles before June in the previous four seasons shows a £1 level-stake profit £20.16 (23 per cent strike-rate).

Turner is the not alone in liking to hit the ground running with juveniles. Here are four others who boast impressive records in March-April two-year-old races since 2008: Richard Fahey (18 wins from 66 runs, 27%, +£13.23), Jim Bolger (11-38, 29%, +£19.25), Alan Bailey (5-16, 31%, +£14) and David Barron (4-16, 25%, +£17.50).

Much of the focus at this time of year is on the first round of Classics, with the English, Irish and French Guineas staged in May, so the vast majority of Group races restricted to three-year-olds run before June are Classic trials.

A trainer with an impressive recent record in three-year-old Group races below top level at this time of year is Bolger. He places horses expertly and conceivably recognises many of the three-year-olds competing against his horses in the earliest Group races are building towards main targets later in the season, so are not always fully tuned up.

Since 2005 Bolger's record in such races is 13 wins from 62 runs (21%, +£29.99) and he has won the following Classic trials at least once in this period: Ballysax, Craven, Derrinstown, Greenham, Musidora, Tetrarch Stakes and both the 1,000 and 2,000 Guineas Trials at Leopardstown.

Thinking big by making runners from the top stables your first port of call when trying to find Guineas winners is proving a sound policy. A telling stat is that a quarter of all Guineas run in England, Ireland and France this century have gone the way of Aidan O'Brien-trained runners.

O'Brien has won the last 15 Irish Flat trainer titles and collectively his record since 2000 in both English Guineas and the Irish and French equivalents, is 22 wins from 202 runs (11%) for a £1 level-stake profit of £10.89.

The Ballydoyle maestro appears to have a particularly strong hand in the colts department this season with the hugely promising pair of Australia and War

Command likely to appear in a Guineas, either at home or overseas.

Andre Fabre has been champion Flat trainer in France on 24 occasions and his horses are also proving profitable in such races this century with five wins from 27 runs generating £11.15 for every £1 staked. Fabre's smart filly Miss France is understandably considered by bookmakers as the most likely winner of this year's English 1,000 Guineas.

The effect of the draw will create lively discussion when Chester stages its feature meeting in the second week of May. Runners drawn low at this historic, right-handed, oval course enjoy a significant advantage at most race distances.

Chester's draw bias is part of racing folklore and is most pronounced in sprints, particularly those featuring big fields. According to my research, at Chester, a horse berthed against the inside rail in a 5f race

War Command forms part of a particularly strong hand for Aidan O'Brien in the colts division

with 16 runners staged on good ground typically enjoys an advantage equating to about five lengths over the horse drawn in the outside stall.

Interestingly, despite the course's reputation as a draw track, well-berthed runners continue to offer value in shorter-distance races. Since the start of the 2005 season, blindly backing runners drawn in the inside stall in sprint handicaps is showing a £1 level-stake profit of £63.46 (33 wins from 140 runs, 24 per cent strike-rate), and this edge is showing no sign of receding with the strategy generating a profit of £30.50 in the last two seasons.

But Chester is not the only British course with a notable draw bias. At Pontefract, where races at all distances feature at least one bend, inside/low-drawn runners can enjoy an advantage and, across the previous two seasons, handicap runners berthed nearest the inside rail are producing a £1 level-stake profit of £36.53 (26-145, 18%).

At Epsom, runners competing in 6f, 7f and 1m½f contests are almost immediately racing on the turn and this means it can be favourable to be drawn closer to the inside (low) at these race distances. This is reflected by the fact that following runners with the lowest draw number in such races, since the start of the 2009-10 season, is returning a £1 level-stake profit of £39.78 (44-232, 19 per cent).

JUNE TO AUGUST

The draw is less important in Epsom's most famous three races – the Derby, Oaks and Coronation Cup – which are all staged over a mile and a half, and the Derby meeting, which takes place in early June, in some respects marks a turning point in the Flat season.

From June through to August the prevalence of fast ground creates an environment where more horses run to form, so punters who use more scientific methods to pick winners often look forward to the summer months as they can have more confidence in horses performing in line with market expectations.

Chester: home of a much documented draw bias

The Derby, Oaks and Coronation Cup each provide a thorough all-round test. Runners initially race uphill in each of these premier middle-distance races. This potentially increases the cost of not settling and was underlined last season when 5-4 favourite Dawn Approach pulled ridiculously hard and unsurprisingly was beaten with three furlongs still left to run.

To win any of these Group 1s a horse needs an abundance of class and stamina, although Epsom's many idiosyncrasies mean that equally speed, balance and temperament are other desirable traits.

Royal Ascot follows hot on the heels of the Epsom Classics, with a coming together of equine talent from all over the world taking place in the middle of June.

Horses trained outside of Britain and Ireland are continually underrated at Royal Ascot and this might be a consequence of the fact many punters are more comfortable in backing horses they are familiar with and so don't give overseas runners the level of respect they often deserve.

In the Group 1 King's Stand run on the first day over the minimum distance of five furlongs, sprinters trained outside of Britain and Ireland are showing a £1 level-stake profit of £55.75 this century (7-39, 18%) and five of the last six overseas winners were stabled in Australia or Hong Kong. Concentrating on sprinters from outside of Europe in this test of speed can continue to reap rewards.

Wesley Ward, who is based in California, routinely sends his fastest two-year-olds to Royal Ascot and they have achieved finishing positions of 1100470021 (+£36.50) in races run over five furlongs.

However, Ward is planning on broadening his horizons at the meeting this season with his three-year-old No Nay Never, who was a decisive winner of the Norfolk Stakes at the meeting last year, being trained with a view to peaking in the mile Group 1 St James's

Palace Stakes. Ward considers No Nay Never the most talented horse he has trained.

The recent record of fancied runners trained in the rest of Europe in 1m-plus Group races at the meeting is also worth flagging. Since 2007, such runners who started no bigger than 8-1 are showing a £1 level-stake profit of £4.25, while five of the 12 who returned SPs of 4-1 or shorter hit the target (+£6.25).

Jockey bookings can carry greater significance at the height of summer when there is so much Flat racing that competition between owners for the services of the best riders is fierce. Last season, Saturday July 13 was a particularly congested day with six meetings and 40 races run in Britain.

At this time of year, an apprentice jockey with a sizeable claim who is good value for their allowance can make a big impact. Demand for the services of established top riders is high, so when connections of a horse who is strongly fancied miss out on bagging their first-choice jockey they will often favour booking a promising apprentice over signing up a journeyman.

It could also be argued that apprentices are inherently more likely to be successful in sprints which are typically a less thorough examination of riding ability as jockeys are often instructed to get their mount from A to B as fast as possible in a straight line.

Since 2008 had you backed every runner sent off at 12-1 or shorter in a British sprint

handicap run in June, July and August worth at least £5,000 to the winner who was ridden by an apprentice claiming at least a 5lb allowance you would have made a level-stake profit of £119.54 (94-601, 16%).

I am looking forward to rolling out the system this summer and we should be keeping our eyes peeled for promising apprentices who are good value for their allowances. You never know, you may discover the next Jason Hart or Oisin Murphy.

The first nurseries are run in July and getting an edge in these handicaps restricted to two-year-olds boils down to finding horses who are favourably treated. There are worse places to start this search than the higher reaches of the handicap because the maxim

of backing topweights in nurseries is based on fact.

Since 2008, around one in seven nursery winners were topweights which is considerably more than you might have expected given that one in every 12 nursery runners in this period shouldered bigger burdens than all of their rivals.

Any edge in blindly backing nursery topweights dried up a long time ago, but the recent performance of highest-rated runners towards the top of the market in 5f nurseries is compelling enough to make juveniles with this profile of interest. Since 2008, topweights in these races who were 7-1 or shorter have returned a £1 level-stake profit of £55.86 (65 wins from 209 bets).

The apprentice angle: it can pay to follow up-and-coming riders, like Oisin Murphy, winner of last season's Ayr Gold Cup with Highland Colori

ONE TO FOLLOW

Montefeltro A Darley castoff, he was snapped up for just 10,000gns by Brian Ellison last August and has since made giant strides. He completed a sparkling hat-trick in the Irish Cesarewitch at the Curragh in October and this low-mileage six-year-old is effective between 1m4f and 2m. He could graduate to Group company. *[Dave Edwards, Topspeed]*

Another approach to consider is following nursery runners from stables who like to target these two-year-old handicaps. Four trainers who fit the bill are Sir Mark Prescott, Saeed Bin Suroor, Charlie Hills and James Tate.

A couple of valuable nurseries feature among an eclectic mix of racing staged across five days at Glorious Goodwood. The meeting is a battleground between the Classic generation and older horses and takes place at a juncture in the calendar when weight-for-age (wfa) allowances that three-year-olds receive can tip the balance in their favour.

This century, the Classic generation are accounting for 31 per cent of the winners of wfa races at Glorious Goodwood from a 21 per cent share of the runners.

Nine of the 14 runnings of the Group 1 Sussex Stakes staged over a mile in this period have gone to three-year-olds and, fancied members of the Classic generation competing in wfa Group races are generally offering value at the meeting in this period, with the record of those sent off at 7-2 or shorter an alluring 33 wins from 91 runs (36%) for a £1 level-stake profit of £16.28.

The Ebor meeting at York is the final big

gathering of the summer and the Knavesmire has a reputation as a place where course specialists are worth following. In recent seasons, had you heeded this advice by concentrating on horses with proven course form in races run over distances between 7f and 1m1f at York you would have been in clover.

The record of course winners at these distances since 2009 is 16 wins from 85 runs (19 per cent strike-rate) for a £1 level-stake profit of £60.50, which compares favourably to the eight per cent strike-rate of runners without a course win in such races.

Glorious Goodwood, where three-year-olds claiming a weight for age allowance have been doing a good job for punters

Dave Martin

SEPTEMBER ONWARDS

The arrival of September is often the time to get seriously interested in runners in Britain wearing the royal blue silks of Godolphin.

We are accustomed to this mega stable finishing the season strongly, and this is reflected by their strike-rates in British Flat races run at different times of the year. Since 2008, they boast a 22 per cent strike-rate from September onwards, which is three per cent better than in races from January through to August.

Breaking down into more detail Godolphin's record with such runners in the last four calendar months of the year reveals a number of interesting angles.

In maidens they show a £1 level-stake profit of £51.69 (177-707, 25%). Following Godolphin in non-two-year-old Listed races also bears fruit (29-141, 21%, +£26.38), while their handicap runners with ratings of 95 or lower in open-age races yields a £1 level-stake profit of £26.45 (44-226, 19%).

Although at Group level Godolphin runners return an overall £1 level-stake loss (-£61), they have regularly enjoyed Group 1 success in the autumn in recent years and last season, the Saeed Bin Suroor-trained Farhh gave the outfit a first win at Ascot's October Champions Day fixture when displaying class and determination to land the Champion Stakes.

Godolphin's record this century in the St Leger is excellent. Their horses have achieved finishing positions of 6411266081064 (+£32) in the final British Classic of the season, which is run at Doncaster in September.

There are often many more suitable opportunities for horses who want softer ground at this stage of the season and sire stats can be useful in determining runners' going preferences as there are stallions who produce disproportionately high numbers of soft-ground winners.

A good example would be progeny of the Pivotal sireline. Most of the stallion's best offspring are fully effective on an easy surface – Farrh, Sariska, Captain Rio, Immortal Verse and Somnus are Group 1 winners on going slower than good – and many of Pivotal's progeny who have gone on to become successful sires in their own right are also producing horses favoured by cut in the ground.

The big end-of-season two-year-old races sort out the final pecking order in the juvenile division and we can expect O'Brien to have a strong presence in these races this season given one in five September-onwards two-year-old races in Britain and Ireland with Group 1 or 2 status since 2000 have gone the way of his runners.

However, blindly supporting these runners results in a £1 level-stake loss of £41.47 and suggests the vast majority are overbet. Top two-year-olds from one of O'Brien's staunch rivals in Ireland seemingly offer a better chance of a positive return. Had you put a pound on each of Bolger's runners in two-year-old Group 1 races staged in Britain and Ireland from September onwards this century you would have enjoyed a profit of £23.32.

Virtually every Saturday through the closing months of the turf season features at least one big handicap. Lots of punters love the challenge of unravelling these competitive contests so they invariably generate a lot of betting interest. They are popular with trainers, too, as the prize-money on offer is sufficient enough for these races to be major targets for some stables.

A trainer who is routinely enjoying success in these races is John Gosden. This century, this Newmarket stable's record in September-onwards British Flat turf handicaps worth at least £20,000 to the winner is a noteworthy nine wins from 52 runs (17 per cent strike-rate) for a £1 level-stake profit of £36. In this period Gosden has won two Cambridgeshires and two November Handicaps.

Another trainer operating from British Flat racing's headquarters with a healthy record at this time of year in handicaps of this value is David Simcock, who has hit the target four times from 26 runs (15%, +£41.50).

otepool.com

TREBLE THE ODDS!

when you get a single winner in your Lucky15!

It's in the breeding – names to look for from a bloodstock perspective

Balansiya (Dermot Weld)
3 b f Shamardal-Baliyana

This filly looked full of potential when sauntering to a seven-length win on her debut in a 7f maiden at Leopardstown at the backend of last season. She raced prominently before readily putting the race to bed when asked for her effort entering the straight and the winning distance could have been bigger.

Balansiya holds an entry in the 1,000 Guineas and her pedigree suggests the mile will be well within her compass. The first foal out of the Group 3-winning miler Baliyana, she descends from the family of Balakheri, winner of the King Edward VII Stakes for Sir Michael Stoute, and Prix du Jockey Club hero Bering.

I'm Yours (Dermot Weld)
3 b f Invincible Spirit-Rebelline

A €420,000 yearling, I'm Yours was unlucky not to win on her debut last year but made amends at the second time of asking when scoring in good style at Leopardstown. A Guineas trial looks the likely starting point this season before a crack at the Irish 1,000 Guineas.

A well-made daughter of Invincible Spirit, I'm Yours should thrive at a mile and could potentially stay a mile and a half, being a daughter of Tattersalls Gold Cup winner Rebelline, the dam of useful bumper performer Pure Science, and descending from the family of Sir Michael Stoute's useful middle-distance runner Telescope and Dubai World Cup winner Moon Ballad.

My Titania (John Oxx)
3 ch f Sea The Stars-Fairy Of The Night

Entered the record books when winning the Group 3 CL Weld Stakes at the Curragh, becoming a first stakes winner for her sire Sea The Stars.

After travelling powerfully My Titania showed a willing attitude to repel the strong challenge of Chicago Girl, the pair pulling five and a half lengths clear of the third. She looks more than capable of providing her sire with a first Classic success in either the 1,000 Guineas or Oaks. She should stay a mile and a half, coming from a family that includes Dress Rehearsal, who was a Grade 3 winner at the trip for William Mott in the US.

Patentar (Marco Botti)
3 b c Teofilo-Poppets Sweetlove

Ready winner of a 7f York maiden last year. The form of that race doesn't look particularly strong, but Marco Botti has been bullish about the colt's prospects for this season and connections are more than hopeful he can develop into a stakes horse.

By Teofilo, a sire capable of producing stock that perform at either ends of the distance spectrum, Patentar's pedigree suggests he'll be best suited by a mile. Out of a winning miler, he is a half-brother to the 5f winner Lady Poppy and is related to top-class sprinter Overdose.

Scotland (Andrew Balding)
3 b c Monsun-Sqillo

Andrew Balding's juveniles often improve for

their initial outing as was the case with Scotland. An encouraging third on his debut, he was the easy winner of an Epsom conditions race, over an extended mile, on his second start, beating dual winner Day Of Conquest in the process.

The unfurnished colt will surely improve at three and for a step up in trip. Although perhaps short of being top class, Scotland should develop into a black-type performer, hailing from a family that includes the exceptional middle-distance runner Shirocco, who is also by Monsun.

Seagull Star (William Haggas)
3 b c Sea The Stars-Dash To The Top

An unexpected but easy winner of a Newmarket maiden last season, a race in which Johann Strauss finished fourth before coming second in the Racing Post Trophy.

Seagull Star holds a Derby entry and looks a live each-way candidate for Epsom's showpiece at 50-1. Although not devoid of speed, Seagull Star should stay – he is out of the Montjeu mare Dash To The Top, who won over a mile at two before landing a Listed race at a mile and a quarter at three.

Sir Walter Scott (Luca Cumani)
4 b c Galileo-Flaming Sea

This lightly raced four-year-old ran once last year, when finishing a never nearer second, after travelling well, in a Listed race at the Curragh in October over 1m4f. Now in the care of Luca Cumani, this colt has the potential to develop into a useful stayer this year. He has the pedigree to mix it at a higher level, being a three-parts brother to Irish Derby winner Frozen Fire, out of a winning half-sister to German Oaks winner Flamingo Road.

MAIDENS

Elusive Guest (George Margarson)
3 b c Elusive City-Mansoura

Elusive Guest is held in high regard by his trainer George Margarson, as you'd expect for a horse who cost €190,000 at Arqana as a yearling. He shaped with promise on his only start last year, travelling well before running green and failing to see out the mile trip in a Windsor maiden. There is plenty of stamina on the female side of his pedigree, but Elusive Guest will be best suited by a mile this year.

King's Land (Saeed Bin Suroor)
3 b/br c New Approach-Kazzia

Very green on his only start in a Newmarket maiden last year, but once the penny dropped he made eyecatching late headway to finish third of 18 runners. Entered in the Derby, King's Land has the pedigree to mix it on the biggest stage, being a son of Derby hero New Approach and Kazzia, who landed the 1,000 Guineas before capturing the Oaks. Expect this horse to win his maiden before going on to much bigger things.

Shama (Sir Michael Stoute)
3 b f Danehill Dancer-Shamadara

A gift from the Aga Khan to the Queen, Shama made a pleasing debut last year when finishing a never-nearer third in a Kempton maiden. He needed every inch of the mile trip and should improve dramatically for a step up to middle distances this year.

Shama is closely related to Shamanova, who landed a 1m7f Listed race for Alain de Royer-Dupre, and is out of Shamadara, a Group 2 winner at 1m4f who finished second in the Irish Oaks.

Strength of the big-race overseas challenge should not be underestimated

EVEN the most committed xenophobe would be well advised these days to have a quick glance at the international form book if they fancy a bet on Europe's major stages this summer. With Royal Ascot leading the way, the welcome appearance of horses trained outside Europe has become a major feature of the summer campaign.

Since the trailblazer Choisir blasted through the royal meeting with his memorable sprint double in 2003, Royal Ascot (and occasionally elsewhere) has been graced by a steady stream of high-profile visitors. They don't all win, of course – for every Black Caviar there's an Animal Kingdom – but win or lose they all add an intriguing extra nuance to the occasion.

At this early stage, before major carnivals in Dubai, Sydney and Singapore, it is tricky to predict any long-range visitors with any confidence. However, Ascot's head of communications and international racing Nick Smith is optimistic about attracting several marquee names – headed by Emirates Melbourne Cup winner Fiorente, who represents Australia's first lady of racing, Gai Waterhouse.

"Initial indications on the international front for Royal Ascot are very positive," reports Smith. "Fiorente is our number-one target – a Melbourne Cup winner for Gai in the Gold Cup at Royal Ascot would be the Animal Kingdom/Black Caviar story for us. Gai has made little secret of her preference to go for it but it is a big group of owners and they have the Sydney spring to think of too.

"The likes of Zoustar and Red Tracer could head Chris Waller's potential team, while the five-furlong sprinters in Australia are emerging now with recent winners Snitzerland and Lankan Rupee obviously high on the list.

"New Zealand's top horse It's A Dundeel, is now in the ownership of John Messara and he has indicated that Royal Ascot could be on the cards after the all-important new Championships meeting at Randwick in April."

Looking further afield, there could be more than one US representative for the St James's Palace Stakes, with last year's Norfolk Stakes winner No Nay Never and, more speculatively, Bobby's Kitten. Smith adds: "Wesley Ward tells me he has the best team of two-year-olds he has had at home and there is increasing interest from other American trainers in sending juveniles, including from Todd Pletcher. I'm also talking to Tom Proctor, who has quite a number of interesting turf horses."

Although Japan is always a tough ask, top three-year-old Asia Express is another potentially exotic contender for the St James's Palace Stakes, as Smith explains.

"Asia Express has emerged as our top target from Japan and connections of Bande are interested in the Gold Cup. There is always the possibility that a three-year-old middle-distance horse could emerge as a King George contender later in the year but attracting their top middle-distance horses remains difficult as they have such a lucrative programme at home running alongside our midsummer.

"Horses like Gold Ship, Gentildonna and Kizuna are all set at this stage for campaigns around Dubai and the Arc, where the prize-money is most compelling."

Looking elsewhere, Hong Kong has enjoyed sprint success with Cape Of Good Hope and Little Bridge. Smith reports: "The Hong Kong sprinters look very strong again and I'll be keeping in contact with the connections of Lucky Nine, Amber Sky and Sterling City, while Mike de Kock will be stabling a lot of horses in Newmarket this year."

Here are ten horses from outside Europe who could hit the headlines if racing in Britain this season:

AMBER SKY Ricky Yiu (Hong Kong)
4g Exceed And Excel - Truly Wicked

Despite the reputation of Hong Kong sprinters, Little Bridge somehow slipped under the radar to some extent when winning the King's Stand two years ago. Blazingly fast, Amber Sky is the rising star of the scene, a straight track specialist who won his sixth race down the Sha Tin's 5f chute in the Group 1 Centenary Sprint Cup in January. Likely to go to the Al Quoz Sprint in Dubai before Royal Ascot comes into view, with the King's Stand an obvious target.

ROYAL ASCOT WINNERS TRAINED OUTSIDE EUROPE

2003	**Choisir, right** (King's Stand, Paul Perry AUS)
	Choisir (Golden Jubilee Paul Perry AUS)
2005	**Cape Of Good Hope** (Golden Jubilee David Oughton HK)
2006	**Takeover Target** (King's Stand Joe Janiak AUS)
2007	**Miss Andretti** (King's Stand Lee Freedman AUS)
2009	**Scenic Blast** (King's Stand Danny Morton AUS)
	Strike The Tiger (Windsor Castle Wesley Ward USA)
	Jealous Again (Queen Mary Wesley Ward USA)
2012	**Little Bridge** (King's Stand Danny Shum HK)
	Black Caviar (Diamond Jubilee Peter Moody AUS)
2013	**No Nay Never** (Norfolk Wesley Ward USA)

ASIA EXPRESS Takahisa Tezuka (Japan)
3c Henny Hughes - Running Bobcat

Japan's two-year-old champion after winning the Asahi Hai Futurity, the only Grade 1 event for juvenile colts on the JRA circuit, at Nakayama in December – with Ryan Moore in the saddle. Now looking at the St James's Palace Stakes, according to Nick Smith, who says: "Our niche appears to be developing as the place for three-year-olds, with the St James's Palace Stakes seen as a crucial breeding race. Asia Express is probably the number one and most likely target in Japan at the moment – they don't see him as a Derby horse after either the Japanese Guineas or NHK Mile Cup."

Melbourne Cup winner Fiorente (centre) could return to Britain this summer for a crack at the Ascot Gold Cup

BOBBY'S KITTEN Chad Brown (USA)
3c Kitten's Joy - Celestial Woods

A more speculative sort for the St James's Palace but well on the Ascot radar and worthy of serious notice if he makes the trip – which looks distinctly possible, given his owner Ken Ramsey is an anglophile who told me that having a winner at the royal meeting is on his 'bucket list'.

As his name suggests, Bobby's Kitten is by Ramsey's excellent stallion Kitten's Joy – already an influence in US turf lines – and he looked a potential superstar on the grass before being sent off favourite for the Breeders' Cup Juvenile Turf, where he was third behind Outstrip and Giovanni Boldini.

Ramsey was aghast at jockey Javier Castellano's efforts that day as he let the horse go off at a ridiculous gallop, rendering him vulnerable in the stretch. A fair effort in the circumstances and remember that Lasix was banned in that race.

FIORENTE Gai Waterhouse (Australia)
6h Monsun - Desert Bloom

High-class performer in Britain, winning soft-ground Princess of Wales's Stakes for Sir Michael Stoute before sale to Australian connections, for whom he repaid hefty purchase price in spades with trainer Gai Waterhouse's first victory in the Melbourne Cup last November.

Renowned for his strong finishing kick these days, he has also won Group races over much shorter trips (as short as a mile) and could stay at home to be freshened up for the Cox Plate. However, connections appear keen for a trip to Royal Ascot, where the Gold Cup looks the most enticing option – "he's had his inoculations, it's definitely on the agenda," says Waterhouse, who was bullish after a sparkling victory at the beginning of March in the Australian Cup at Flemington.

Next up is the prestigious Queen Elizabeth Stakes at the new Sydney Championships meeting in April. "He's a six-year-old but he's only just reaching his peak," adds Waterhouse. "He's an absolutely super horse."

IT'S A DUNDEEL Murray Baker (New Zealand)
4c High Chaparral - Stareel

New Zealand's No.1 racehorse is a five-time Group 1 winner whose class shone out in a six-length victory last April in Australasia's foremost Classic, the AJC Australian Derby at Randwick in Sydney, where he was winning his third Group 1 in a month.

He touched off the much-vaunted Coolmore mare Atlantic Jewel in the Underwood Stakes at Caulfield at the start of a four-year-old campaign focusing on a return to Randwick for the inaugural Championships meeting in April, after which Royal Ascot beckons with the Queen Anne or Prince of Wales's Stakes on the agenda.

"He's definitely come back a stronger horse – it's scary how much he has improved," says jockey James McDonald.

LANKAN RUPEE Mick Price (Australia)
4g Redoute's Choice - Estelle Collection

The new star of the Australian sprinting scene who confirmed his rise to the top with a scintillating victory over a top-class field in the prestigious Newmarket Handicap at Flemington in March to complete a five-timer (six out of seven since being gelded) a fortnight after his first Group 1 success in the Oakleigh Plate. "I haven't had a horse quicken like that," said jockey Chad Schofield after a totally dominant display. Sure to be on the Royal Ascot radar, although the TJ Smith Stakes on April 12 at the Championships in Sydney will come first.

NO NAY NEVER Wesley Ward (USA)
3c Scat Daddy - Cat's Eye Witness

Lit up Royal Ascot last year with his sensational Norfolk Stakes victory before completing an unbeaten hat-trick in the Group 1 Prix Morny at Deauville in August. Although defeat at odds of 2-5 on his seasonal debut at Gulfstream Park in Florida on March 1 might not have been what the doctor ordered, it should perhaps be remembered that he had never before run on conventional dirt, having made his career debut last year on the Polytrack at Keeneland.

A return to Europe is still on the agenda, but Wesley Ward will have some thinking to do about his target as his undoubted speed suggests the mile of the St James's Palace Stakes could be a stretch, which brings the Jersey (and other races) into the equation.

SHEA SHEA Mike de Kock (South Africa)
6g National Emblem - Yankee Clipper

Dual Grade 1 winner in native South Africa, won the Al Quoz Sprint in Dubai and is unlucky not to have won a Group 1 in Europe already after narrow defeats in the King's

Stand (has beaten the winner Sole Power on each of five other meetings) and Nunthorpe. Looked as good as ever with a second straight victory in the Group 3 Meydan Sprint on Super Saturday. Has twice broken 5f track record at Meydan and looked to be in pole position to repeat last year's World Cup night win before returning to Europe.

VERCINGETORIX Mike de Kock (South Africa)
4c Silvano - National Vixen

Winner of the Grade 1 Daily News 2000 at home in South Africa, where he was a champion three-year-old, he extended his unbeaten sequence to six career starts when drawing away for his second top-level victory in the Jebel Hatta, the principal trial for the Dubai Duty Free at Meydan on Super Saturday. Still difficult to assess the merit of his form (runner-up Vancouverite is an unexposed French Group 2 winner) and he was favoured by the way the race panned out

but likely to be a major player in the De Kock European squad.

ZOUSTAR Chris Waller (Australia)
3c Northern Meteor - Zouzou

Described as the next big thing by Sydney's champion trainer Chris Waller, Australia's top three-year-old sprinter is set to spend the summer in Britain after the sale of a significant share to Sheikh Fahad.

Twice a Group 1 winner at home, including a dominant performance in the Coolmore Stud Stakes over 6f, Zoustar will bid to add to his tally in Sydney before being shipped to Europe, where the Diamond Jubilee offers an early target.

"This colt represents everything that is great about Australian horses," says Sheikh Fahad. "He's strong, masculine and incredibly fast and I'm very excited about the prospects of him racing in Europe and ultimately retiring to stud."

No Nay Never won last season's Norfolk Stakes and is set for a return to Royal Ascot this season

Treve the big gun in France but plenty of new names coming through

J**OHN OXX was apt to say that choosing his favourite Sea The Stars race was like choosing among his children.**

That French racing was dominated by the children of Alec Head in 2013 is undeniable and, while it might seem invidious to place the achievements of Criquette Head-Maarek's *Treve* over brother Freddy's magnificent campaign with Moonlight Cloud, it will be last season's scintillating Arc winner who carries the family banner into 2014.

Unbeaten and largely unchallenged to date, Treve will have the comfort of starting out her season on level terms against her fellow elders, with Head-Maarek highlighting the Prix Ganay and the Prince of Wales's Stakes as her likely targets for the first half of the season.

The real test will come after a summer break when, if all goes to plan, Treve will return to Longchamp to defend her all-age crowns in the Prix Vermeille and the Prix de l'Arc de Triomphe.

One of the defining images of last season's post-Arc ceremonies was of Head-Maarek sharing a horse-drawn carriage with Sheikh Joaan Al Thani and his two sons.

His Al Shaqab racing operation has become synonymous with high-profile purchases of proven talent. But this year Al Shaqab can look forward to the fruits of its first heavyweight entry into the yearling market two years ago.

As early as last summer, retained jockey Frankie Dettori pointed to the massive untapped potential among Sheikh Joaan's two-year-olds. A host of middle distance propects are spread across the stables of Alain de Royer-Dupre, Mikel Delzangles and Francis Graffard among others, most of whose development at two was confined to the training gallops of Chantilly.

Royer-Dupre has nine three-year-olds in training for Sheikh Joaan, only one of whom raced last year. And a casual glance at the pedigrees etched onto stable doors at his yard on the Chemin des Aigles hints at enormous potential.

To name just three, Royer-Dupre can gaze out at *Al Jassassiyah*, who is a sister to Oaks heroine Was (and thus a half-sibling of the €5,000,000gns filly who broke the European sales record last October at Tattersalls); 2012 Arqana top lot *Edkhan*, a son of Sea The Stars out of Royer-Dupre's Grand Prix Jean Romanet winner Alpine Rose; and another product of the 2009 Arc winner's first crop, *Jarada*, a filly out of Dylan Thomas's half sister Love To Dance.

Perhaps among those three there is a readymade replacement for last season's Irish Oaks winner Chicquita, now being primed by Aidan O'Brien to capitalise on the painstaking groundwork laid by Royer-Dupre.

Not that life is likely to be any less interesting in the yard for which the trainer is also responsible up the road at Aiglemont, where a sub-standard 2013 has resulted the Aga Khan recalling the former prodigal son

SCOTT BURTON: VIEW FROM FRANCE

Christophe Soumillon as first jockey.

Soumillon is headline news wherever he goes and it is likely that one of the more forseeable narratives to the season will be his progress, as well as that of the man he replaced.

Christophe Lemaire still has much to offer and, as well as riding many of the Sheikh Mohammed Al Thani horses like *Flotilla*, the 34-year-old is likely to become a very in-demand freelance.

With his excellent strike-rate in Britain, particularly at Newmarket, Lemaire could conceivably evolve into a more frequent visitor, especially following the retirement of Johnny Murtagh.

Gerard Augustin-Normand's influence on French racing may not reach back nearly as far as that of the Aga Khan and his family but 2014 could also be a pivotal year for the financier.

Augustin-Normand first made a splash in 2009 with Le Havre, who followed up a second place in the Poule d'Essai by going one better in the Prix du Jockey Club.

Le Havre's first crop are three-year-olds this season and Augustin-Normand has supported the stallion with plenty of expensively-purchased mares.

Unbeaten filly *La Hoguette* looked the best offspring of Le Havre to race in Augustin-Norman's cream and mauve silks at two but she won't be the owner's only Classic hope this spring.

Flotilla: Breeders' Cup winner can find more success this season under Christophe Lemaire

As a half-brother to St James's Palace winner Most Improved, *Ectot* was always going to attract attention if he showed some ability. With a Group 1 success to his name in the Criterium International, Ectot plainly has plenty of that and Elie Lellouche will aim the son of Hurricane Run at the Prix de Fontainebleau as a dress rehearsal for the French Guineas.

Counter to some recent seasons, French trainers managed to land four of the five Group 1 juvenile prizes on offer in 2013, with only American interloper No Nay Never spoiling the clean sweep in the Prix Morny.

Alongside Ectot, Saint-Cloud's other end of season highlight went to the Rouget-trained *Prince Gibraltar*. In common with many of his predecessors, Prince Gibraltar will need to prove he handles a sounder surface than encountered on that occasion if he is to progress into a genuine contender for the Prix du Jockey Club.

The ground was also pretty testing a month earlier on Arc day but, there is little suggestion that either *Karakontie* or *Indonesienne* – winners of the Prix Jean-Luc Lagardere and the Prix Marcel Boussac – will require such conditions to excel this term.

Indonesienne's win over the classy Lesstalk In Paris owed plenty to her tenacity, with the pair fighting out a protracted duel in the Longchamp straight. In fact, the conclusion which might be inferred both from that run and her second to Qipco 1,000 Guineas favourite Miss France, is that Indonesienne is going to need further than a mile in time if she is to build on her Boussac win.

Karakontie showed he handles all types of ground in a campaign which demonstrated improvement in each of his four starts. Jonathan Pease started him off in the shallow waters of Compiegne, where he had to overcome none other than Ectot to shed his maiden.

On breeding the son of Bernstein might be expected to excel at around the 1m2½f of the Jockey Club but, as he demonstrated in his Group 3 prep race for the Lagardere, Karakontie isn't short of pace.

His principal victim in the Lagardere was the Spanish-trained Noozhoh Canarias, the choice that day of none other than Soumillon. The ground hindered his chances at Longchamp and trainer Enrique Leon Penate is now eyeing an audacious challenge for the Qipco 2,000 Guineas at Newmarket.

While Noozhoh Canarias could provide Spain with their most high-profile international runner since Equiano shocked Royal Ascot in 2008 for Mauricio Delcher-Sanchez, German trainers have proved rather more regular diners at Europe's top table in recent seasons.

Peter Schiergen has already scaled the summit once with Danedream and, in the shape of the 2013 Deutches Derby hero *Lucky Speed*, the Cologne-based trainer could have another horse capable of challenging for higher honours beyond his own frontier.

SOMETIMES WE ALL NEED A REMINDER

With the **NEW** Horse Tracker feature on the Racing Post iPad app you can follow, make notes on and receive alerts for horses that catch your eye.

Free 30-day trial. On the app store now.

Casting the net far and wide to find a dozen to back throughout the year

I ALWAYS find making a list of horses to follow a bit of a headache. You can feel a bit silly when you have missed something obvious but, on the other hand, if it's obvious you don't need me or anyone else to tell you.

Everyone is clearly looking forward to seeing what Kingman, Australia and Kingston Hill can do this term but, having played it too safe and paid for it by putting Sprinter Sacre in the Guide to the Jumps, I've decided to be a little more adventurous this time.

Some of those below will hopefully develop into Classic contenders – I'm pretty keen on the John Oxx Filly My Titania – while others will just be handicappers.

Let's hope they show us enough to make us some money by backing them throughout the season.

BETIMES John Gosden

This New Approach half-sister to several winners was one of several horses given experience by John Gosden in a far busier December than usual, and she made some impact on her debut. Always travelling well in a 7f maiden on Lingfield's Polytrack, she was never going to do anything other than win easily and scooted clear by four lengths from a Mark Johnston-trained runner who was awarded a mark of 76 after winning two starts later. Where she goes is open to question, as while that race was at 7f and she got it easily, most of her siblings are sprint winners (including the useful Aahayson), and rider Rab Havlin said she would have had no trouble going back in trip.

CARLO BUGATTI Aidan O'Brien

There are obviously stacks of Aidan O'Brien-trained three-year-olds to choose from and

Carlo Bugatti (right): could develop into a big player over middle distances

you don't really need to be told about Australia, who heads the market for the Derby and is right up there for the Guineas. Carlo Bugatti represents the brilliant Montjeu, who sadly died in 2012, and has the potential to develop into a top 1m4f performer. He ran only once last season, defying a lack of experience and the worst of the draw to edge out a Dermot Weld-trained favourite with the pair well clear. Stablemate Buonarroti was fourth, some nine lengths adrift, and won a maiden by eight lengths next time before finishing fifth in the Racing Post Trophy. All in all, it was a fine first effort and there has to be more to come. Expect him to go for at least one of the Derby trials.

LAT HAWILL Marco Botti

Having fetched just 10,000gns in October 2012, this son of Invincible Spirit had obviously shown plenty as just six months later he went for a whopping 230,000gns to Qatar Racing. The owners had to wait a further six months to find out whether that was money well spent and the signs are good giving Lat Hawill showed a tidy change of gear to win a Newcastle maiden by an ever-widening eight lengths. He's a half-brother to 2m winner Chocala, but clearly has plenty of speed, so it will be interesting to see what the plans are.

LEADING LIGHT Aidan O'Brien

Last year's St Leger winner had many pundits thinking he could play a big part in the Prix de l'Arc de Triomphe but it was a red-hot contest and I wouldn't read too much into a heavy defeat. Staying is this colt's game, as he had already proved when a game winner of the Queen's Vase, a race the previous year's winner Estimate took before following up in the Gold Cup itself 12 months on. Leading Light is already favourite to do the same and the staying division, in need of another star, has probably found one.

MARVELLOUS Aidan O'Brien

Lovely pedigree, being by Galileo out of a Cherry Hinton-winning full sister to Giants Causeway and, having been called a "nice filly for next year" by trainer Aidan O'Brien, it will be disappointing if she doesn't develop into a high-class performer. Had only one run last season in a competitive 15-runner maiden at Navan, where she defied the widest draw and a market drift to win by half a length. The form is probably not great, but Marvellous was so green she had to be ridden along for almost three-quarters of the race, yet she responded gamely and ran arrow-straight to the line. She wasn't flashy, but you had to love that attitude and if she improves you know she's going to dig deep for you.

MUTASHADED Roger Varian

Roger Varian clearly holds this lightly raced colt in high regard as following a win off just 79 in a Sandown handicap in May, he was thrown into the Group 2 King Edward VII Stakes at Royal Ascot just a month later. Despite being the lowest-rated runner in the race by a minimum of 7lb, he went off a well supported 11-2 second favourite before finishing third, after which his trainer said he

was disappointed he hadn't won. He also said the horse had a bright future, so it will be interesting to see what happens this year as he hasn't run since.

MY PAINTER Charlie Hill

This one won't be winning any Classics but Charlie Hills's three-year-old looks to be on a very tasty mark based on her desperately unlucky second at Chester at the end of August. That day she was slow to start and received a bump and then stumbled on the bend after a furlong and completely lost her place. Chester is not a course at which you can expect to find trouble and win and she did really well to stay on for third even though the front two had long gone. She wasn't so good when chasing too strong a pace next time, but that got her qualified for handicaps and I'll be staggered if she is not much better than an opening mark of 72.

MY TITANIA John Oxx

If Sea The Stars was going to make an impact as a sire it was always likely he would do so with three-year-olds rather than juveniles and this filly, with the same connections as her sire, is top of my list of those likely to shine for him. Entered in the 1,000 Guineas and Oaks, she was given a very similar first season as her sire, having run second in her maiden, won one afterwards and then took the fillies' Group 3 on the same card that Sea The Stars closed his campaign on by winning the Beresford. Like her old man she showed a good turn of foot that day only to idle close home and the half-length winning margin over Chicago Girl (pair five and a half lengths clear) was misleading. With normal improvement she's a Classic contender.

OUR OBSESSION William Haggas

This Shamardal filly has had her problems as she has been restricted to just two starts on each of her first two seasons to race, but career Racing Post Ratings of 67-85-96-108 tell you she is very much going the right way. A soft-ground winner at two, her runs last year came on fast ground at York, but she

clearly had no problem with it as she won both, hacking up off 84 in a handicap in July and then winning winning the Listed Galtres Stakes as a well-backed 3-1 favourite. Connections believe she will be even better as a four-year-old, so let's hope we see more of her this term.

SUMMER SCHOOL Mark Johnston

Mark Johnston is another trainer who bloods plenty of his better horses on the all-weather over the winter and he has a potentially very decent older filly on his hands in Summer School, who has a lovely fast-ground pedigree. She only made her three-year-old debut in December having reportedly had a couple of setbacks but, sent off at odds-on, she sauntered clear in a 1m4f Wolverhampton maiden and had the rest strung out as though it was a jumps race. The form is probably still nothing special, but she appeared to do it at half-pace, so she's worth keeping on side.

TIZLOVE REGARDLESS Mark Johnston

A slow starter for Mark Johnston, this son of Breeders' Cup Classic winner Tiznow started his career in September but needed six starts to get off the mark and eventually did so in lowly 1m handicap off a mark of 58 at Lingfield in February. He followed up raised to 1m2f three days later and this big, scopey horse is just the type to keep on improving and run up a sequence.

TRUE STORY Saeed Bin Suroor

Entered in the 2,000 Guineas and Derby, this son of Manduro was very green as a two-year-old, but his form has worked out remarkably well. He was actually favoured in the market when second to stablemate Outstrip at Newmarket in June, but defeat by one and a half lengths to a subsequent Champagne Stakes and Breeders' Cup winner was no mean first effort. Next time he was a ridiculously easy winner of his maiden on the same course despite still running green. The second, third and fifth are now rated 99, 97 and 96, so with more to come True Story could develop into a major force for Godolphin.

Retirement Plan Unraced as a juvenile and almost unsighted on his debut he showed he had learned plenty when breaking the ice at Doncaster in June. Lady Cecil's colt was a convincing winner of a Goodwood handicap seven weeks later and the Warren Place colt surely has a lot more to offer. [*Dave Edwards, Topspeed*]

Our Obsession: has won three of her four starts and is expected to improve this season at four

What you need to know if you want to win big in the latest Ten to Follow

SPRING is with us, the Flat season is kicking into gear and so is the Ten to Follow competition. It starts on May 3 with a fortune up for grabs for the overall winner and £30,000 to be won in monthly prizes. And remember, you are allocated ten selections with one of those being your star horse whose Tote dividend will be doubled for points scored.

Each list of ten horses costs £10 to enter online at racingpost.com/ttf, or you can find an entry form in the Racing Post (£12/€14). There are 250 horses to currently choose from with the possibility more could be added before the competition starts, so keep up to date with any further additions through the Totesport website and the Racing Post.

Some 24 Group 1 contests carry an additional 25-point bonus with 12 points to the runner-up, so this is a competition for quality campaigners in the top races. Here is a five-point plan that can help you pick the right ten . . .

1. DON'T GET SUCKED IN BY EARLY-SEASON FORM

More horses could be added to the competition before it starts on 2,000 Guineas day. These are likely to be horses who have shown improved form over recent months, which enables us to put in those who have already shown their wellbeing and are clearly

improving – but don't get too carried away.

We are in the very early stages of the season and a lot of the big yards have barely got going. The Dubai Carnival and the Classic trials are important markers, but the O'Briens, Stoutes and Gosdens are not going to seriously set the wheels in motion for their outfits until May, so those top races run in March and April might not be as meaningful as we think.

2. NEVER UNDERESTIMATE OLDER HORSES

There are five bonus races before Royal Ascot with four of them confined to the Classic generation. Given that it is important to get off to a good start, the inclination could be to focus on the three-year-olds to bag the big points. But it might be wiser to use them sparingly as older horses are more likely to be the finished article.

UNBEATABLE ADVICE

RSA Chase hero **Lord Windermere**, whose first big target is the Hennessy, seems underrated and there is no doubt he's progressive. There will be plenty of big points up for grabs in the races he contests.

You can always take a chance with one or two old stalwarts in the Ten to Follow given the extra Tote dividend points on offer (50 maximum), but don't be too wasteful it's the quality horses who come to the fore.

Our strategy expert advised 20-1 Gold Cup winner Lord Windermere as his Ten to Follow star horse in the Racing Post in November

JAMES HILL: TEN TO FOLLOW STRATEGY

There will be plenty of three-year-olds targeted at the Classics but there is only one winner of each race and finding the right one isn't easy. With the older horses we are much more likely to realise their potential and limitations – those who are established and those who are set to reach the top.

Al Kazeem was a good example of this last year. He had raced only once in 2012 but was clearly improving and with an injury-free season he amassed 147 points, the highest of any horse in the competition. You don't want to miss the likes of him by putting in too many three-year-olds into your list as not all of them will be superstars.

3. PICK THE IMPROVER AS YOUR STAR SELECTION

This is Flat racing and we're dealing with very young horses who are improving fast. There are plenty of established names among the older horses and the top juveniles now going for Classic glory, but if their progression has plateaued then they won't be as good as last term. Therefore it is important to go for the improving type, so make that your priority for your star selection.

Take Declaration Of War, who had dividends of £9.70 and £9.90 for his two Group 1 victories last term – and he's from Ballydoyle. That's what a horse who improves a stone in a season can do to your score. Look for a progressive type.

4. LOOK TO FOREIGN SHORES

If you want to be different and get an edge with one or two selections don't look at the Cup races or the sprints – they're very competitive and there are few mega points on offer in either sphere. What might be better is to look for a top-class foreign raider winning races in their native country with the potential to bag a big Group 1 abroad.

Points are awarded for Group-race winners in France, Germany and Italy, and the last two years have shown how useful it is that such races are eligible in the competition with both Novellist and Dandream having been big points scorers, bagging Group contests in Germany before coming over and winning the King George at Ascot.

5. PATIENCE IS KEY

This competition runs into October and there are plenty of bonus points on offer all the way through, so if a horse you like has had a bad first run, don't give up on it as there are likely to be bigger days in the summer for them and for you. Best of luck.

That's the way to do it: Declaration Of War scored plenty of points last year

Ten with big-race credentials who can bag plenty of bonus points

BERKSHIRE Paul Cole

The 2,000 Guineas is the first aim for Berkshire this season, but he should improve massively when stepped up in trip, so the Derby looks his best chance of Classic glory. He was a big juvenile who always promised to grow into his frame at three, yet he still managed to destroy what proved to be a red-hot field in the Chesham Stakes at Royal Ascot with top-class prospects Bunker and Ihtimal filling the places. He had been given a long break before returning with a less impressive success in the Royal Lodge and may well prove much better than that.

FLINTSHIRE Andre Fabre

Andre Fabre looked to be treading a familiar path to Arc glory with Flintshire last season, typical of the sort of progressive three-year-old with whom he has won the race many times in the past, but soft ground went against him as it also had in the Prix Niel. He had shot to the head of the Arc market with a terrific victory in the Grand Prix de Paris and remains a seriously good prospect. He could win some valuable races in France either side of a potential King George bid and will be a threat to Treve and the best three-year-olds in the Arc granted a quicker surface.

GEOFFREY CHAUCER Aidan O'Brien

You're always taking a chance with a middle-distance colt from Ballydoyle as there are so many in the yard who could show sudden improvement and elevate themselves up the pecking order, but this one will surely be part of the Derby team and has every chance of winning at Epsom. A half-brother by Montjeu to the mighty Shamardal, he won both starts last year and eased to victory over Oklahoma City and Altruistic (both placed behind Kingston Hill later) in the Beresford Stakes, which often throws up a future star.

MAGICIAN Aidan O'Brien

This horse's versatility makes him particularly interesting and he is likely to prove best at a mile and a quarter, over which there are numerous Ten to Follow bonus opportunities. He dropped to a mile to win the Irish 2,000 Guineas last season before suffering a setback that affected him in the St James's Palace, and he then returned five months later over an extra half-mile to land the Breeders' Cup Turf. The turn of foot he produced that day marked him out as a serious talent.

MY TITANIA John Oxx

John Oxx's filly won both of her races last season with the minimum of fuss, giving the impression she had a lot more to offer. She showed a good turn of foot and did little in front according to her rider when winning a Group 3 on the second occasion. She will relish stepping up to a mile and will probably stay further, making the Oaks a possibility after she's gone off as one of the leading players in the 1,000 Guineas.

SHIFTING POWER Richard Hannon

In a year in which there is no strong favourite for the 2,000 Guineas like Dawn Approach

DYLAN HILL: TEN TO FOLLOW

last season, it is important to include a few three-year-olds in a bid to mop up the early bonus points. The Classic generation will get cracking earlier than most older horses with so much of their campaign decided by mid-June, and any Guineas principals will find other big points available at the Irish Guineas meeting and Royal Ascot. One who makes the list on that basis is Shifting Power, who provides good back-up to my main Guineas fancy War Command. He was very green as a two-year-old so should have plenty of improvement, yet still showed smart form when maintaining an unbeaten record at Newmarket on his final start. The Hannon yard also has a stunning recent record with three-year-old milers.

SKY LANTERN (below) Richard Hannon

Winner of four Group 1 races and unlucky not to have more in the locker as she would surely have beaten Elusive Kate in the Falmouth Stakes had that filly not dragged her across the July course. Sky Lantern comprehensively took her revenge in the Sun Chariot Stakes after an inconclusive first attempt at a mile and a quarter in the Nassau Stakes when she didn't have much luck in running. She looks sure to win more races at the top level.

TAPESTRY Aidan O'Brien

This filly should probably be unbeaten having been the victim of Kiyoshi's waywardness when second in the Moyglare Stud Stakes last season. Rizeena won the race fairly comfortably in the end, but Tapestry seems to need a bit of time to hit top gear so the interference she suffered when just getting going probably cost her more than it seemed at the time. She has every chance of making amends in the 1,000 Guineas and is then likely to head to the Oaks, giving her two stabs at Classic glory, and should continue to be a force in top fillies' races.

TREVE Criquette Head-Maarek

Last year's runaway Arc winner looks a must for the list. No bonus race has a more likely winner at this stage than the flying Treve, who was sensational in landing the Longchamp showpiece last season. She is also due to come to Royal Ascot for the Prince of Wales's Stakes and will be enormously hard to beat wherever she turns up.

WAR COMMAND Aidan O'Brien

It's not often you get a Coventry and Dewhurst winner who receives as little credit as War Command, presumably because he didn't quite fulfil the enormous hype that followed his runaway victory at Royal Ascot. However, he still got the job done in the Dewhurst despite finding the good to soft ground against him, so really he has failed to deliver just once when Aidan O'Brien claims to have left him undercooked for the Phoenix Stakes. Whatever the reasons for that flop, he remains of vast potential on quicker ground and looks a leading contender for the 2,000 Guineas with Australia and Kingman both having far more to prove.

Australia leads the way as Ireland look to have plenty of Classic prospects

AUSTRALIA Aidan O'Brien

"Everyone probably knows we always thought he was the best horse we've ever had," said Aidan O'Brien last October. The Ballydoyle master's remarks were amazing and it will be fascinating to see if the product of a mating between two greats (Galileo and Ouija Board) can justify the hype.

There was clear progression from him at two: beaten on his debut and no more than workmanlike in a maiden win, he achieved a rating of 117 after trouncing Free Eagle in a Group 3 at Leopardstown on Champion Stakes day. Australia entered the spring as a warm favourite for the Derby and looks likely to need at least 1m2f.

BALANSIYA Dermot Weld

This smashing daughter of Shamardal was Weld's first winner since given juveniles by the Aga Khan, in whose colours she runs. The going was soft on that evening at Leopardstown when she landed her debut by seven lengths eased down. However, Weld stressed that better ground would be ideal. She is a fascinating outsider for the the 1,000 Guineas. While she has an entry in the Irish Oaks and is out of a Dalakhani mare, she may not be guaranteed to get 1m4f.

GEOFFREY CHAUCER Aidan O'Brien

This one has gone beneath the radar in some respects – certainly fellow Ballydoyle three-year-old Australia has impressed the bookmakers more. However, this likeable colt, a half-brother to Shamardal, is dangerous to underestimate this term. Winner of a three-runner maiden on his debut, the son of Montjeu then scored readily in the Group 2 Beresford Stakes, in which Oklahoma City – rated 109 – was a well-held second. Geoffrey Chaucer looks an ideal Ballysax-Beresford-Epsom type.

FREE EAGLE Dermot Weld

Free Eagle seemed to be put in his place by Australia on Champion Stakes day but it was a defeat that Weld seemed to be happy enough to forgive.

Moyglare Stud's home-bred oozed brilliance on his debut, winning eased down at Leopardstown, with a subsequent easy maiden winner in fourth.

A half-brother to the Medicean mare Sapphire who won over 1m4f at Group 2 level, Free Eagle rates a Derby contender, even if he clearly has to re-establish his credentials after his hammering by Australia.

JOHANN STRAUSS Aidan O'Brien

There were some long faces in the Naas betting ring after Johann Strauss, such an eyecatcher when fourth on his Newmarket debut, was beaten at 2-7 on his second start. Punters were shocked that the High Chaparral bay could be beaten that day but he showed far more when a strong-travelling second in the Racing Post Trophy.

Generally a 25-1 chance for the Derby, Johann Strauss is bred to stay at least 1m2f but has an entry in the Irish 2,000 Guineas and may be quite versatile regarding distances. He travels like he could get away with a mile, even in top company.

LEADING LIGHT Aidan O'Brien

Leading Light ended his three-year-old campaign with a struggle in the Arc but it did little to deter those who consider O'Brien's colt a top stayer of the future. With a distinctly lazy manner evident in many of his outings, Leading Light seems to conserve energy for late in his races and he never looked like being caught when winning the Leger in September.

He is hardly guaranteed to get 2m4f – certainly on pedigree it is far from set in stone – but Leading Light must have every chance because of how he races and, given his three-year-old form, he rates the one to beat in the 2014 Gold Cup. The Irish Leger, with a heavily enhanced purse this term, looks made for him too.

MY TITANIA John Oxx

Sea The Stars ended 2013 by leaving the impression he had not proven himself fully as a top-class stallion but that there was every chance he would do so with more time. The best of his progeny, My Titania, won a Group 3 at the Curragh in September and ought to make a smart three-year-old.

SLADE POWER Eddie Lynam

The five-year-old sprinter has raced just 16 times and his story remains to be told for the excellent Lynam. Although he has yet to win at Group 1 level, he can make the breakthrough in 2014 and is ground-versatile as regards ground.

TRADING LEATHER Jim Bolger

Trading Leather was fortunate that he was a three-year-old in 2013 and not 2012, the former being the hottest summer in living memory and the latter being the wettest. Getting the quick ground he craves, the Teofilo bay battled gamely to win the Irish Derby and ran similar races in defeat in all-age Group 1s. He is a hardy type and it was notable his trainer said at the end of 2013 that he expected the horse to be much better next season.

VENUS DE MILO (below) Aidan O'Brien

The daughter of Duke Of Marmalade was seriously progressive in her debut season, going from a maiden win to finishing half-a-length second to Chiquita in the Irish Oaks under two months later. A hardy type, she could be even better again over staying distances.

A guide to runners from across the Channel who can get among the points

WITH only 25 or so French-trained horses to choose from, a Ten to Follow list which is to feature at least some Gallic flare ought not to be quite such an arduous task to assemble.

But exactly the same rigor is required in naming a Francophile squad for the competition, where selection must be concentrated on horses who have a chance of running in at least one bonus race.

The Qipco 1,000 Guineas has been by far the most fruitful objective among British Group 1s for French trainers over the last 20 or 30 years and, in *Miss France* and *Vorda*, the country can boast two live contenders, both with winning form at Newmarket.

Philippe Sogorb deserves enormous credit for the way he campaigned Vorda last season, earning his nascent training career its first Group 1 prize in the Cheveley Park. Sogorb must now prove his precocious champion can stay ahead of the later-maturing types.

Miss France heads most ante-post lists for the Guineas on the back of an impressive Group 3 success at Newmarket on her third and final start at two.

Having already beaten subsequent Prix Marcel Boussac heroine Indonesienne at Chantilly, Andre Fabre clearly has a very talented filly on his hands. However, she pulled ferociously on her first encounter with the Rowley Mile and, in somewhat the reverse case to Vorda, will need to have done some mental maturing over the winter if she is to make the most of her undoubted talent.

Trainer Jean-Claude Rouget called *Lesstalk In Paris's* Longchamp defeat in the Boussac his biggest regret of last season and she might easily turn out to be the best of the French milers. But neither the trainer nor owner Jean-Louis Tepper seem inclined towards Newmarket, which would mean hoping for success in the Poule d'Essai followed by a tilt at the Coronation Stakes – all in all Lesstalk In Paris might end up spending too much time in the city for which she is named.

The selection among the French Classic three-year-olds is *Royalmania*, who could only finish fourth in the Boussac on slow ground, having looked far from the finished article on her previous start at Chantilly. But it is impossible to get away from her eight-length debut success at Deauville, the first of three runs over a mile.

That she is quoted in the betting for the Investec Oaks shows that Royalmania is likely to end up staying further than trainer Freddy Head's recent star females Goldikova and Moonlight Cloud.

Head has never been afraid of travelling his good horses abroad and Royalmania's clear preference for a sound surface could make Britain an attractive option at some stage.

Like stablemate Miss France, *Galiway* has already made the trip across to Britain at two, when failing to cope with either the heavy Newbury ground or the ill-fated Piping Rock.

But, having been pitched into Group 3 company on just his second start, Galiway remains an exciting prospect and should ensure – alongside Royalmania – the famous blue and white Goldikova silks of Alain and Gerard Wertheimer enjoy plenty of success.

Unbeaten Arc heroine *Treve* picks herself as team captain among the older horses.

The choice of another filly to join her is a tricky one, since the owner-breeders who still dominate French racing are apt to retire their best broodmare prospects should they show any sign of beginning to go off the boil.

One late-maturing type who may be given more time to flourish is the Aga Khan's *Narniyn*, who must be one of the biggest fillies in training and who was only just getting the hang of racing when beating a decent field at Saint-Cloud last October.

Flintshire has already enjoyed one moment in the sun, thanks to his authoritative display in what might not have been a vintage edition of the Grand Prix de Paris. His subsequent runs in the Prix Niel and the Arc proved nothing more than his distaste for a soft surface and it is surely significant that Khalid Abdullah and Andre Fabre believe there is more to come.

Fear of a wet autumn means connections may be reluctant to put all their eggs back in the Arc basket, meaning the likes of the Coronation Cup and the King George could come into the reckoning for the son of Dansili.

Vorda's exploits last season might have given Sogorb more of a taste for travel and, although he needs to be delivered desperately late, there are few better sprinters in Europe than *Catcall* on his day.

The choice of a stayer to round out the list is an easy one. At four *Top Trip* proved almost good enough to deprive the Queen of her cherished victory in the Gold Cup.

With the anglophile Francois Doumen likely to plan his season around a return visit to Ascot (and remember Top Trip also ran at York last May), the homebred son of Dubai Destination is the French-trained horse most likely of any on the list to satisfy the prime selection criterion.

Top Trip (right) is a smart stayer who could clock points for his supporters this season

ENTER NOW AT

ENTER NOW AT
RACINGPOST.com/TTF

HOW TO ENTER

Select ten horses from the list starting on page 108 and published at racingpost.com/ttf to compete in the 2014 Totepool/Racing Post Ten to Follow competition which runs from Saturday, May 3 to Saturday, October 18, 2014. There are two ways to enter:
1. Online at racingpost.com/ttf (£10 per stable);
2. Complete a postal entry form published in the Racing Post (£12 /€14 per stable).
Entries open Saturday, April 19, 2014. Online entries close at noon on Saturday, May 3, 2014. Postal entries close on Thursday, May 1, 2014.

SCORING

Selections winning Flat races under the Rules of Racing (excluding NH Flat races) in Great Britain or Ireland or Group races in France, Germany or Italy during the period of the competition will be awarded points as follows:
Group 1 winner 25; Group 2 winner 20; Group 3 winner 15; Listed race winner 12; any other race 10.
In the event of a dead-heat, points will be divided by the number of horses dead-heating with fractions rounded down. No points for a walkover. The official result on the day will be used for the calculation of points with any subsequent disqualifications disregarded.

BONUS POINTS

An additional 25 points will be awarded to the winner and 12 points to the runner-up in each of these races:

2,000 Guineas	*Newmarket, May 3*
1,000 Guineas	*Newmarket, May 4*
Oaks	*Epsom, June 6*
Coronation Cup	*Epsom, June 7*
Derby	*Epsom, June 7*
Queen Anne Stakes	*Royal Ascot, June 17*
St James Palace Stakes	*Royal Ascot, June 17*
Prince Of Wales Stakes	*Royal Ascot, June 18*
Ascot Gold Cup	*Royal Ascot, June 19*
Coronation Stakes	*Royal Ascot, June 20*
Diamond Jubilee Stakes	*Royal Ascot, June 21*
Irish Derby	*Curragh, June 28*
Eclipse Stakes	*Sandown, July 5*
July Cup	*Newmarket, July 12*
King George VI & QE Stakes	*Ascot, July 26*
Sussex Stakes	*Goodwood, July 30*
Nassau Stakes	*Goodwood, August 2*
International Stakes	*York, August 20*
Nunthorpe Stakes	*York, August 22*
Irish Champion Stakes	*Leopardstown, September 13*
St Leger	*Doncaster, September 13*
Prix De L'arc De Triomphe	*Longchamp, October 5*
Champion Stakes	*Ascot, October 18*
Queen Elizabeth II Stakes	*Ascot, October 18*

Any of the above races which take place outside the dates of the competition will not be included in the competition. Tote dividend points will be awarded according to the official Tote win and Tote place dividend odds – including a £1 unit stake – as follows: Win dividend – straight

conversion from £'s to points. For example for a £9.40 win dividend the horse is awarded 9.40 points, £15.30 is awarded 15.30 points etc. Horses finishing first will not receive the place dividend. Horses who finished placed will only receive the Tote place dividend points (unless finishing second in the bonus races detailed above). This will be on the same criteria as above – i.e. £7.20 equates to 7.20 points. The maximum Tote dividend points earned by a horse in a race is 50 points. So if a horse was returned at a Tote win dividend of £67.50, the number of points earned would be 50. See Star Horse section below for more details on the 50-point cap. If no Tote win/ Tote place dividend is declared, the starting price will determine any Tote dividend points using standard each-way terms. Should neither a Tote win dividend nor a starting price be returned, Tote dividend points will not apply.

STAR HORSES

Players nominate one horse to be their Star Horse in each entry. This horse scores double points on the Tote dividend points system, detailed above, for a win or place in any race. For example a horse wins and returns the following dividend: £6.20. As the horse is the Star Horse the return will be doubled for a total combined return of 12.40 points. The maximum combined Tote dividend + Star Horse points is capped at 50 for any one horse in any race. Therefore the maximum total number of points earned by a horse, in a £30,000+ bonus race is 100 points – ie. 25 prize-money points + 25 bonus race points + a maximum of 50 Tote dividend + star horse points.

PRIZE-MONEY

There will not be a guaranteed minimum dividend pay out. All stake monies will be aggregated and paid out in dividends after a 30 per cent deduction to cover administration costs. The remaining 70 per cent of all stakes will be divided as follows to the overall winners: winner 70%, second 10%, third 5%, fourth 4.5%, fifth 3%, sixth 2.5%, seventh 2%, eighth 1.5%, ninth 1%, tenth 0.5%. In the event of a tie for any places, the dividend(s) for the places concerned will be shared. In addition to the overall winners, the highest scoring entry in the prize periods below will win the following prizes: **May 3-31 £5,000; June £5,000; July £5,000; August £5,000; September £5,000; October 1-18 £5,000**. In the event of a tie for any places, the dividends for the places concerned will be shared.

LEAGUES

Ten to Follow players are automatically entered into separate public TTF leagues dependent upon where you place your entry, e.g if you enter via the Racing Post you are in the Post's public league and so on.

Each of the profiles listed on the following pages contains the number to put on your entry form; age, colour, sex, sire, dam and dam's sire; trainer; career form figures to March 5, 2014; owner; current Racing Post rating; details of career wins; summary of achievements and, where known, possible running plans

YOU CAN NOW PLACE MULTIPLE BETS ON MULTIPLE HORSES IN MULTIPLE RACES
(WITHOUT THE USE OF MULTIPLE HANDS)

Choose from a multitude of multiples when you
bet with our bookies William Hill and Ladbrokes
on the Racing Post App. The chance for a bigger
payout has never been so close to hand.

BET
WITH YOUR
HEAD

001 Afsare

7 b g Dubawi - Jumaireyah (Fairy King)

Luca Cumani   Sheikh Mohammed Obaid Al Maktoum

PLACINGS: **11/65244/42122/8211-**   RPR **121**

Starts	1st	2nd	3rd	4th	Win & Pl
18	6			3	£388,592

8/13	Gdwd	1m Cls1 Gp2 good	£56,710
8/13	Sals	1m Cls1 Gp3 good	£42,533
7/12	Sand	1m2f Cls1 List gd-sft	£18,714
6/10	Asct	1m2f Cls1 List 3yo gd-fm	£28,385
6/10	Donc	1m2¹/₂f Cls2 3yo gd-fm	£19,428
5/10	NmkR	1m Cls4 Mdn 3yo gd-fm	£5,181

Lightly raced for his age and better than ever last season; finally made breakthrough at Pattern level when benefiting from drop to a mile for first time since three-year-old campaign, with biggest win coming in Celebration Mile at Goodwood; should win more good races.

002 Ahzeemah (Ire) *(below, right)*

5 b g Dubawi - Swiss Roll (Entrepreneur)

Saeed Bin Suroor   Godolphin

PLACINGS: **13/243121/221222129-**   RPR **117**

Starts	1st	2nd	3rd	4th	Win & Pl
19	5	9	2	2	£507,631

8/13	York	2m¹/₂f Cls1 Gp2 gd-sft	£85,065
3/13	Meyd	1m6f Gp3 good	£73,620
95	9/12	Asct	1m4f Cls2 81-100 3yo Hcap gd-fm	£97,035
86	7/12	Asct	1m2f Cls3 78-95 Hcap gd-sft	£8,093
10/11	Ling	7f Cls4 Mdn 2yo stand	£3,235

Had finished first or second in 11 successive races until managing only ninth in Long Distance Cup at Ascot in October; had progressed out of handicaps

003 Al Thakhira

3 b f Dubawi - Dahama (Green Desert)

Marco Botti   HE Sheikh Joaan Bin Hamad Al Thani

PLACINGS: **110-**   RPR **110+**

Starts	1st	2nd	3rd	4th	Win & Pl
3	2				£42,608

10/13	NmkR	7f Cls1 Gp2 2yo gd-sft	£39,697
9/13	Yarm	6f Cls5 Mdn 2yo soft	£2,911

Bred for speed but saw out 7f strongly on good to soft ground when easily winning a weak Rockfel Stakes at Newmarket; flopped badly when encountering quicker conditions for first time in Breeders' Cup Juvenile Fillies Turf; Guineas possible but has to prove she stays a mile.

004 Albasharah (USA)

5 b m Arch - Desert Gold (Seeking The Gold)

Saeed Bin Suroor   Godolphin

PLACINGS: **11/153U-**   RPR **114+**

Starts	1st	2nd	3rd	4th	Win & Pl
6	3		1		£25,076

88	5/13	Donc	1m2¹/₂f Cls3 83-95 Hcap gd-sft	£7,439
80	10/12	Kemp	1m Cls4 78-85 3yo Hcap stand	£4,075
10/12	Nott	1m2f Cls5 Mdn 3yo soft	£2,264

Missed second half of last season having had blind removed late and reared in stalls when odds-on for

a Listed race at York, capping luckless campaign having finished full of running in fifth in Wolferton Handicap at Royal Ascot after failing to find room; should have lots more to offer.

005 Aljamaaheer (Ire)
5 ch h Dubawi - Kelly Nicole (Rainbow Quest)

Roger Varian — **Hamdan Al Maktoum**

PLACINGS: **1/41333/23218-** — RPR **119+**

Starts	1st	2nd	3rd	4th	Win & Pl
11	3	2	4	1	£209,100
	7/13	Asct	1m Cls1 Gp2 gd-fm		£56,710
	5/12	NmkR	7f Cls1 List 3yo gd-fm		£18,714
	10/11	Yarm	6f Cls5 Mdn 2yo good		£3,151

Has a poor strike-rate for horse of such ability but began to fulfil potential last season, winning Summer Mile at Ascot following close second to Declaration Of War in Queen Anne Stakes; missed end of season after disappointing effort in Prix Jacques le Marois.

006 Along Came Casey (Ire)
6 b m Oratorio - Secretariat's Tap (Pleasant Tap)

Dermot Weld (Ir) — **Mrs C L Weld**

PLACINGS: **674210/6P512/12317-** — RPR **111+**

Starts	1st	2nd	3rd	4th	Win & Pl
16	4	3	1	1	£91,016
	8/13	Gowr	1m1½f List good		£26,423
	6/13	Leop	1m List gd-fm		£21,138
82	9/12	Gowr	1m1½f 70-88 Hcap gd-sft		£7,475
	8/11	Gowr	1m1½f Mdn good		£7,138

Proved herself a very smart mare when kept to quick ground last season, winning two Listed races by wide margins and twice getting placed in Group 3 company (beaten only a head by Fiesolana on first occasion); should be capable of winning at that level.

007 Altano (Ger)
8 b g Galileo - Alanda (Lando)

Andreas Wohler (Ger) — **Frau Dr I Hornig**

PLACINGS: **221161/18412/153518-** — RPR **116**

Starts	1st	2nd	3rd	4th	Win & Pl
29	12	6	2	2	£327,706
	10/13	Lonc	2m4f Gp1 soft		£139,366
	5/13	Hopp	2m Gp3 good		£26,016
	9/12	Dort	1m6f Gp3 good		£26,667
	5/12	Hopp	2m Gp3 good		£26,667
	10/11	Siro	1m6f Gp3 good		£34,483
	8/11	Claf	1m6½f v soft		£12,931
	7/11	Duss	1m3f Hcap good		£4,310
	4/11	Mulh	1m4f Hcap good		£2,586
	9/10	Badn	1m6f Hcap soft		£4,425
	8/10	Colo	1m3f Hcap good		£3,540
	7/10	Colo	1m3f Hcap good		£2,124
	1/10	Neus	1m1½f stand		£885

Thorough stayer who may well have won last season's Ascot Gold Cup but for being given too much to do (finished fast in fifth) and made amends when winning Prix du Cadran over same trip at Longchamp; slightly less effective over shorter, though still came third in Goodwood Cup.

008 Altruistic (Ire)
3 ch c Galileo - Altesse Imperiale (Rock Of Gibraltar)

Johnny Murtagh (Ir) — **Andrew Tinkler**

PLACINGS: **133-** — RPR **104**

Starts	1st	2nd	3rd	4th	Win & Pl
3	1	-	2	-	£43,857
	8/13	Naas	7f Mdn 2yo yield		£8,134

Finished third in two top juvenile races over a mile last season, particularly catching the eye when staying on late in Racing Post Trophy having appeared to be struggling on soft ground; seems sure to stay at least 1m4f.

009 Amazing Maria (Ire)
3 gr f Mastercraftsman - Messias Da Silva (Tale Of The Cat)

Ed Dunlop — **Sir Robert Ogden**

PLACINGS: **7311-** — RPR **106+**

Starts	1st	2nd	3rd	4th	Win & Pl
4	2	-	1	-	£36,295
	8/13	Gdwd	7f Cls1 Gp3 2yo good		£22,684
	8/13	Gdwd	7f Cls2 Mdn 2yo good		£12,938

Twice won well at Goodwood last season, romping home in a maiden by six lengths and following up in similarly comprehensive fashion in Group 3 Prestige Stakes; unsuited by drop to 6f previously; expected to be even better when getting quicker ground; has plenty of scope.

010 Ambivalent (Ire)
5 b m Authorized - Darrery (Darshaan)

Roger Varian — **Ali Saeed**

PLACINGS: **18/13150/23192-** — RPR **111**

Starts	1st	2nd	3rd	4th	Win & Pl
12	4	2	2	-	£214,722
	6/13	Curr	1m2f Gp1 gd-fm		£97,561
	8/12	Newb	1m4f Cls1 List gd-fm		£18,714
72	6/12	Nott	1m2f Cls5 56-75 3yo Hcap good		£2,264
	9/11	Wolv	1m½f Cls5 Mdn 2yo stand		£3,235

Found a soft Group 1 opportunity when winning Pretty Polly Stakes at the Curragh last season, making all over 1m2f; ran several decent races at a slightly lower level when placed three times but ran below best when failing to cope with Goodwood track in Nassau Stakes.

011 Anjaal
3 ch c Bahamian Bounty - Ballymore Celebre (Peintre Celebre)

Richard Hannon — **Hamdan Al Maktoum**

PLACINGS: **8114-** — RPR **110**

Starts	1st	2nd	3rd	4th	Win & Pl
4	2	-	-	1	£70,203
	7/13	NmkJ	6f Cls1 Gp2 2yo gd-fm		£45,368
	6/13	Bevl	5f Cls5 Auct Mdn 2yo gd-fm		£3,235

Finished fast when getting up late to win July Stakes at Newmarket last season; seen only once subsequently having been pulled out of Champagne Stakes due to soft ground and may also have found conditions too slow when fourth in Dewhurst; bred to get much further.

012 Annecdote

4 b f Lucky Story - May Fox (Zilzal)

Jonathan Portman				Tom Edwards & Partners
PLACINGS: 42141/611414-				RPR **107**

Starts	1st	2nd	3rd	4th	Win & Pl
11				4	£96,481
	8/13	Gdwd	7f Cls1 Gp3 good		£34,026
91	6/13	Asct	1m Cls1 List 91-105 3yo Hcap gd-fm		£34,026
83	5/13	Newb	7f Cls4 72-83 3yo Hcap gd-fm		£5,175
78	9/12	NmkR	7f Cls2 68-91 2yo Hcap good		£12,450
	8/12	Sals	7f Cls5 Mdn Auct 2yo soft		£2,588

Progressive last season, winning Sandringham Handicap at Royal Ascot and successfully stepping up to Group 3 level at Goodwood; may have found good to soft ground against her when fourth on final start at Doncaster (had run only once on ground slower than good when winning maiden).

013 Ascription (Ire)

5 b g Dansili - Lady Elgar (Sadler's Wells)

Hugo Palmer				V I Araci
PLACINGS: 03419/6261210-				RPR **113**

Starts	1st	2nd	3rd	4th	Win & Pl
12		3	2	1	1	£33,238
98	9/13	Donc	1m Cls3 93-107 Hcap gd-sft		£16,173
83	7/13	Gdwd	1m Cls3 74-90 Hcap gd-sft		£9,704
70	7/12	Hayd	1m Cls5 60-75 3yo Hcap soft		£2,911

Gelded after first three runs last season and immediately went from strength to strength, winning two out of three handicaps and climbing from 83 to 109; best with plenty of cut, although also ran well to finish second at Goodwood on good to firm; may thrive over stiff 7f.

014 Astaire (Ire)

3 b c Intense Focus - Runway Dancer (Dansili)

Kevin Ryan				Mrs Angie Bailey
PLACINGS: 16111-				RPR **116**

Starts	1st	2nd	3rd	4th	Win & Pl
5		4	-	-	-	£249,383
	10/13	NmkR	6f Cls1 Gp1 2yo gd-sft		£119,034
	8/13	York	6f Cls1 Gp2 2yo soft		£113,420
	7/13	NmkJ	6f Cls3 2yo gd-fm		£8,410
	5/13	York	6f Cls3 Auct Mdn 2yo good		£7,439

Won four out of five races last season, improving throughout and signing off with a narrow all-the-way win over Hot Streak in Middle Park Stakes; far

015 Astonishing (Ire)

4 b f Galileo - Amazing Krisken (Kris S)

Sir Michael Stoute				Lady Rothschild
PLACINGS: 6/31221-				RPR **110+**

Starts	1st	2nd	3rd	4th	Win & Pl
6		2	2	1	-	£31,267
	9/13	NmkR	1m4f Cls1 List good		£22,684
	7/13	Kemp	1m4f Cls5 Mdn stand		£2,588

Did remarkably well to win a Listed race at Newmarket by seven lengths on final start having suffered second defeat in a handicap off 92 just five days earlier; form seems questionable but was helped by settling better and should continue to improve with experience.

016 Australia ♯ ♪

3 ch c Galileo - Ouija Board (Cape Cross)

Aidan O'Brien (Ir)				
			D Smith, Mrs J Magnier, M Tabor & T Ah Khing
PLACINGS: 211-				RPR **118+**

Starts	1st	2nd	3rd	4th	Win & Pl
3		2	1	-	-	£43,304
	9/13	Leop	1m Gp3 2yo good		£31,707
	7/13	Curr	7f Mdn 2yo gd-fm		£9,256

Leading Classic hope after six-length romp in a Group 3 at Leopardstown; hard to be dogmatic about strength of form (main rival seemed well below best) but third finished much closer in Royal Lodge Stakes; more of a Derby horse but may have enough speed to go close in 2,000 Guineas.

017 Avenue Gabriel

3 b f Champs Elysees - Vas Y Carla (Gone West)

Paul Deegan (Ir)				Lady O'Reilly
PLACINGS: 13315-				RPR **104**

Starts	1st	2nd	3rd	4th	Win & Pl
5		2	-	2	-	£52,316
	9/13	Curr	1m List 2yo good		£26,423
	6/13	Curr	7f Mdn 2yo good		£9,256

Improved for step up to a mile when winning Listed race at the Curragh after two placed efforts in Group company over 7f, overcoming a hefty bump having been boxed in; unable to quicken off slow pace when fifth in Fillies' Mile; should do better in more strongly run race.

from certain to stay a mile, although pedigree offers hope; likes cut but has won on good to firm.

018 Balansiya (Ire)
3 b f Shamardal - Baliyana (Dalakhani)

Dermot Weld (Ir)   H H Aga Khan

PLACINGS: 1-   RPR 89+

Starts	1st	2nd	3rd	4th	Win & Pl
1	1	-	-	-	£9,256
	11/13	Leop	7f Mdn 2yo soft		£9,256

Out of a Group 3 winner over a mile and looked a very smart recruit when winning only start in a Leopardstown maiden in November by an eased-down seven lengths on soft ground; described as a good-ground filly by her trainer so should improve in quicker conditions.

019 Baltic Knight (Ire)
4 b c Baltic King - Night Of Joy (King's Best)

Richard Hannon   Thurloe Thoroughbreds XXX

PLACINGS: 5121/13217-   RPR 113

Starts	1st	2nd	3rd	4th	Win & Pl
9	4	2	1	-	£48,588
	6/13	York	1m Cls1 List gd-fm		£20,983
	4/13	Newb	7f Cls2 82-99 3yo Hcap gd-sft		£11,828
95	10/12	Sals	7f Cls4 2yo gd-sft		£4,528
	8/12	Kemp	7f Cls5 Auct Mdn 2yo stand		£2,264

Progressed well for much of last season; faced an impossible task when conceding 9lb to Remote at Doncaster but ran a fine race to beat rest well off mark of 103 and then won a Listed race at York in good style; well below that form when last seen at Goodwood in August.

020 Barley Mow (Ire)
3 b c Zamindar - Harvest Queen (Spinning World)

Richard Hannon   Lady Rothschild

PLACINGS: 125-   RPR 109

Starts	1st	2nd	3rd	4th	Win & Pl
3	1	1	-	-	£18,018
	8/13	Newb	7f Cls4 Mdn 2yo good		£4,075

Unable to build on debut victory but shaped with promise on both subsequent runs; bumped into a top-class prospect in Be Ready next time, beating the rest well, and didn't get a clear run when a fast-finishing fifth in Prix Jean Luc Lagardere; should improve on quicker ground.

021 Be Ready (Ire)
3 ch c New Approach - Call Later (Gone West)

Saeed Bin Suroor   Godolphin

PLACINGS: 21-   RPR 108+

Starts	1st	2nd	3rd	4th	Win & Pl
2	1	1	-	-	£20,794
	9/13	Donc	7f Cls1 List 2yo gd-sft		£15,312

Held in highest regard and justified being thrust into Listed company for debut when second to Somewhat at Newbury; improved again when winning a very strong race for that grade by three lengths from Barley Mow at Doncaster; has lots of scope and could be top class.

022 Belle De Crecy (Ire)
5 b m Rock Of Gibraltar - Bloemfontain (Cape Cross)

Johnny Murtagh (Ir)   Andrew Tinkler

PLACINGS: 2/32112412-   RPR 112

Starts	1st	2nd	3rd	4th	Win & Pl
9	3	4	1	1	£195,026
	9/13	Curr	1m2f Gp2 good		£52,846
90	7/13	Curr	1m1f 72-94 Hcap gd-fm		£11,098
	7/13	Rosc	1m2f Mdn gd-fm		£4,488

Ran just once as a three-year-old for Richard Hannon in 2012 but progressed well for new yard last season; made big leap forward when winning a Group 2 at the Curragh and ran equally well when second in Champion Fillies and Mares Stakes at Ascot on first run over 1m4f.

023 Berkshire (Ire)
3 b c Mount Nelson - Kinnaird (Dr Devious)

Paul Cole   H R H Sultan Ahmad Shah

PLACINGS: 311-   RPR 111+

Starts	1st	2nd	3rd	4th	Win & Pl
3	2	-	1	-	£91,361
	9/13	NmkR	1m Cls1 Gp2 2yo gd-fm		£56,710
	6/13	Asct	7f Cls1 List 2yo gd-fm		£34,026

Easy winner of a red-hot Chesham Stakes last season; missed several subsequent targets due to preference for quick ground and less impressive when landing Royal Lodge Stakes, although he showed good battling qualities to hold off Somewhat; should stay middle distances.

024 Big Time (Ire)
3 br c Kheleyf - Beguine (Green Dancer)

John Joseph Murphy (Ir)   Mrs C C Regalado-Gonzalez

PLACINGS: 122-   RPR 113

Starts	1st	2nd	3rd	4th	Win & Pl
3	1	2	-	-	£54,756
	5/13	Naas	6f 2yo yld-sft		£8,415

Twice came close to bagging a major juvenile prize last season but beaten half a length by Sudirman on both occasions over 6f at the Curragh; form seems slightly questionable after that colt's subsequent defeats, though this horse may well have more to offer over further.

025 Biographer
5 b h Montjeu - Reflective (Seeking The Gold)

David Lanigan   B E Nielsen

PLACINGS: 212121/42746-   RPR 112

Starts	1st	2nd	3rd	4th	Win & Pl
11	3	4	-	2	£62,320
	10/12	Asct	1m6f Cls1 List 3yo soft		£19,849
88	8/12	Ffos	1m4f Cls3 76-88 Hcap gd-sft		£6,792
	6/12	Donc	1m4f Cls5 Mdn gd-sft		£2,911

Ran well in several top staying races last season

having signed off progressive 2012 with Listed win at Ascot; finished second in that grade at Sandown and beaten three lengths or less in Doncaster Cup and Long Distance Cup at Ascot; may make mark in similar races.

026 Bold Sniper
4 b g New Approach - Daring Aim (Daylami)
Sir Michael Stoute — **The Queen**
PLACINGS: 711317- — RPR **105**

Starts	1st	2nd	3rd	4th	Win & Pl
6	3	-	1	-	£45,392
93	7/13	Asct	1m4f Cls2 84-94 3yo Hcap gd-fm		£31,125
81	6/13	Leic	1m2f Cls4 76-83 3yo Hcap good		£4,690
	5/13	Thsk	1m4f Cls5 Mdn soft		£2,588

Progressive middle-distance handicapper last season; staying-on third when sent off favourite for 1m4f handicap at Royal Ascot and made amends when winning over same course and distance next time; failed to handle track at Goodwood on final start and may well resume progress.

027 Bracelet (Ire)
3 b f Montjeu - Cherry Hinton (Green Desert)
Aidan O'Brien (Ir) — **Michael Tabor, Derrick Smith & Mrs John Magnier**
PLACINGS: 81- — RPR **90+**

Starts	1st	2nd	3rd	4th	Win & Pl
2	1	-	-	-	£9,256
	6/13	Leop	7f Mdn 2yo gd-yld		£9,256

Out of Oaks fifth Cherry Hinton (whose only previous foal won Rockfel Stakes) and may well have Epsom race on agenda if progressing well this spring; comfortable winner of a 7f maiden at Leopardstown in June and seems sure to appreciate further, especially on quicker ground.

028 Brendan Brackan (Ire)
5 b g Big Bad Bob - Abeyr (Unfuwain)
Ger Lyons (Ir) — **Anamoine Limited**
PLACINGS: 126146/05261012-30 — RPR **114+**

Starts	1st	2nd	3rd	4th	Win & Pl
16	4	3	1	1	£135,314
	9/13	Curr	1m Gp3 good		£31,707
104	7/13	Gway	1m¹/₂f 83-114 Hcap yield		£56,098
92	9/12	Curr	1m 78-94 Hcap yield		£11,104
	6/12	DRoy	7f Mdn gd-fm		£5,750

Pulled off long-term plan when winning Topaz Mile at Galway last season, remarkably succeeding by eight and a half lengths off mark of 104; proved ability in higher grade when winning in Group 3 company, although was unable to defy 5lb penalty in a Listed race next time.

029 Brown Panther
6 b h Shirocco - Treble Heights (Unfuwain)
Tom Dascombe — **A Black & Owen Promotions Limited**
PLACINGS: 4111522/417238/1158- — RPR **117**

Starts	1st	2nd	3rd	4th	Win & Pl
18	7	3	1	2	£397,487
	8/13	Gdwd	2m Cls1 Gp2 good		£56,710
	6/13	Pont	1m4f Cls1 List good		£22,684
	6/12	Pont	1m4f Cls1 List soft		£18,714
91	6/11	Asct	1m4f Cls2 85-99 3yo Hcap gd-sft		£31,155
81	5/11	Hayd	1m4f Cls3 76-90 3yo Hcap good		£9,970
73	5/11	Ches	1m4¹/₂f Cls3 73-85 3yo Hcap gd-fm		£9,066
	11/10	Sthl	7f Cls6 Mdn Auct 2yo stand		£1,619

Won Goodwood Cup last season when able to run

over 2m on decent ground for first time; had previously won Pontefract Castle Stakes for second successive year but was otherwise without a win since Royal Ascot in 2011; should find more chances over staying trips.

030 Brown Sugar (Ire) *(below, left)*

3 b c Tamayuz - Lady Livius (Titus Livius)

Richard Hannon   De La Warr Racing

PLACINGS: 2101519-   RPR **110**aw

Starts	1st	2nd	3rd	4th	Win & Pl
7	3	1	-	-	£63,759
9/13	Kemp	6f Cls1 Gp3 2yo stand....................................			£22,684
7/13	Gdwd	5f Cls1 Gp3 2yo gd-sft.....................................			£28,355
6/13	Sals	6f Cls5 Mdn 2yo gd-fm...................................			£3,235

Dual Group 3 winner last season over 5f and 6f, defying a penalty to land Sirenia Stakes on all-weather at Kempton; ran equally well in between when beaten just three lengths in fifth in a red-hot Prix Morny but well below best when ninth in Middle Park Stakes.

031 Bunker (Ire)

3 br c Hurricane Run - Endure (Green Desert)

Richard Hannon
      Sheikh Joaan Al Thani, Morecombe, Anderson & Hughes

PLACINGS: 121-   RPR **107**+

Starts	1st	2nd	3rd	4th	Win & Pl
3	2	1	-	-	£37,845
8/13	Deau	7f List 2yo good................................			£22,358
5/13	Hayd	6f Cls5 Mdn 2yo good			£2,588

Regarded as a work in progress when still immature last season but did well to win two out of three starts, suffering only defeat behind Berkshire

in Chesham Stakes; went one better when beating Karakontie in a Listed race at Deauville; likely to be trained for the Derby.

032 Buonarroti (Ire)

3 b c Galileo - Beauty Is Truth (Pivotal)

Aidan O'Brien (Ir)
      Derrick Smith, Mrs John Magnier & Michael Tabor

PLACINGS: 415-   RPR **102**

Starts	1st	2nd	3rd	4th	Win & Pl
3				1	£14,979
10/13	Tipp	1m1f Mdn 2yo yield............................			£7,293

Eight-and-a-half-length winner of same Tipperary race as subsequent St Leger hero Leading Light and should also come into his own when sent over much longer trips; dropped a furlong to run in Racing Post Trophy and ran fair race in fifth having made much of the running.

033 Cable Bay (Ire)

3 b c Invincible Spirit - Rose De France (Diktat)

Charles Hills   Julie Martin & David R Martin & Partner

PLACINGS: 4124322-   RPR **115**

Starts	1st	2nd	3rd	4th	Win & Pl
7	1	3	1	2	£135,809
6/13	Leic	6f Cls4 Mdn 2yo good			£3,881

Knocking on the door at Pattern level last season when second in three Group races; produced best effort on final start when chasing home War Command in Dewhurst Stakes, although fellow principals may have underperformed; likely to start in a 2,000 Guineas trial.

034 Cafe Society (Fr)

4 b g Motivator - Mishina (Highest Honor)

David Simcock   S Bamber, J Barnett & M Caine

PLACINGS: 1/231252-   RPR 97 +

Starts	1st	2nd	3rd	4th	Win & Pl
7	3	3	1	-	£28,280
76	6/13	Sals	1m4f Cls3 72-88 3yo Hcap gd-fm		£9,704
	10/12	Wolv	1m¹/₂f Cls6 Auct Mdn 2yo stand		£2,181

Won only once when competing exclusively in 1m4f handicaps last season but shaped with plenty of promise, including when set too much to do when close second to Bold Sniper; has lots of size and regarded by trainer as potentially his best ever middle-distance horse.

035 Camborne

6 b g Doyen - Dumnoni (Titus Livius)

John Gosden   HRH Princess Haya Of Jordan

PLACINGS: 1/10611725/2411-   RPR 116

Starts	1st	2nd	3rd	4th	Win & Pl
13	6	2	-	1	£143,773
	9/13	Newb	1m3f Cls1 Gp3 soft		£34,026
108	9/13	Donc	1m6¹/₂f Cls2 94-108 Hcap gd-sft		£25,876
97	6/12	Asct	1m4f Cls2 94-103 Hcap gd-sft		£43,575
84	6/12	Donc	1m4f Cls4 67-84 Hcap gd-sft		£5,175
80	4/12	Ling	1m2f Cls4 72-84 Hcap stand		£4,075
	11/11	Kemp	1m2f Cls6 Auct Mdn 3-4yo stand		£1,617

Late developer who ran only once before four-year-old campaign and hit new heights at end of last season; good winner of Mallard Handicap off 108 and coped well with drop in trip to win

Newbury Arc Trial; needs soft ground (well below best on both runs on quicker than good to soft).

036 Cambridge

3 b f Rail Link - Alumni (Selkirk)

Charles Hills   K Abdullah

PLACINGS: 1-   RPR 86 +

Starts	1st	2nd	3rd	4th	Win & Pl
1	1	-	-	-	£3,234
	10/13	Nott	1m¹/₂f Cls5 Mdn 2yo good		£3,235

Half-sister to Listed winner Dux Scholar who faced several fillies with decent form when sent off at 16-1 for her only start in a Nottingham maiden last October, but belied her odds to win well with first two pulling clear; has scope to improve into a top middle-distance performer.

037 Cape Peron *(below, right)*

4 b g Beat Hollow - Free Offer (Generous)

Henry Candy   The Earl Cadogan

PLACINGS: 3/11521-   RPR 113 +

Starts	1st	2nd	3rd	4th	Win & Pl
6	3	1	1	-	£62,318
	10/13	Chan	1m List soft		£21,138
87	5/13	Donc	1m Cls3 76-87 3yo Hcap gd-sft		£8,410
	4/13	Newb	1m Cls4 Mdn 3yo gd-sft		£5,175

Unlucky not to land a major handicap last season before routing rivals by four lengths when stepping into Listed company for first time at Chantilly in October; had found good to firm ground too fast

when a creditable fifth in Royal Hunt Cup before close second off 101 in Betfred Mile.

038 Carla Bianca (Ire)

3 gr f Dansili - Majestic Silver (Linamix)

Dermot Weld (Ir)   Moyglare Stud Farm

PLACINGS: 24-   **RPR 102**

Starts	1st	2nd	3rd	4th	Win & Pl
2	-	1	-	1	£7,634

Showed great promise in two runs last season despite not winning; made a fine debut to push Australia close (five lengths clear of third) and defied inexperience to finish fair fourth in Moyglare Stud Stakes, staying on late; seems sure to get another crack at Group 1 level in time.

039 Caspar Netscher

5 b h Dutch Art - Bella Cantata (Singspiel)

David Simcock   Charles Wentworth

PLACINGS: 231158/191654/24420-   **RPR 112**

Starts	1st	2nd	3rd	4th	Win & Pl
21	5	4	2	4	£345,204

5/12	Colo	1m Gp2 3yo good	£83,333
4/12	Newb	7f Cls1 Gp3 3yo soft	£31,191
9/11	Newb	6f Cls1 Gp2 2yo good	£34,026
8/11	York	6f Cls1 Gp2 2yo gd-sft	£82,880
5/11	Bevl	5f Cls5 Mdn 2yo gd-fm	£2,423

Returned to training from failed stud career midway through last season having won Mill Reef and Gimcrack Stakes for Alan McCabe; unable to

match those feats, though still finished good second to Garswood in Lennox Stakes; could do better after more settled winter.

040 Casual Smile

3 ch f Sea The Stars - Casual Look (Red Ransom)

Andrew Balding   W S Farish

PLACINGS: 232-   **RPR 89**

Starts	1st	2nd	3rd	4th	Win & Pl
3	-	2	1	-	£3,945

Beautifully-bred filly out of trainer's 2003 Oaks winner; placed on all three starts last season, going close every time and doing best when third in novice race at Ascot; sure to improve at three (like her sire) and seems bound to appreciate middle distances; may be an Oaks filly.

041 Cat O'Mountain (USA)

4 br g Street Cry - Thunder Kitten (Storm Cat)

Charlie Appleby   Godolphin

PLACINGS: 411/43511-10   **RPR 114+aw**

Starts		1st	2nd	3rd	4th	Win & Pl
10		5	-	1	2	£62,126
100	1/14	Meyd		1m3f 97-105 Hcap stand		£39,759
93	9/13	Kemp		1m3f Cls3 82-95 3yo Hcap stand		£7,159
88	9/13	Kemp		1m3f Cls3 86-94 Hcap stand		£7,159
82	10/12	Kemp		1m Cls4 70-82 2yo Hcap stand		£3,429
	8/12	Kemp		1m Cls5 Mdn 2yo stand		£2,264

Looked hugely progressive at end of last season when winning two handicaps at Kempton and

continued winning run at Meydan this spring; unbeaten on all-weather surfaces at that stage but has something to prove on turf (beaten on all four starts).

042 Catcall (Fr)

5 b g One Cool Cat - Jurata (Polish Precedent)

Philippe Sogorb (Fr)   Mme Gerard Samama

PLACINGS: 13/22112832-5   RPR **117**

Starts	1st	2nd	3rd	4th	Win & Pl
11	3	4	2	-	£174,258
	5/13	Lonc	5f Gp3 good		£32,520
	3/13	Fntb	5½f List soft		£21,138
	10/12	Toul	7f 3yo gd-sft		£11,250

Had first four runs over at least 7f but found niche at 5f last season, developing into France's leading sprinter; yet to win above Group 3 level but should have landed Prix de l'Abbaye when hitting front too soon having suffered similar fate on previous start; can win top sprints.

043 Century (Ire) *(below, centre)*

3 b c Montjeu - Mixed Blessing (Lujain)

Aidan O'Brien (Ir)   Mrs John Magnier, Michael Tabor & Derrick Smith

PLACINGS: 10-   RPR **87+**

Starts	1st	2nd	3rd	4th	Win & Pl
2	1	-	-	-	£9,256
	10/13	Curr	1m Mdn 2yo good		£9,256

Out of a Princess Margaret winner but seemed more about stamina when staying on powerfully to win an often informative mile maiden at the

Curragh in October; stable's leading hope on prices for Racing Post Trophy but floundered in soft ground; capable of much better.

044 Certify (USA)

4 b f Elusive Quality - Please Sign In (Doc's Leader)

Charlie Appleby   Godolphin

PLACINGS: 1111/14   RPR **113+**

Starts	1st	2nd	3rd	4th	Win & Pl
6	5	-	-	1	£242,719
1/14	Meyd	1m Gp2 good			£72,289
9/12	NmkR	1m Cls1 Gp1 2yo good			£92,721
9/12	Donc	1m Cls1 Gp2 2yo good			£39,697
8/12	NmkJ	7f Cls1 Gp3 2yo gd-fm			£25,520
7/12	NmkJ	6f Cls4 Mdn 2yo soft			£6,469

Missed last season having been banned for a positive drugs test in April when among favourites for 1,000 Guineas but made winning return in Dubai this spring; had been a top-class two-year-old when unbeaten in four races, culminating with wide-margin victory in Fillies' Mile.

045 Charm Spirit (Ire)

3 b c Invincible Spirit - L'Enjoleuse (Montjeu)

Freddy Head (Fr)   HH Sheikh Abdulla Bin Khalifa Al Thani

PLACINGS: 213-   RPR **112**

Starts	1st	2nd	3rd	4th	Win & Pl
3	1	1	1	-	£50,247
	9/13	Lonc	7f 2yo good		£13,821

Given too much to do when third in Prix Jean Luc Lagarde last season having made all when winning a conditions race over same 7f trip at Longchamp previously; had made debut over a

mile and likely to be much better when reverting to that distance and beyond.

046 Chicquita (Ire)
4 b f Montjeu - Prudenzia (Dansili)

Aidan O'Brien

PLACINGS: 3/F21-   RPR **114+**

Starts	1st	2nd	3rd	4th	Win & Pl
4	1	1	1	-	£377,471
7/13	Curr	1m4f Gp1 3yo gd-fm			£188,618

May stay in training despite being sold for €6m in November; won last season's Irish Oaks, building on fine second to Treve in Prix de Diane; should progress again if ironing out waywardness (fell when jinking right on second run and has since hung badly left).

047 Chief Barker (Ire)
3 b c Azamour - Millay (Polish Precedent)

Richard Hannon   Middleham Park Racing XXIII

PLACINGS: 1116-   RPR **101+**

Starts	1st	2nd	3rd	4th	Win & Pl
4	3	-	-	-	£25,787
77	9/13	Hayd	1m Cls1 List 2yo gd-sft		£14,461
	8/13	NmkJ	1m Cls4 65-77 2yo Hcap good		£3,881
	8/13	Sand	1m Cls5 Mdn 2yo good		£3,881

Claimed notable scalp of Chriselliam when completing hat-trick in a Listed race at Haydock, though perhaps flattered as runner-up challenged too soon; well below that form next time in Racing Post Trophy but expected to improve on quicker ground; good middle-distance prospect.

048 Cirrus Des Aigles (Fr)
8 b g Even Top - Taille De Guepe (Septieme Ciel)

Corine Barande-Barbe (Fr)   **Jean-Claude-Alain Dupouy**

PLACINGS: 15/2112d12/54251123-4   RPR **126**

Starts	1st	2nd	3rd	4th	Win & Pl
54	18	19	6	4	£4,778,055
10/13	Lonc	1m2f Gp2 soft			£92,683
9/13	MsnL	1m2f Gp3 gd-sft			£32,520
10/12	Lonc	1m2f Gp2 heavy			£95,000
4/12	Lonc	1m2¹/₂f Gp1 heavy			£142,850
3/12	Meyd	1m4f Gp1 good			£1,935,484
10/11	Asct	1m2f Cls1 Gp1 good			£737,230
8/11	Deau	1m4¹/₂f Gp2 v soft			£98,276
8/11	Deau	1m2f Gp3 heavy			£34,483
7/11	Vich	1m2f Gp2 v soft			£34,483
6/11	Lonc	1m2f Gp3 gd-sft			£34,483
10/10	Lonc	1m2f Gp2 v soft			£65,575
9/10	Lonc	1m2f List good			£23,009
10/09	Lonc	1m4f Gp2 gd-sft			£71,942
9/09	Lonc	1m2f Gp3 3yo good			£38,835
8/09	Le L	1m2f List 3yo gd-sft			£26,699
5/09	Lonc	1m2¹/₂f 3yo soft			£27,760
5/09	Lonc	1m2f 3yo good			£14,078
1/09	Cagn	1m 3yo stand			£9,709

Winner of 13 Group races, including three at Group 1 level; below best for much of last season (often takes time to peak and may have taken longer to recover from ligament strain at end of 2012) but bounced back to win twice and go close to recapuring Champion Stakes crown.

ONE TO FOLLOW

Derbyshire Raced three times in maidens without finishing better than sixth. Hinted at fair ability, however, and an initial mark of 64 could prove generous. *[Simon Turner, Racing Post Ratings]*

049 Coach House (Ire)

3 b c Oasis Dream - Lesson In Humility (Mujadil)

Aidan O'Brien (Ir)
Mrs John Magnier, Michael Tabor & Derrick Smith

PLACINGS: **21123-**   RPR **104**

Starts	1st	2nd	3rd	4th	Win & Pl
5	2	2	1	-	£61,419
5/13	Curr	5f List 2yo gd-fm.......................................£27,744
5/13	Tipp	5f Mdn 2yo soft..£7,012

Missed second half of last season following disappointing third in Railway Stakes but had previously looked a smart prospect; won a Listed race at the Curragh before beating all bar brilliant No Nay Never in Norfolk Stakes at Royal Ascot; could be a top sprinter.

050 Code Of Honor

4 b c Zafeen - Verbal Intrigue (Dahar)

Saeed Bin Suroor   Sheikh Majid Bin Mohammed Al Maktoum

PLACINGS: **811/491532-72**   RPR **112+**

Starts	1st	2nd	3rd	4th	Win & Pl
11	3	2	1	1	£79,481
90	7/13	Sand	1m2f Cls3 74-93 Hcap gd-fm...............£12,450
85	10/12	Donc	7f Cls3 67-85 2yo Hcap soft.................£7,439
	9/12	Newb	7f Cls4 Mdn 2yo gd-fm.........................£4,722

Won on soft ground in 2012 but produced his best performances last season on good to firm, winning a 1m2f handicap at Sandown and going down by a short head to Educate in the Cambridgeshire; subsequently left Henry Candy's yard and started Godolphin career at Meydan.

051 Come To Heel (Ire)

3 ch f Elnadim - Give A Whistle (Mujadil)

David Wachman (Ir) M Buckley, D Graham & Mrs P Shanahan

PLACINGS: **114-**   RPR **105**

Starts	1st	2nd	3rd	4th	Win & Pl
3	2	-	-	1	£39,097
8/13	Curr	5f List 2yo good...£21,138
8/13	Cork	6f Mdn 2yo good.......................................£8,134

Smart juvenile last season, winning a Listed race at the Curragh before finishing fourth in Cheveley Park Stakes (stayed on strongly having initially looked green when asked to quicken); looks full of speed and should progress into a high-class sprinter.

052 Conduct (Ire)

7 gr g Selkirk - Coventina (Daylami)

William Haggas   Highclere T'Bred Racing Royal Palace

PLACINGS: **11/2/531-**   RPR **111**

Starts	1st	2nd	3rd	4th	Win & Pl
6	3	1	1	-	£56,309
96	11/13	Donc	1m4f Cls2 82-104 Hcap soft.................£40,463
85	9/10	Newb	1m2f Cls3 76-89 Hcap good...................£6,476
	9/10	Sand	1m1f Cls5 Mdn 3yo good......................£3,238

Out of a 2m winner and relished step up to 1m4f

when storming home by five lengths off mark of 96 in November Handicap; has been hugely fragile (was having only sixth career start) but clearly capable at higher level if staying sound; seems sure to stay longer trips.

053 Cristoforo Colombo (USA)

4 b c Henrythenavigator - La Traviata (Johannesburg)

Aidan O'Brien (Ir)
Mrs John Magnier, Michael Tabor & Derrick Smith

PLACINGS: **132S4/58177-**   RPR **107+**

Starts	1st	2nd	3rd	4th	Win & Pl
10	2	1	1	1	£59,739
10/13	Dund	6f stand..£8,415
5/12	Navn	6f Mdn 2yo good...................................£8,338

Beaten just a length by Dawn Approach in Coventry Stakes as a juvenile; yet to fulfil potential since then but not helped by missing most of last season through injury following fifth in 2,000 Guineas; stayed on fairly well when getting favoured fast ground in Breeders' Cup Mile.

054 Danadana (Ire)

6 b h Dubawi - Zeeba (Barathea)

Luca Cumani   Sheikh Mohammed Obaid Al Maktoum

PLACINGS: **53/125/81191/15621-**   RPR **117**

Starts	1st	2nd	3rd	4th	Win & Pl
15	6	2	1	-	£193,057
	9/13	Veli	1m2¹/₂f List fast...£93,496
	5/13	Ches	1m2¹/₂f Cls1 Gp3 good.................................£34,026
101	8/12	York	1m2¹/₂f Cls2 82-101 Hcap gd-fm.............£16,173
94	6/12	Rdcr	1m2f Cls2 80-100 Hcap gd-fm.................£16,173
85	5/12	NmkR	1m2f Cls3 77-88 Hcap good....................£7,763
	4/11	Newc	1m2f Cls5 Mdn gd-fm................................£2,331

Sharply progressive handicapper in 2012 when winning three times on good to firm but got preferred conditions only once last season when stretched too far by step up to 1m4f; still did well to win Ormonde Stakes and nearly defied Group 3 penalty when second at York, both over 1m2f.

055 Dank

5 b m Dansili - Masskana (Darshaan)

Sir Michael Stoute   James Wigan

PLACINGS: **2/191215/13111-**   RPR **116+**

Starts	1st	2nd	3rd	4th	Win & Pl
12	7	2	1	-	£1,099,202
	11/13	SnAt	1m2f Gd1 firm...£674,847
	8/13	Arlt	1m1¹/₂f Gd1 firm.....................................£267,791
	7/13	Curr	1m1f Gp2 gd-fm.......................................£52,846
	5/13	NmkR	1m1f Cls1 Gp3 gd-fm..............................£34,026
	9/12	Sand	1m Cls1 Gp3 gd-fm..................................£31,191
88	7/12	Asct	1m Cls3 73-90 Hcap firm..........................£8,410
	4/12	Kemp	1m Cls5 Mdn 3yo stand.............................£3,558

Excelled in United States last autumn with two Grade 1 wins, most notably in Breeders' Cup Filly & Mare Turf; yet to show same ability in Europe but capable of better than her close third in Duke of Cambridge Stakes at Royal Ascot; unproven on ground slower than good.

056 Dark Crusader (Ire)

4 b/br f Cape Cross - Monty's Girl (High Chaparral)

Tony Martin (Ir)　　　　Newtown Anner Stud Farm Ltd

PLACINGS: 0/5781116-　　　　　　　　RPR 101+

Starts	1st	2nd	3rd	4th	Win & Pl
8	3	-	-	-	£59,247
90	8/13	York	1m6f Cls2 78-97 3yo Hcap soft		£46,688
83	7/13	Gway	1m4f 65-89 3yo Hcap yield		£7,293
64	7/13	Klny	1m3f 47-69 3yo Hcap gd-fm		£4,768

Rapid improver last summer, completing hat-trick in Melrose Stakes at York off 26lb higher mark than when breaking duck at Killarney; disappointed next time at Ascot when long season may have taken toll (had begun with two runs on all-weather at Dundalk during winter).

057 Darwin (USA)

4 b c Big Brown - Cool Ghoul (Silver Ghost)

Aidan O'Brien (Ir)

　　　　　　Derrick Smith, Mrs John Magnier & Michael Tabor

PLACINGS: 14/113-　　　　　　　　RPR 114+

Starts	1st	2nd	3rd	4th	Win & Pl
5	3	-	1	1	£79,156
	7/13	Curr	7f Gp3 gd-fm		£33,293
	6/13	Naas	1m 3yo gd-fm		£8,699
	10/12	Belm	6f 2yo fast		£26,323

Exciting US import who won first two starts for new yard last season, claiming a notable scalp in Gordon Lord Byron in a Group 3 at the Curragh; didn't show same turn of foot on good ground and may need fast conditions to produce best.

058 Dazzling (Ire)

3 b f Galileo - Secret Garden (Danehill)

Aidan O'Brien (Ir)　　　　　　Michael Tabor

PLACINGS: 163-　　　　　　　　RPR 96

Starts	1st	2nd	3rd	4th	Win & Pl
3	1	-	1	-	£12,182
	9/13	Curr	1m Mdn 2yo gd-fm		£9,256

Twice beaten at short prices in Listed races over a mile at the Curragh last season having won well over course and distance on debut; clearly expected to do better and has fine pedigree (out of Listed-winning dam of Classic hero Roderic O'Connor); potential Oaks filly.

059 Dutch Masterpiece

4 b g Dutch Art - The Terrier (Foxhound)

Gary Moore　　　　　　R A Green

PLACINGS: 1711/571110-　　　　　　　　RPR 113+

Starts	1st	2nd	3rd	4th	Win & Pl
10	6	-	-	-	£66,519
	8/13	Curr	5f Gp3 good		£31,707
98	6/13	NmkJ	5f Cls2 81-100 3yo Hcap good		£12,450
89	6/13	Ches	5f Cls3 74-93 3yo Hcap good		£7,763
86	10/12	Hayd	5f Cls2 68-86 2yo Hcap heavy		£7,633
80	10/12	Wind	5f Cls4 63-85 2yo Hcap soft		£3,558
	7/12	Sthl	5f Cls5 Mdn 2yo stand		£3,409

Progressive sprinter last season, following up pair of handicap wins with Group 3 victory at the Curragh only to disappoint in first-time blinkers when favourite for Prix de l'Abbaye; unlikely to be chanced on ground quicker than good; hasn't appeared to stay on both attempts at 6f.

060 Earnshaw (USA)

3 gr c Medaglia D'Oro - Emily Bronte (Machiavellian)

Andre Fabre (Fr)　　　　　　Godolphin

PLACINGS: 112-　　　　　　　　RPR 112

Starts	1st	2nd	3rd	4th	Win & Pl
3	2	1	-	-	£88,739
	10/13	StCl	1m Gp3 2yo v soft		£32,520
	9/13	Chan	1m 2yo good		£9,756

Won leading trial for Criterium International at Saint-Cloud in hugely impressive fashion but only second in that Group 1 when beaten by Ectot; may have run into a very smart rival that day and remains a leading contender for French Classics.

061 Ectot ↗

3 b c Hurricane Run - Tonnara (Linamix)

Elie Lellouche (Fr)　　　G Augustin-Normand & Mme E Vidal

PLACINGS: 21111-　　　　　　　　RPR 114

Starts	1st	2nd	3rd	4th	Win & Pl
5	4	1	-	-	£211,910
	11/13	StCl	1m Gp1 2yo v soft		£116,138
	9/13	Lonc	1m Gp3 2yo soft		£32,520
	8/13	Deau	1m List 2yo good		£49,593
	7/13	Claf	7f 2yo sft-hvy		£9,756

Progressed throughout last season to win Group 1 Criterium International on final start and suffered only defeat in five races to subsequent Group 1 winner Karakontie on his debut; very effective in testing conditions but below best when scrambling home on only run on good.

062 Educate

5 b g Echo Of Light - Pasithea (Celtic Swing)

Ismail Mohammed　　　　　　Sultan Ali

PLACINGS: 7155011/10100351-6　　　　　　RPR 117+

Starts	1st	2nd	3rd	4th	Win & Pl
16	6	-	1	-	£162,277
104	9/13	NmkR	1m1f Cls2 93-105 Hcap gd-fm		£99,600
93	5/13	Ling	1m2f Cls2 92-98 Hcap soft		£12,291
88	3/13	Donc	1m Cls2 76-90 Hcap soft		£28,013
80	10/12	York	1m2½f Cls4 69-80 3yo Hcap heavy		£6,469
76	9/12	Sand	1m Cls4 68-79 Hcap gd-fm		£4,075
	6/12	Yarm	1m2f Cls6 Auct Mdn 3yo gd-fm		£1,617

Superb winner of last season's Cambridgeshire when defying mark of 104; had won two handicaps (including Spring Mile) earlier in campaign and suffered serious trouble in running on two occasions in between; raced keenly when fifth in Celebration Mile on only try in Pattern company.

063 Ektihaam (Ire)

5 b g Invincible Spirit - Liscune (King's Best)

Roger Varian   Hamdan Al Maktoum

PLACINGS: 119/1202/31S8-   RPR **121**

Starts	1st	2nd	3rd	4th	Win & Pl
11	4	2	1	-	£88,880
	5/13	Asct	1m4f Cls1 List gd-fm.................................£20,983		
	4/12	Newb	1m2f Cls3 3yo soft...£6,536		
	9/11	Donc	7f Cls2 2yo good...£10,894		
	7/11	Newb	7f Cls4 Mdn 2yo gd-fm....................................£4,237		

Has had lots of problems since Dante second in 2012 but proved himself a high-class gelding when winning a Listed race at Ascot by six lengths on first attempt at 1m4f last season; slipped up early in Hardwicke Stakes next time and well below best in King George.

064 Elik (Ire)

4 b f Dalakhani - Elopa (Tiger Hill)

Sir Michael Stoute   Nurlan Bizakov

PLACINGS: 73/24132-   RPR **105**

Starts	1st	2nd	3rd	4th	Win & Pl
7	1	2	2	1	£56,105
	5/13	Gdwd	1m2f Cls1 List 3yo good................................£23,680		

Developed into a useful middle-distance filly from just a handful of starts last season; finished good third in Ribblesdale Stakes and comfortably beat all bar Wild Coco when stepped up to 1m6f in Lillie Langtry Stakes at Goodwood; still lightly raced and should have more to offer.

065 Elliptique (Ire)

3 br c New Approach - Uryale (Kendor)

Andre Fabre (Fr)   Rothschild Family

PLACINGS: 1321-   RPR **106**

Starts	1st	2nd	3rd	4th	Win & Pl
4	2	1	1	-	£74,227
	10/13	Lonc	1m1f Gp3 2yo v soft..................................£32,520		
	7/13	Deau	7¹/₂f 2yo stand...£13,821		

Suffered both defeats last season behind Group 1 winner Ectot before making amends by impressively landing a Group 3 over 1m1f at Longchamp, coming from last to first and asserting strongly in closing stages; looks a very useful middle-distance prospect.

066 Encke (USA)

5 b h Kingmambo - Shawanda (Sinndar)

Charlie Appleby   Godolphin

PLACINGS: 21/1231/

Starts	1st	2nd	3rd	4th	Win & Pl
6	3	2	1	-	£355,973
	9/12	Donc	1m6¹/₂f Cls1 Gp1 3yo good.......................£311,905		
	7/12	Sand	1m2f Cls3 82-93 Hcap gd-sft £6,792		
	10/11	NmkR	1m Cls4 Mdn 2yo gd-fm................................£5,175		

Missed last season in fallout from Godolphin drugs scandal; had won St Leger in 2012 when last seen, denying Camelot a historic victory by taking a big step forward on previous form (placed in Great Voltigeur and Gordon Stakes); likely to run in Group 1 races at around 1m4f.

067 Ernest Hemingway (Ire)

5 br h Galileo - Cassydora (Darshaan)

Aidan O'Brien (Ir)

Mrs John Magnier, Michael Tabor & Derrick Smith

PLACINGS: 1702/41136-   RPR **116+**

Starts	1st	2nd	3rd	4th	Win & Pl
9	3	1	1	1	£78,135
	8/13	Leop	1m4f Gp3 gd-fm.......................................£31,707		
	6/13	Curr	1m6f Gp3 gd-fm.......................................£30,488		
	4/12	Dund	1m2¹/₂f Mdn 3yo stand...................................£6,900		

Made huge improvement when stepped up to staying trips and encountering good to firm ground for first time, winning Curragh Cup by five lengths from Royal Diamond; beat same rival far more narrowly over 1m4f but disappointed twice later, including when sixth in Irish St Leger.

068 Esoterique (Ire)

4 b f Danehill Dancer - Dievotchka (Dancing Brave)

Andre Fabre (Fr)   Baron Edouard De Rothschild

PLACINGS: 1127-   RPR **114**

Starts	1st	2nd	3rd	4th	Win & Pl
4	2	1	-	-	£126,317
	4/13	Lonc	1m1f Gp3 3yo good...................................£32,520		
	4/13	StCl	1m 3yo soft...£10,163		

Sent off favourite for last season's Poule d'Essai des Pouliches just over a month after making her debut and ran a fine race when just touched off by Flotilla; failed to stay when seventh in Prix de Diane next time but remains a top-class prospect when switched back to a mile.

069 Estimate (Ire) *(below)*

5 b m Monsun - Ebaziya (Darshaan)

Sir Michael Stoute — The Queen

PLACINGS: 7/1133/117- RPR **113**

Starts	1st	2nd	3rd	4th	Win & Pl
8	4	-	2	-	£285,267
6/13	Asct	2m4f Cls1 Gp1 gd-fm			£198,485
5/13	Asct	2m Cls1 Gp3 good			£34,026
6/12	Asct	2m Cls1 Gp3 3yo soft			£34,026
5/12	Sals	1m4f Cls5 Mdn 3yo gd-sft			£4,205

Fairytale winner of last season's Ascot Gold Cup, relishing extra distance and maintaining tremendous record at track having won both previous starts there; had won Queen's Vase on soft ground but found conditions too testing when disappointing favourite in Long Distance Cup.

070 Excellent Result (Ire)

4 b c Shamardal - Line Ahead (Sadler's Wells)

Saeed Bin Suroor — Godolphin

PLACINGS: 34/91714-41 RPR **103**

Starts	1st	2nd	3rd	4th	Win & Pl
9	3	-	1	3	£160,923
99	2/14	Meyd	1m6f 95-109 Hcap good		£54,217
94	9/13	Asct	1m4f Cls2 88-100 3yo Hcap good		£97,035
	5/13	Sand	1m2f Cls5 Mdn 3-4yo gd-fm		£3,881

Has been a slow learner but looked much improved when returning from a break to win a fiercely competitive three-year-old handicap at Ascot in September, showing a smart turn of foot over 1m4f; seemed less effective when dropped in trip next time; type to improve again at four.

071 Eye Of The Storm (Ire)

4 ch c Galileo - Mohican Princess (Shirley Heights)

Aidan O'Brien (Ir) — Michael Tabor, Derrick Smith & Mrs John Magnier

PLACINGS: 13/22113- RPR **114**

Starts	1st	2nd	3rd	4th	Win & Pl
7	3	2	2	-	£101,452
9/13	Curr	2m List gd-fm			£22,195
9/13	List	1m4f List heavy			£22,459
9/12	Gway	1m¹/₂f Mdn 2yo heavy			£10,350

Missed much of last season after a close second in Sandown Classic Trial but soon thrived on return, winning back-to-back Listed races in September over 1m4f and 2m; confirmed liking for longer trip with fine third in Long Distance Cup at Ascot; should be a top-class stayer.

072 Festive Cheer (Fr)

4 b c Montjeu - Bold Classic (Pembroke)

Aidan O'Brien (Ir) — Michael Tabor, Derrick Smith & Mrs John Magnier

PLACINGS: 51/303- RPR **115+**

Starts	1st	2nd	3rd	4th	Win & Pl
5	1	-	2	-	£113,067
8/12	Dund	7f Mdn 2yo stand			£5,750

Bitterly disappointing in Derby but showed true colours with terrific third behind Trading Leather in Irish Derby, looking unlucky having been blocked at a key stage; also beaten just a head when third in Prix Hocquart; may well have more to offer after just five outings.

073 Fiesolana (Ire) *(above, front left)*

5 b m Aussie Rules - Tidal Reach (Kris S)

Willie McCreery (Ir)   K Leavy, L Cribben & Mrs A McCreery

PLACINGS: 5231/1416/21116151-   RPR **116**

Starts		1st	2nd	3rd	4th	Win & Pl
16		8	2	1	1	£221,804
	10/13	NmkR	7f Cls1 Gp2 gd-sft			£51,039
	8/13	Tipp	7¹/₂f Gp3 good			£33,028
	7/13	Fair	7f Gp3 good			£40,955
	6/13	Leop	6f Gp3 gd-yld			£31,707
93	5/13	Curr	1m 78-105 Hcap gd-fm			£24,390
	5/12	StCl	1m 3yo good			£14,167
	3/12	Bord	1m 3yo good			£11,250
	12/11	Agno	1m2f 2yo heavy			£4,369

Sold for 960,000gns in December but kept in training in bid to land Group 1 win; modest fifth on only start in that grade in Matron Stakes having won three of previous four starts (all Group 3 races) but took further step forward when winning Challenge Stakes at Newmarket last time.

074 Flintshire

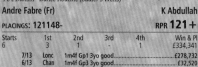

4 b c Dansili - Dance Routine (Sadler's Wells)

Andre Fabre (Fr)   K Abdullah

PLACINGS: 121148-   RPR **121+**

Starts		1st	2nd	3rd	4th	Win & Pl
6		3	1		1	£334,341
	7/13	Lonc	1m4f Gp1 3yo good			£278,732
	6/13	Chan	1m4f Gp3 3yo good			£32,520
	5/13	Chan	1m2f 3yo good			£10,163

Unraced as a juvenile but progressed rapidly last season and looked a leading Arc contender after winning Grand Prix de Paris; disappointing twice

subsequently on soft ground (had also suffered only previous defeat on soft at odds-on); should do better back in quicker conditions.

075 Flotilla (Fr)

4 b f Mizzen Mast - Louvain (Sinndar)

Mikel Delzangles (Fr)
**   H H Sheikh Mohammed Bin Khalifa Al Thani**

PLACINGS: 61541/186-42   RPR **115+**

Starts		1st	2nd	3rd	4th	Win & Pl
10		3	1	-	2	£615,164
	5/13	Lonc	1m Gp1 3yo good			£209,049
	11/12	SnAt	1m Gd1 2yo firm			£348,387
	7/12	Claf	7f 2yo v soft			£10,000

Brilliant dual Group 1 winner having landed Poule d'Essai des Pouliches last season to add to Breeders' Cup success as a juvenile; had excuses for both subsequent defeats having not seen out longer trip in Prix de Diane and failed to act on soft ground in Prix du Moulin.

076 Flying Officer (USA)

4 b g Dynaformer - Vignette (Diesis)

John Gosden   George Strawbridge

PLACINGS: 17/1-   RPR **105+**

Starts		1st	2nd	3rd	4th	Win & Pl
3		2	-	-	-	£11,320
88	6/13	Wind	1m2f Cls3 82-88 3yo Hcap gd-fm			£7,439
	9/12	Sand	1m Cls5 Mdn 2yo gd-fm			£3,881

Restricted to just three starts over two seasons and ran only once last season, but made a big impression

when running away with a Windsor handicap; capable of landing a good middle-distance handicap before probably stepping up in class.

077 Francis Of Assisi (Ire)

4 b g Danehill Dancer - Queen Cleopatra (Kingmambo)

Aidan O'Brien (Ir)   Mrs John Magnier

PLACINGS: 81/101-   RPR **109+**

Starts	1st	2nd	3rd	4th	Win & Pl
5	3	-	-	-	£39,446
	11/13	Leop	7f List soft...£21,138
93	3/13	Curr	7f 80-100 3yo Hcap heavy £10,833
	10/12	Naas	6f Mdn 2yo heavy £7,475

Limited to just three runs last season through injury but looked a high-class prospect when winning twice (needed the run after long absence on other start and may not have liked quick ground); signed off with a comfortable Listed win in November; could be a very smart miler.

078 Free Eagle (Ire)

3 b c High Chaparral - Polished Gem (Danehill)

Dermot Weld (Ir)   Moyglare Stud Farm

PLACINGS: 12-   RPR **104+**

Starts	1st	2nd	3rd	4th	Win & Pl
2	1	1	-	-	£17,682
	8/13	Leop	1m Mdn 2yo good £8,415

Made a huge impression on debut when thumping Orchestra in a quality maiden at Leopardstown but failed to build on that next time over same course

and distance when easily brushed aside by Australia; likely to prove better than that and could start in a Derby trial.

079 Galiway

3 b c Galileo - Danzigaway (Danehill)

Andre Fabre (Fr)   Wertheimer & Frere

PLACINGS: 12-   RPR **100+**

Starts	1st	2nd	3rd	4th	Win & Pl
2	1	1	-	-	£18,356
	9/13	StCl	1m 2yo soft..£9,756

Found out by drop in trip to 7f when never threatening in Horris Hill Stakes at Newbury, but stayed on well to finish second to Piping Rock; expected to improve significantly by top trainer (was reported to be very green) and due to be trained for French Classics.

080 Garswood

4 b c Dutch Art - Penchant (Kyllachy)

Richard Fahey   D W Armstrong & Cheveley Park Stud

PLACINGS: 3412/174163-   RPR **113**

Starts	1st	2nd	3rd	4th	Win & Pl
10	3	1	2	2	£165,401
	7/13	Gdwd	7f Cls1 Gp2 gd-sft...................................£85,065
106	4/13	NmkR	7f Cls1 List 100-113 3yo Hcap good...........£20,983
	9/12	Ayr	5f Cls1 List 2yo heavy £14,178

Excellent performer over 7f on soft ground; won Group 2 at Goodwood last season before fine third to Moonlight Cloud in Prix de la Foret; outpaced over 6f when sixth in Haydock Sprint Cup; could return to a mile having found ground too quick when seventh in 2,000 Guineas.

081 Geoffrey Chaucer (USA)

3 b c Montjeu - Helsinki (Machiavellian)
Aidan O'Brien (Ir)
Mrs John Magnier & Michael Tabor & Derrick Smith
PLACINGS: **11-** RPR **108+**

Starts	1st	2nd	3rd	4th	Win & Pl
2	2	-	-	-	£62,101
9/13	Curr	1m Gp2 2yo good			£52,846
7/13	Leop	1m Mdn 2yo gd-fm			£9,256

Clearly held in high regard having been sent off just 4-7 against smart stablemate Oklahoma City in Beresford Stakes and went some way to justify reputation with smooth victory; may not be as effective on softer ground (missed intended engagement in Racing Post Trophy).

082 Giovanni Boldini (USA)

3 b/br c War Front - Dancing Trieste (Old Trieste)
Aidan O'Brien (Ir)
Mrs John Magnier, Michael Tabor & Derrick Smith
PLACINGS: **1312-** RPR **115+**

Starts	1st	2nd	3rd	4th	Win & Pl
4	2	1	1	-	£158,579
10/13	Dund	7f List 2yo stand			£25,102
9/13	Dund	7f 2yo stand			£8,415

Put in his place by Toormore in National Stakes on only his second start but looked green that day and seemed to make major strides subsequently, most notably when just pipped by Outstrip in Breeders' Cup Juvenile Turf; may also have preferred much faster conditions.

083 Gordon Lord Byron (Ire)

6 b g Byron - Boa Estrela (Intikhab)
Tom Hogan (Ir) Morgan J Cahalan
PLACINGS: **3421214/17342311274-** RPR **121**

Starts	1st	2nd	3rd	4th	Win & Pl
34	9	8	8	4	£783,920
9/13	Hayd	6f Cls1 Gp1 gd-sft			£141,775
8/13	Leop	1m Gp3 good			£31,707
3/13	Dund	6f stand			£8,415
10/12	Lonc	7f Gp1 heavy			£142,850
8/12	York	7f Cls1 List gd-sft			£28,355
5/12	Cork	6f gd-sft			£8,625
90	5/12	Tipp	5f 70-96 Hcap heavy		£7,475
78	11/11	Dund	6f 77-95 Hcap stand		£7,733
	10/11	Dund	6f Mdn stand		£4,759

Has won Group 1 races in each of last two seasons over 6f and 7f, most recently when coping best with soft ground to run away with Haydock Sprint Cup; equally effective in quicker conditions having

finished second in same race on firm ground in 2012; stays a mile on good ground.

084 Grandeur (Ire)

5 rg g Verglas - Misskinta (Desert Sun)
Jeremy Noseda Miss Yvonne Jacques
PLACINGS: **1/4127131121/42717-1** RPR **118**

Starts	1st	2nd	3rd	4th	Win & Pl
18	8	4	1	2	£337,249
	2/14	Ling	1m2f Cls1 List stand		£25,520
	9/13	Gdwd	1m2f Cls1 List good		£22,684
	12/12	Holl	1m4f Gd2 firm		£96,774
	11/12	SnAt	1m1f Gd2 3yo firm		£58,065
	9/12	Newb	1m1f Cls3 gd-fm		£7,159
99	8/12	Gdwd	1m2f Cls2 76-99 3yo Hcap good		£28,013
88	5/12	Gdwd	1m2f Cls2 83-90 3yo Hcap gd-fm		£12,938
	8/11	Brig	7f Cls5 Auct Mdn 2yo gd-fm		£3,170

Globetrotting middle-distance performer who also showed ability to compete at a high level in Britain last season, particularly when pushing Mukhadram close in a Group 2 at York; comfortable winner when dropped to Listed grade at Goodwood; much prefers quick ground.

085 Graphic (Ire)

5 ch g Excellent Art - Follow My Lead (Night Shift)
William Haggas The Royal Ascot Racing Club
PLACINGS: **0/35600/97434114115-** RPR **112**

Starts	1st	2nd	3rd	4th	Win & Pl
22	6	1	2	4	£96,895
102	11/13	Nott	1m¹/₂f Cls2 95-107 Hcap stand		£19,407
97	10/13	York	1m Cls2 85-99 Hcap good		£16,173
90	9/13	Kemp	1m Cls2 87-110 Hcap stand		£31,125
82	8/13	Hayd	1m Cls3 79-95 Hcap gd-fm		£8,086
	9/11	Kemp	7f Cls4 2yo stand		£3,429
	6/11	Sals	7f Cls4 Mdn 2yo gd-fm		£3,918

Hugely progressive during second half of last season when winning four handicaps out of five (only defeat when excellent fourth in Cambridgeshire); may have had enough for year when fifth on first run at Listed level; has most form on good to firm ground but also effective on soft.

086 Great White Eagle (USA)

3 b c Elusive Quality - Gender Dance (Miesque's Son)
Aidan O'Brien (Ir)
Michael Tabor, Derrick Smith & Mrs John Magnier
PLACINGS: **118-** RPR **107+**

Starts	1st	2nd	3rd	4th	Win & Pl
3	2	-	-	-	£40,121
9/13	Curr	6f Gp3 2yo gd-fm			£31,707
8/13	Naas	6f 2yo yield			£8,415

Bitterly disappointing when 2-1 favourite for Middle Park Stakes, failing to pick up in eighth; well worth another chance on strength of Group 3 win on quicker ground at the Curragh, coming from almost last to first down unfavoured middle of the track, though bare form was moderate for the grade.

087 Gregorian (Ire)

5 gr h Clodovil - Three Days In May (Cadeaux Genereux)

John Gosden   HRH Princess Haya Of Jordan

PLACINGS: 1/15032012/21351386-   RPR **118**

Starts	1st	2nd	3rd	4th	Win & Pl
19	5	3	3	-	£309,032
	8/13	Newb	7f Cls1 Gp2 good		£56,710
	5/13	Epsm	1m¹/₂f Cls1 Gp3 gd-sft		£34,026
	9/12	Haml	1m¹/₂f Cls3 heavy		£9,057
88	4/12	Newb	7f Cls3 78-88 3yo Hcap soft		£6,536
	10/11	Donc	7f Cls5 Mdn 2yo good		£3,299

Highly tried last season, winning a Group 3 at Epsom in June and subsequently competing exclusively at a higher level; gained biggest win when claiming scalp of Soft Falling Rain in Hungerford Stakes and came closest to a Group 1 victory when third in Queen Anne Stakes.

088 Guerre (USA)

3 b/br c War Front - Golden Toast (Hennessy)

Aidan O'Brien (Ir)
     Derrick Smith, Mrs John Magnier & Michael Tabor

PLACINGS: 12-   RPR **98**

Starts	1st	2nd	3rd	4th	Win & Pl
2	1	1	-	-	£16,276
	9/13	Curr	6f Mdn 2yo good		£10,098

Beaten at odds-on in a Listed race at the Curragh in September having won over course and distance but lost little in defeat when outpaced by Shining Emerald with several fair yardsticks some way

behind; could have done with longer trip and should do well over at least a mile.

089 Guest Of Honour (Ire)

5 b h Cape Cross - Risera (Royal Academy)

Marco Botti   Giuliano Manfredini

PLACINGS: 4511/2221397-   RPR **116+**

Starts	1st	2nd	3rd	4th	Win & Pl
11	3	3	1	1	£64,905
	5/13	Wind	1m¹/₂f Cls1 List good		£22,684
79	12/12	Kemp	1m Cls4 72-84 Hcap stand		£4,075
	11/12	Wolv	1m¹/₂f Cls5 Mdn stand		£2,911

Raced mainly on all-weather early in career but flourished when switched to turf last season, easily winning a Listed race at Windsor and going close in Summer Mile at Ascot; didn't let himself down on firm ground in Arlington Million and disappointed again on good to firm at Ascot.

090 Harris Tweed

7 b g Hernando - Frog (Akarad)

William Haggas   B Haggas

PLACINGS: 32243/1344203/23112-   RPR **118**

Starts	1st	2nd	3rd	4th	Win & Pl
26	7	7	5	3	£353,225
	8/13	Gdwd	1m6f Cls1 List good		£22,684
105	7/13	Gdwd	1m6f Cls2 93-108 Hcap gd-sft		£46,688
	4/12	Newb	1m4f Cls1 Gp3 soft		£31,191
	9/10	NmkR	1m6f Cls1 List 3yo soft		£19,870
	9/10	Ches	1m4¹/₂f Cls1 List soft		£21,926
86	6/10	Muss	1m4¹/₂f Cls2 81-104 3yo Hcap gd-fm		£49,848
	4/10	Ripn	1m2f Cls5 Mdn 3yo gd-fm		£2,914

Seemed to have lost his way early last season but gained first win for more than a year when landing a Goodwood handicap by six lengths and continued to progress after; nearly made all in Long Distance

Cup at Ascot when pipped on line and should run in top staying races.

091 Hartnell *(below)*

3 b c Authorized - Debonnaire (Anabaa)

Mark Johnston
Sheikh Hamdan Bin Mohammed Al Maktoum

PLACINGS: 9212113-					RPR **103**
Starts	1st	2nd	3rd	4th	Win & Pl
7	3	2	1	-	£41,435
	11/13	NmkR	1m2f Cls3 2yo soft...........................£6,225		
88	10/13	Donc	1m Cls3 68-88 2yo Hcap soft....................£6,469		
	9/13	Ffos	1m Cls5 Mdn 2yo soft.........................£2,911		

Improved with every run last season, progressing from taking three attempts to win a maiden to finishing third in a Group 1 at Saint-Cloud on final

start; suffered first two defeats on only runs on good ground or quicker so likely to prove best with plenty of cut; potential Leger horse.

092 Havana Cooler (Ire)

4 ch c Hurricane Run - Unquenchable (Kingmambo)

Luca Cumani
Leonidas Marinopoulos

PLACINGS: 2/1133-					RPR **102**
Starts	1st	2nd	3rd	4th	Win & Pl
5	2	1	2	-	£25,935
83	7/13	NmkJ	1m4f Cls3 76-90 Hcap gd-fm..................£9,704		
	4/13	Ripn	1m2f Cls5 Mdn 3yo good £3,235		

Did well in several top staying handicaps last season for one with so little experience; beat Pether's Moon at Newmarket before failing to confirm form at Goodwood (didn't handle track)

and did better when third in Melrose Stakes at York; should improve after just five runs.

093 Heaven's Guest (Ire)

4 b g Dark Angel - Bakewell Tart (Tagula)

Richard Fahey   J K Shannon & M A Scaife

PLACINGS: 821/27114100417-   RPR **109**

Starts		1st	2nd	3rd	4th	Win & Pl
14		5	2	-	2	£197,136
100	10/13	Asct	7f Cls2 95-109 Hcap gd-sft			£93,375
94	7/13	Nmkl	6f Cls2 82-103 3yo Hcap gd-fm			£62,250
86	5/13	Epsm	7f Cls2 81-94 3yo Hcap gd-sft			£15,563
79	5/13	Haml	6f Cls4 71-79 3yo Hcap gd-sft			£6,469
	10/12	Catt	5f Cls5 Mdn 2yo soft			£3,170

Won three handicaps out of four, including notable scalp of Moviesta, when climbing from 79 to 100 early last season; twice below best at Goodwood

subsequently, but stayed on well at end of Ayr Gold Cup and relished step up to 7f to win another valuable handicap at Ascot.

094 Heeraat (Ire)

5 b h Dark Angel - Thawrah (Green Desert)

William Haggas   Hamdan Al Maktoum

PLACINGS: 6/36334115/14262104-   RPR **116**

Starts		1st	2nd	3rd	4th	Win & Pl
19		5	2	4	3	£115,260
	7/13	Newb	6f Cls1 Gp3 gd-fm			£34,026
101	4/13	Newb	5f Cls2 91-105 Hcap gd-sft			£12,450
94	9/12	York	6f Cls2 83-97 3yo Hcap gd-fm			£12,938
89	8/12	York	5f Cls2 76-90 App 3yo Hcap gd-sft			£16,173
	8/11	Pont	6f Cls4 Mdn 2yo gd-fm			£4,399

Finished 2012 on upward curve and earned step up into Pattern company with another handicap

ONE TO FOLLOW **York Glory** Kevin Ryan's Wokingham winner gets better with age. The six-year-old earned a career-best RPR of 114 for last season's big win and can strike beyond handicap company this year. *[Simon Turner, Racing Post Ratings]*

win at Newbury on return; produced best effort at higher level at same track when winning 6f Group 3 and very consistent otherwise, finishing out of first four only in Group 1 company.

095 Highland Colori (Ire)

6 b g Le Vie Dei Colori - Emma's Star (Darshaan)

Andrew Balding   Evan M Sutherland

PLACINGS: 5162270/40106311412-   RPR **116**

Starts	1st	2nd	3rd	4th	Win & Pl
26	4	4	1	2	£181,447

10/13	Donc	7f Cls3 soft	£8,093
104 9/13	Ayr	6f Cls2 97-110 Hcap gd-sft	£96,488
8/13	Wwck	7f Cls3 good	£7,439
92 6/13	Nmkj	7f Cls2 76-95 Hcap gd-fm	£7,763
88 8/12	Nmkj	7f Cls2 86-102 Hcap gd-fm	£12,450
85 5/12	Sand	1m Cls3 82-93 Hcap gd-fm	£6,848
80 5/12	NmkR	7f Cls4 66-81 Hcap gd-fm	£5,175
75 5/12	Wind	6f Cls4 67-79 Hcap soft	£4,205
7/11	Sthl	5f Cls5 Mdn 3yo stand	£2,264

Has won on good to firm but is much more effective on soft and made most of preferred conditions and proven stamina when winning Ayr Gold Cup last season; equally good at 7f and wasn't beaten far in a Group 2 at Newmarket before good second to Jack Dexter at Doncaster.

096 Hillstar

4 b c Danehill Dancer - Crystal Star (Mark Of Esteem)

Sir Michael Stoute   Sir Evelyn De Rothschild

PLACINGS: 41/221346-   RPR **119**

Starts	1st	2nd	3rd	4th	Win & Pl
8	2	2	1	2	£283,564

6/13	Asct	1m4f Cls1 Gp2 2yo gd-fm	£99,243
10/12	Leic	7f Cls4 Mdn 2yo soft	£4,334

Beaten favourite twice in handicaps last season but won King Edward VII Stakes when running over 1m4f for first time and followed up with fine third in King George; returned to 1m2f for next two runs at Group 1 level when outpaced both times; should appreciate stepping back up in trip.

097 Hot Streak (Ire)

3 ch c Iffraaj - Ashirah (Housebuster)

Kevin Ryan   Qatar Racing Limited

PLACINGS: 115312-   RPR **115**

Starts	1st	2nd	3rd	4th	Win & Pl
6	3	1	1	-	£110,706

10/13	Asct	5f Cls1 Gp3 2yo gd-sft	£22,684
8/13	York	5f Cls1 List 2yo soft	£28,355
7/13	York	6f Cls4 Auct Mdn 2yo gd-fm	£6,469

Top-class juvenile sprinter last season who looked outstanding when running away with Cornwallis Stakes at Ascot; also effective over an extra furlong (fine second to Astaire in Middle Park) but looks all

about speed and likely to prove best when reverting to minimum trip.

098 Hunter's Light (Ire)

6 ch h Dubawi - Portmanteau (Barathea)

Saeed Bin Suroor   Godolphin

PLACINGS: 11/6371121/1176304-4   RPR **116**+aw

Starts	1st	2nd	3rd	4th	Win & Pl
23	9	2	3	2	£666,953

3/13	Meyd	1m2f Gp1 stand	£147,239
2/13	Meyd	1m1¹/₂f Gp2 stand	£92,025
11/12	Capa	1m2f Gp1 heavy	£79,167
9/12	Veli	1m2f Gp2 stand	£95,833
8/12	Hayd	1m2¹/₂f Cls1 Gp3 gd-fm	£31,191
11/11	Ling	1m2f Cls1 List stand	£17,013
9/11	Gdwd	1m2f Cls1 List soft	£17,013
7/11	Haml	1m3f Cls1 List 3yo good	£23,680
5/11	NmkR	1m2f Cls5 Mdn 3yo good	£3,238

Developed into top-class middle-distance performer in Dubai last year when winning second Group 1 after success in Italy; beaten in next five races, all at top level, but would have gone close in Arlington Million but for interference and was good fourth in Champion Stakes.

099 Ihtimal (Ire)

3 b f Shamardal - Eastern Joy (Dubai Destination)

Saeed Bin Suroor   Godolphin

PLACINGS: 223113-11   RPR **113**+aw

Starts	1st	2nd	3rd	4th	Win & Pl
8	4	2	2	-	£277,456

2/14	Meyd	1m1¹/₂f Gp3 3yo stand	£90,361
2/14	Meyd	1m List 3yo stand	£90,361
9/13	Donc	1m Cls1 Gp2 2yo gd-sft	£39,697
8/13	Nmkj	7f Cls1 Gp3 2yo gd-fm	£28,355

Progressive last season, gaining biggest win in May Hill Stakes at Doncaster on good to soft; had all other runs on good to firm and won well in Sweet Solera Stakes but couldn't quicken as effectively in Fillies' Mile when third to Chriselliam; won UAE 1,000 Guineas in February.

100 Indian Maharaja (Ire)

3 b c Galileo - Again (Danehill Dancer)

Aidan O'Brien (Ir)

Michael Tabor, Derrick Smith & Mrs John Magnier

PLACINGS: 11-   RPR **102**+

Starts	1st	2nd	3rd	4th	Win & Pl
2	2	-	-	-	£33,235

8/13	Tipp	7¹/₂f List 2yo good	£25,102
7/13	Gowr	1m Mdn 2yo gd-fm	£8,134

First foal of Irish 1,000 Guineas winner Again; easily won a Listed race last season over 7f at the Curragh, although form is highly questionable (five opponents lost all ten subsequent starts

ONE TO FOLLOW **Art Of War** Raced only once last year – over 7f at Ascot in September – but Tom Dascombe's gelding showed a lot of promise in finishing second and should not be long in winning. *[Simon Turner, Racing Post Ratings]*

between them with two beaten favourites next time); full of potential over middle distances.

101 Indonesienne (Ire)

3 b f Muhtathir - Mydarshaan (Darshaan)

Christophe Ferland (Fr)   Wertheimer & Frere

PLACINGS: 121-   RPR **111**

Starts	1st	2nd	3rd	4th	Win & Pl
3	2	1	-	-	£150,585
	10/13	Lonc	1m Gp1 2yo soft		£139,366
	7/13	Buch	1m 2yo good		£6,504

Faced a hugely tough task when second to Miss France at Chantilly conceding 4lb and proved her class when landing Prix Marcel Boussac from Lesstalk In Paris; stayed on relentlessly that day and looks likely to stay further having had all three starts over a mile.

102 Integral

4 b f Dalakhani - Echelon (Danehill)

Sir Michael Stoute   Cheveley Park Stud

PLACINGS: 11712-   RPR **116**

Starts	1st	2nd	3rd	4th	Win & Pl
5	3	1	-	-	£89,433
	8/13	Sand	1m Cls1 Gp3 gd-fm		£23,463
	7/13	Sand	1m Cls1 List 3yo gd-fm		£20,983
	5/13	Gdwd	1m Cls5 Mdn good		£3,235

Made debut on May 31 so did well to progress rapidly last season, finishing second to Sky Lantern in Sun Chariot Stakes less than four months later; has gained all three wins over a mile but seemed to stay 1m2f in Nassau Stakes when not getting clear run; sure to improve.

103 Intibaah

4 b g Elnadim - Mawaared (Machiavellian)

Brian Meehan   Hamdan Al Maktoum

PLACINGS: 0110/2021-   RPR **113**

Starts	1st	2nd	3rd	4th	Win & Pl
8	3	2	-	-	£28,022
100	10/13	Asct	6f Cls2 85-103 3yo Hcap soft		£12,450
84	8/12	Ffos	6f Cls4 79-84 2yo Hcap soft		£3,429
	7/12	Wolv	6f Cls5 Mdn 2yo stand		£2,264

Easy winner of a competitive sprint handicap at Ascot on final start of last season, appearing to relish soft ground, though had also run well when second in a Listed race over course and distance earlier in season; pipped on line over 7f previously; still lightly raced and should improve.

104 Jack Dexter

5 b/br g Orientor - Glenhurich (Sri Pekan)

Jim Goldie   Johnnie Delta Racing

PLACINGS: 1153741110/10641321-   RPR **119**

Starts	1st	2nd	3rd	4th	Win & Pl
19	8	2	2	2	£281,552
	11/13	Donc	6f Cls1 List soft		£21,904
	6/13	Newc	6f Cls1 Gp3 gd-sft		£34,026
	3/13	Donc	6f Cls1 List soft		£20,983
97	10/12	Donc	5f Cls2 90-106 Hcap soft		£31,125
93	10/12	Asct	7f Cls2 87-99 App Hcap soft		£32,345
84	9/12	Ayr	6f Cls4 75-84 Hcap heavy		£12,450
78	5/12	Ches	6f Cls3 75-88 3yo Hcap soft		£9,057
	4/12	Thsk	6f Cls5 Auct Mdn 3-4yo soft		£2,943

Highly progressive sprinter over last two seasons, remarkably maintaining upward curve with virtually

every run; has won three times at Group 3 and Listed level and did well in higher grade when second in Champions Sprint and fourth in King's Stand Stakes at Ascot.

105 Johann Strauss

3 b c High Chaparral - Inchmina (Cape Cross)

Aidan O'Brien (Ir)   Derrick Smith

PLACINGS: 422-   RPR **110**

Starts	1st	2nd	3rd	4th	Win & Pl
3	-	2	-	1	£58,787

Highly talented but not straightforward on evidence of last season, even getting beaten at 2-7 in a Naas maiden after an eyecatching debut; showed his true form when running on well to finish second in Racing Post Trophy; seems sure to improve and looks a terrific prospect.

106 Joyeuse

3 b f Oasis Dream - Kind (Danehill)

Lady Cecil   K Abdullah

PLACINGS: 1316-   RPR **105+**

Starts	1st	2nd	3rd	4th	Win & Pl
4	2	-	1	-	£32,922
9/13	Sals	6f Cls1 List 2yo gd-fm			£19,849
5/13	Ling	6f Cls5 Mdn 2yo gd-sft			£3,068

Looked full of promise last season without quite fulfilling potential; given time to develop after finishing third in Albany Stakes and may have needed run when scrambling home in Listed race at Salisbury, but struggled to cope with fast ground when disappointing in Cheveley Park.

107 Just The Judge (Ire)

4 br f Lawman - Faraday Light (Rainbow Quest)

Charles Hills   Qatar Racing Limited & Sangster Family

PLACINGS: 111/21306-   RPR **111+**

Starts	1st	2nd	3rd	4th	Win & Pl
8	4	1	1	-	£327,351
5/13	Curr	1m Gp1 3yo gd-fm			£141,463
10/12	NmkR	7f Cls1 Gp2 2yo gd-sft			£34,026
8/12	Newb	7f Cls1 List 2yo gd-fm			£13,043
6/12	Newb	7f Cls4 Mdn 2yo gd-sft			£3,558

Proved herself a top miler early last season, winning Irish 1,000 Guineas and twice placed behind brilliant Sky Lantern (second in 1,000 Guineas and lost that position close home in Coronation Stakes having tried to match winner); out of sorts later but lost a shoe in Nassau Stakes.

ONE TO FOLLOW

Indy Annihilated the opposition on his debut at Doncaster in November in a time that stacked up really well up against the rest of the card. He could be a colt going places. *[Dave Edwards, Topspeed]*

108 Karakontie (Jpn)

3 b c Bernstein - Sun Is Up (Sunday Silence)

Jonathan Pease (Fr)   Niarchos Family

PLACINGS: 1211-   RPR **117+**

Starts	1st	2nd	3rd	4th	Win & Pl
4	3	1	-	-	£213,813
10/13	Lonc	7f Gp1 2yo soft			£162,593
9/13	Lonc	7f Gp3 2yo good			£32,520
7/13	Comp	7f 2yo v soft			£9,756

Outstayed main rival to win Prix Jean Luc Lagardere over 7f at Longchamp on final start last season; form looks questionable for top level but had also won two of three previous races, suffering only defeat by a short-head to Bunker; could be a big player in French Classics.

109 Kenhope (Fr)

4 b f Kendargent - Bedford Hope (Chato)

Henri-Alex Pantall (Fr)   Guy Pariente

PLACINGS: 21250/1103234-   RPR **110**

Starts	1st	2nd	3rd	4th	Win & Pl
12	3	3	2	1	£205,040
4/13	Lonc	1m Gp3 3yo v soft			£32,520
3/13	StCl	1m 3yo v soft			£13,821
9/12	MsnL	7f 2yo good			£10,000

Group 3 winner early last season and did well when tried exclusively at higher level subsequently; did best when second in Coronation Stakes to Sky Lantern and given too much to do when only fourth in Matron Stakes having been sent off favourite; sold for €900,000 but stays in training.

110 Kingman

3 b c Invincible Spirit - Zenda (Zamindar)

John Gosden   K Abdullah

PLACINGS: 11-   RPR **112+**

Starts	1st	2nd	3rd	4th	Win & Pl
2	2	-	-	-	£26,565
8/13	Sand	7f Cls1 Gp3 2yo gd-fm			£22,684
6/13	NmkJ	7f Cls4 Mdn 2yo good			£3,881

Missed end of last season after requiring minor surgery on a joint but had already done enough in two starts to confirm himself a top contender for 2,000 Guineas; made a big impression on Newmarket debut and followed up with easy win in Solario Stakes; could be special.

111 Kingsbarns (Ire)

4 b c Galileo - Beltisaal (Belmez)

Aidan O'Brien (Ir)
Mrs John Magnier, Michael Tabor & Derrick Smith

PLACINGS: 11/63-   RPR **118**

Starts	1st	2nd	3rd	4th	Win & Pl
4	2	-	1	-	£250,578
10/12	Donc	1m Cls1 2yo soft			£122,494
10/12	Navn	1m Mdn 2yo soft			£8,338

Missed nearly all of last season having won Racing

Post Trophy as a juvenile; well below best on return in Irish Champion Stakes (only run on ground quicker than soft) but did much better when third in Queen Elizabeth II Stakes; could be a major contender in top races over 1m2f.

112 Kingsgate Native (Ire) *(below, right)*

9 b g Mujadil - Native Force (Indian Ridge)

Robert Cowell				Cheveley Park Stud

PLACINGS: 06740/7290/21020530-   RPR **117**

Starts	1st	2nd	3rd	4th	Win & Pl
37	5	7	3	3	£752,626

5/13	Hayd	5f Cls1 Gp2 firm		£51,039
5/10	Hayd	5f Cls1 Gp2 gd-fm		£56,770
7/09	Gdwd	5f Cls1 Gp3 good		£39,739
6/08	Asct	6f Cls1 Gp1 gd-fm		£212,888
8/07	York	5f Cls1 Gp1 good		£136,158

Top-class sprinter in his prime (Group 1 winner in 2007 and 2008) and produced best form for two years when winning Temple Stakes for second time last season; ran to similar level when placed in three Group 3 races, including on soft ground at Newbury despite all wins coming on faster.

113 Kingston Hill

3 rg c Mastercraftsman - Audacieuse (Rainbow Quest)

Roger Varian				Paul Smith

PLACINGS: 111-   RPR **119+**

Starts	1st	2nd	3rd	4th	Win & Pl
3	3	-	-	-	£176,926

10/13	Donc	1m Cls1 Gp1 2yo soft		£149,714
10/13	NmkR	1m Cls1 Gp3 2yo gd-sft		£22,684
9/13	Newb	7f Cls4 Mdn 2yo soft		£4,528

Made rapid progress at end of last season, running away with Racing Post Trophy having made

Pattern breakthrough in Autumn Stakes just two weeks earlier; looks a leading Derby contender and could take in 2,000 Guineas first; yet to race on ground quicker than good to soft.

114 Kiyoshi

3 b f Dubawi - Mocca (Sri Pekan)

Charles Hills				Qatar Racing Limited

PLACINGS: 4112d3-   RPR **111**

Starts	1st	2nd	3rd	4th	Win & Pl
5	2	-	2	1	£80,101

6/13	Asct	6f Cls1 Gp3 2yo gd-fm		£39,697
5/13	Gdwd	6f Cls5 Mdn 2yo gd-fm		£3,881

Failed to build on impressive win in Albany Stakes at Royal Ascot last season, though did herself no favours by hanging badly right at times; disappointing third in Cheveley Park Stakes but connections remain confident of better when stepped up in trip on softer ground.

115 Lat Hawill (Ire)

3 b c Invincible Spirit - Arbella (Primo Dominie)

Marco Botti				Qatar Racing & Essafinaat

PLACINGS: 1-   RPR **92+**

Starts	1st	2nd	3rd	4th	Win & Pl
1	1	-	-	-	£4,075

10/13	Newc	7f Cls4 Mdn 2yo gd-fm		£4,075

Powerfully-built colt whose price rocketed from 10,000gns as a yearling to 230,000gns last year; justified the price with a breathtaking eight-length win in a 7f maiden at Newcastle on his only run last October; half-brother to 1m6f/2m winner Chocala and sure to stay much further.

116 Leading Light (Ire) *(below, winning)*

4 b c Montjeu - Dance Parade (Gone West)

Aidan O'Brien (Ir)

Derrick Smith, Mrs John Magnier & Michael Tabor

PLACINGS: 41/11110-   RPR 118+

Starts	1st	2nd	3rd	4th	Win & Pl
7	5	-	-	1	£433,110
9/13	Donc	1m6½f Cls1 Gp1 3yo gd-sft			.£340,260
6/13	Asct	2m Cls1 Gp3 3yo gd-fm			.£42,533
5/13	Curr	1m2f Gp3 3yo gd-fm			.£31,707
5/13	Navn	1m2f 3yo yield			.£10,569
10/12	Tipp	1m1f Mdn 2yo heavy			.£7,475

Excellent winner of St Leger last season when making full use of proven stamina having won Queen's Vase over 2m earlier; never a factor having been supplemented for Arc but may be given another chance over 1m4f with option of stepping back up to staying distances later.

117 Lesstalk In Paris (Ire)

3 b f Cape Cross - Top Toss (Linamix)

Jean-Claude Rouget (Fr)   Sarl Ecurie J-L Tepper

PLACINGS: 112-   RPR 109

Starts	1st	2nd	3rd	4th	Win & Pl
3	2	1	-	-	£102,097
9/13	Chan	1m Gp3 2yo soft			.£32,520
8/13	Deau	7½f 2yo gd-sft			.£13,821

Unlucky not to win Prix Marcel Boussac last season, doing enough to stand out as France's best juvenile filly having raced far too keenly in front and nearly held off Indonesienne; had overcome trouble to win a Group 3 at Chantilly and should have lots more to offer.

118 Libertarian

4 b c New Approach - Intrum Morshaan (Darshaan)

Charlie Appleby   Godolphin

PLACINGS: 141284-   RPR 118

Starts	1st	2nd	3rd	4th	Win & Pl
6	2	1	-	2	£422,208
5/13	York	1m2½f Cls1 Gp2 3yo good			.£85,065
4/13	Pont	1m2f Cls4 Mdn 3yo gd-sft			.£5,175

Unraced as a juvenile but quickly went from strength to strength for Elaine Burke last season, finishing second in the Derby only to flop on final run for yard in Irish version; reportedly took time to come to hand after move to Godolphin but did well to finish close fourth in St Leger.

119 Lightning Spear

3 ch c Pivotal - Atlantic Destiny (Royal Academy)

Ralph Beckett   Qatar Racing Limited

PLACINGS: 1-   RPR 85+aw

Starts	1st	2nd	3rd	4th	Win & Pl
1	1	-	-	-	£2,911
8/13	Kemp	7f Cls5 Mdn 2yo stand			.£2,911

Half-brother to several winners including former Derby hope Ocean War (11th at 12-1 in 2011) and could also be heading for Epsom if progressing well this spring; well on top close home when winning only start at Kempton and has plenty of scope for improvement.

ONE TO FOLLOW

High Secret This three-year-old gelding raced three times in 12 days for Sir Mark Prescott last season, quickly earning a handicap mark. He finished no better than eighth but showed enough to suggest he'll be a lot better than a mark of 52. *[Simon Turner, Racing Post Ratings]*

120 Lightning Thunder

3 b f Dutch Art - Sweet Coincidence (Mujahid)

Olly Stevens			Mohd Al Kubasi & Pearl Bloodstock Ltd		

PLACINGS: **1124-**   RPR **109**

Starts	1st	2nd	3rd	4th	Win & Pl
4	2	1	-	1	£29,330

9/13	Donc	6f Cls2 2yo gd-sft	£12,450
8/13	Newb	6f Cls4 Mdn 2yo good	£4,528

Had excuses for odds-on defeat in Rockfel Stakes (scoped dirty and showed signs of being in-season) and remains a fine prospect on previous form; won a strong conditions race at Doncaster and finished well clear of rest when second to Miss France in Oh So Sharp Stakes.

121 Lockwood

5 gr g Invincible Spirit - Emily Bronte (Machiavellian)

Saeed Bin Suroor			Godolphin

PLACINGS: **32/14166/40431129-**   RPR **116**

Starts	1st	2nd	3rd	4th	Win & Pl
15	4	2	2	3	£133,751

8/13	Gdwd	7f Cls1 Gp3 good	£34,026
8/13	Thsk	7f Cls3 good	£9,704
7/12	MsnL	6f Gp3 gd-sft	£33,333
4/12	Lonc	7f 3yo soft	£12,083

Group 3 winner for Andre Fabre in 2012 and did well following switch to new trainer last season, winning at same level at Goodwood and nearly following up in Park Stakes at Doncaster when just beaten by Viztoria; best with plenty of cut; yet to win in four races over a mile.

122 Long John (Aus)

4 b g Street Cry - Hosiery (Night Shift)

Charlie Appleby			Godolphin

PLACINGS: **11131319-1**   RPR **115**

Starts	1st	2nd	3rd	4th	Win & Pl
9	6	-	2	-	£609,624

2/14	Meyd	1m Gp3 3yo stand	£90,361
10/13	Caul	1m Gp1 3yo good	£389,744
9/13	Flem	7f List 3yo good	£46,154
4/13	Flem	7f List 2yo good	£46,154
4/13	Sann	6¹/₂f 2yo Hcap good	£13,462
3/13	Bndg	6¹/₂f 2yo Hcap soft	£6,731

High-class performer in Australia last year, justifying favouritism to win Group 1 Caulfield Guineas before disappointing when stepped up in trip for Cox Plate; subsequently switched to Godolphin and made stunning debut when hacking up in UAE 2,000 Guineas in February.

123 Lucky Kristale

3 b f Lucky Story - Pikaboo (Pivotal)

George Margarson			Graham Lodge Partnership

PLACINGS: **11611-**   RPR **110+**

Starts	1st	2nd	3rd	4th	Win & Pl
5	4	-	-	-	£137,847

8/13	York	6f Cls1 Gp2 2yo gd-fm	£85,065
7/13	NmkJ	6f Cls1 Gp2 2yo gd-fm	£45,368
5/13	Yarm	6f Cls5 2yo gd-fm	£3,235
5/13	NmkR	6f Cls5 Mdn Auct 2yo good	£3,235

Dual Group 2 winner last season, claiming notable scalp of Rizeena (possibly below best) at Newmarket and comfortably following up under a penalty in Lowther Stakes at York; missed Prix

Morny and Cheveley Park after dirty scopes; expected to stay a mile by connections.

124 Maarek

7 b g Pivotal - Ruby Rocket (Indian Rocket)

Evanna McCutcheon (Ir) Lisbunny Syndicate

PLACINGS: 1161313212/15290110- RPR **118**

Starts	1st	2nd	3rd	4th	Win & Pl
34	11	5	2	4	£553,442

	10/13	Lonc	5f Gp1 soft £162,593
	9/13	Newb	5f Cls2 Gp3 soft £34,026
	4/13	Naas	5f List soft £21,138
	10/12	Asct	6f Cls1 Gp2 soft £141,775
	9/12	Curr	6f Gp3 yield..£31,146
	6/12	Newc	6f Cls1 Gp3 heavy £31,191
102	5/12	NmkR	6f Cls2 82-104 Hcap gd-sft £27,390
97	4/12	Naas	6f 73-97 Hcap gd-yld £10,833
89	9/11	Curr	6f 79-103 Hcap heavy £25,216
79	6/11	Curr	5f 61-85 Hcap soft £6,246
69	4/11	Navn	6f 47-70 Hcap gd-yld £4,759

Top-class sprinter who won Prix de l'Abbaye last season with powerful late run, relishing soft ground; had lost his way earlier in campaign before bouncing back to form with Group 3 win at Newbury following switch to current yard; has also proved equally effective over 6f.

125 Magician (Ire) ♘

4 b c Galileo - Absolutelyfabulous (Mozart)

Aidan O'Brien (Ir)
  Michael Tabor, Derrick Smith & Mrs John Magnier

PLACINGS: 9217/1191- RPR **123+**

Starts	1st	2nd	3rd	4th	Win & Pl
8	4	1	-	-	£1,198,646

	11/13	SnAt	1m4f Gd1 firm £1,012,270
	5/13	Curr	1m Gp1 3yo gd-fm £141,463
	5/13	Ches	1m2¹/₂f Cls1 Gp3 3yo gd-sft..........................£34,026
	10/12	Curr	1m Mdn 2yo heavy £9,488

Missed much of last season through injury but still made a huge impression with Group 1 wins in Irish 2,000 Guineas and Breeders' Cup Turf (after five-month absence), showing great class and versatility; may prove even better at intermediate trip of 1m2f; should win top races.

126 Mandour (USA)

5 ch h Smart Strike - Mandesha (Desert Style)

Alain de Royer-Dupre (Fr) Princess Zahra Aga Khan

PLACINGS: 2/13/131492- RPR **118**

Starts	1st	2nd	3rd	4th	Win & Pl
9	3	2	2	1	£124,094

	7/13	Sand	1m2f Cls1 List gd-fm......................................£20,983
	4/13	Lonc	1m¹/₂f good..£11,382
	4/12	MsnL	1m2f 3yo gd-sft £12,083

Showed high-class form at around 1m2f last season, winning a strong Listed race at Sandown (on good to firm ground) and finishing placed in Prix d'Ispahan and Prix Dollar (both on soft); last of nine in Prix Foy on only attempt at 1m4f but may be worth another chance at that trip.

127 Mango Diva

4 b f Holy Roman Emperor - Mango Mischief (Desert King)

Sir Michael Stoute Antoniades Family

PLACINGS: 2/12911- RPR **104**

Starts	1st	2nd	3rd	4th	Win & Pl
6	3	2	-	-	£73,882

	9/13	Gowr	1m1¹/₂f Gp3 good..£36,992
	8/13	Sals	1m2f Cls1 List gd-fm.......................................£24,102
	5/13	Kemp	1m Cls5 Mdn 3yo stand £3,881

Progressed well on turf last season having had both maiden runs on all-weather at Kempton; won at Listed level at third attempt when appreciating step up to 1m2f and followed up in a Group 3 at Gowran Park, winning comfortably despite 1lb overweight; should improve.

128 Manndawi (Fr)

4 gr c Dalakhani - Mintly Fresh (Rubiano)

Alain de Royer-Dupre (Fr) H H Aga Khan

PLACINGS: 31425- RPR **116**

Starts	1st	2nd	3rd	4th	Win & Pl
5	1	1	1	1	£133,463

	5/13	MsnL	1m4f 3yo v soft..£10,163

Highly tried last season, running a cracker when second to Flintshire in Grand Prix de Paris, but disappointed when favourite for a Listed race on final start; half-brother to 1m7f winner and Ascot Gold Cup fourth Manighar so should do well over longer trips.

129 Maputo

4 b c Cape Cross - Insijaam (Secretariat)

Charlie Appleby Godolphin

PLACINGS: 2/11101110-3 RPR **116**

Starts	1st	2nd	3rd	4th	Win & Pl
10	6	1	1	-	£129,989

	8/13	Curr	1m2f Gp3 gd-fm £31,707
	7/13	Haml	1m3f Cls1 List 3yo gd-fm................................£23,680
95	7/13	NmkJ	1m2f Cls2 76-96 3yo gd-fm £43,575
88	6/13	NmkJ	1m2f Cls3 77-92 3yo Hcap gd-fm £7,763
82	5/13	Rdcr	1m2f Cls4 74-82 3yo Hcap gd-fm £6,469
	5/13	Haml	1m¹/₂f Cls5 Mdn 3-5yo soft..............................£3,881

Won six out of eight races last season for Mark Johnston up to Group 3 level, looking most impressive when winning a Newmarket handicap by six lengths; flopped in Prix Dollar but may not have acted on soft ground (only previous win on going slower than good to firm came in a maiden).

130 Marvellous (Ire)

3 b f Galileo - You'resothrilling (Storm Cat)

Aidan O'Brien (Ir)
  Derrick Smith, Mrs John Magnier & Michael Tabor

PLACINGS: 1- RPR **86**

Starts	1st	2nd	3rd	4th	Win & Pl
1	1	-	-	-	£8,134

	10/13	Navn	1m Mdn 2yo yield...£8,134

First foal of Cherry Hinton winner You'resothrilling

but looks to have inherited more of her sire's stamina after winning her only start at Navan; expected to be too green by connections (very easy to back) but passed several rivals in closing stages; could be a Classic filly.

131 Mekong River (Ire)
3 b c Galileo - Simply Perfect (Danehill)

Aidan O'Brien (Ir)
Mrs John Magnier, Michael Tabor & Derrick Smith

PLACINGS: 11114-					RPR **104+**
Starts	1st	2nd	3rd	4th	Win & Pl
5	4	-	-	1	£65,146

	11/13	Leop	1m1f List 2yo soft	£21,138
93	9/13	List	1m 81-98 2yo Hcap yld-sft	£15,854
87	8/13	Klny	1m¹/₂f 81-87 2yo Hcap good	£8,415
	8/13	Gowr	7f Mdn 2yo good	£8,134

Given little chance of getting trip when setting off too fast on heavy ground in 1m2f Group 1 at Saint-Cloud (was 2-1 favourite); had won all four previous starts, following up nursery double with brilliant six-length win in Listed race at Leopardstown; still a top middle-distance prospect.

132 Miracle Of Medinah *(below)*
3 ch c Milk It Mick - Smart Ass (Shinko Forest)

Mark Usher
The High Jinks Partnership

PLACINGS: 64111971-					RPR **105**
Starts	1st	2nd	3rd	4th	Win & Pl
8	4	-	-	1	£55,616

9/13	NmkR	7f Cls1 Gp3 2yo good	£22,684
7/13	Newb	6f Cls1 List 2yo gd-fm	£14,461
6/13	Sals	6f Cls3 Auct 2yo gd-fm	£7,763
6/13	Ling	6f Cls5 Mdn 2yo stand	£2,727

Underestimated throughout last season, gaining

Group 3 and Listed victories at 25-1 and 33-1; twice disappointed in between but showed class by winning Somerville Tattersall Stakes at Newmarket, beating subseqent Dewhurst runner-up Cable Bay; best on fast ground.

133 Miss France (Ire)
3 b f Dansili - Miss Tahiti (Tirol)

Andre Fabre (Fr)
Ballymore Thoroughbred Ltd

PLACINGS: 911-					RPR **112+**
Starts	1st	2nd	3rd	4th	Win & Pl
3	2	-	-	-	£34,472

9/13	NmkR	7f Cls1 Gp3 2yo gd-fm	£22,684
8/13	Chan	1m 2yo good	£11,789

Cosy winner of Oh So Sharp Stakes at Newmarket last season when gaining valuable experience of Rowley Mile for likely 1,000 Guineas bid; had also beaten Prix Marcel Boussac winner Indonesienne in conditions race at Chantilly previously; looks an exciting filly.

134 Montiridge (Ire)
4 b c Ramonti - Elegant Ridge (Indian Ridge)

Richard Hannon
Mitaab Abdullah

PLACINGS: 112/3121152-					RPR **117**
Starts	1st	2nd	3rd	4th	Win & Pl
10	5	3	1	-	£136,127

8/13	Gdwd	1m Cls1 Gp3 3yo good	£34,026
7/13	NmkJ	1m Cls1 List 3yo gd-fm	£22,684
5/13	Sand	1m Cls1 List 3yo gd-sft	£20,983
9/12	Sand	7f Cls4 2yo gd-fm	£3,881
7/12	Newb	7f Cls4 Mdn 2yo soft	£4,561

Very smart miler just below top level last season, winning a Group 3 and two Listed races; showed a similarly strong level of form when second to Soft

Falling Rain in a Group 2 at Newmarket last time; looks capable of winning in that grade and could even progress again.

135 Moohaajim (Ire)

4 b c Cape Cross - Thiella (Kingmambo)

Marco Botti   **Sheikh Mohammed Bin Khalifa Al Maktoum**

PLACINGS: **1512/30-**   RPR **104+**

Starts	1st	2nd	3rd	4th	Win & Pl
6	2	1	1	-	£94,011
	9/12	Newb	6f Cls1 Gp2 2yo gd-fm		£34,026
	7/12	Asct	6f Cls2 Mdn 2yo good		£12,938

Top-class juvenile in 2011 when winning Mill Reef Stakes and finishing second in Middle Park; trained for 2,000 Guineas last season but finished well down field having been third in Greenham (travelled best); missed rest of season after a setback; likely to return to sprinting.

136 Morawij

4 ch c Exceed And Excel - Sister Moonshine (Piccolo)

Roger Varian   **Sheikh Ahmed Al Maktoum**

PLACINGS: **141286/613-**   RPR **111**

Starts	1st	2nd	3rd	4th	Win & Pl
9	3	1	1	1	£55,643
	6/13	Sand	5f Cls1 List 3yo good		£20,983
	7/12	Sand	5f Cls1 List 2yo good		£13,043
	5/12	Hayd	6f Cls5 Mdn 2yo gd-fm		£2,264

Had an abbreviated campaign last season but confirmed himself a smart sprinter in just three races; followed decent return with Listed win at Sandown and ran well when beaten just a length

by Slade Power in a Curragh Group 3; disappointed on only start over 6f since debut win.

137 Mount Athos (Ire)

7 b g Montjeu - Ionian Sea (Slip Anchor)

Marco Botti   **Dr Marwan Koukash**

PLACINGS: **144484/11150/158239-**   RPR **120**

Starts	1st	2nd	3rd	4th	Win & Pl
28	8	1	2	5	£606,733
	5/13	Ches	1m5¹/₂f Cls1 Gp3 gd-sft		£42,533
	8/12	Newb	1m5¹/₂f Cls1 Gp3 gd-fm		£31,191
108	7/12	York	1m6f Cls1 List 94-108 Hcap good		£19,536
103	5/12	NmkR	1m6f Cls2 82-103 Hcap gd-fm		£18,675
94	4/11	Dund	1m4f 74-95 Hcap stand		£11,207
84	8/10	York	1m6f Cls2 83-104 3yo Hcap gd-fm		£42,094
70	7/10	Folk	1m4f Cls5 51-70 3yo Hcap gd-fm		£2,730
64	7/10	Hayd	1m2¹/₂f Cls5 58-70 Hcap gd-fm		£2,590

Best known for attempts to win Melbourne Cup, finishing third and fifth in last two seasons; has also produced a couple of striking performances in Britain (two Group 3 wins came by combined total of more than 12 lengths), although twice came up short at higher level last season.

138 Moviesta (USA)

4 b g Hard Spun - Miss Brickyard (A.P. Indy)

Bryan Smart   **Redknapp, Salthouse & Fiddes**

PLACINGS: **321/8112210-**   RPR **115**

Starts	1st	2nd	3rd	4th	Win & Pl
10	4	3	1	-	£114,821
	8/13	Gdwd	5f Cls1 Gp2 good		£56,710
87	5/13	York	5f Cls3 76-90 3yo Hcap soft		£9,704
83	4/13	Donc	6f Cls3 75-88 3yo Hcap gd-fm		£7,439
	9/12	Wolv	5f Cls5 Mdn 2yo stand		£2,264

Ran too badly to be true when well fancied for

Nunthorpe Stakes at York but had improved with every run last season previously; won two handicaps and just touched off twice before bridging gap to Group 2 class in King George Stakes at Goodwood; could be a top sprinter.

139 Mshawish (USA)

4 b c Medaglia D'Oro - Thunder Bayou (Thunder Gulch)

Mikel Delzangles (Fr)   Al Shaqab Racing

PLACINGS: 5/124417-21   RPR 119+

Starts	1st	2nd	3rd	4th	Win & Pl
9				2	£257,030
2/14	Meyd	1m Gp2 good			£90,361
8/13	Deau	1m List 3yo good			£22,358
4/13	StCl	1m 3yo v soft			£11,789

Ran well in top company last season when finishing fourth in Prix du Jockey-Club and St James's Palace Stakes; subsequently kept to a mile and benefited from drop in grade when winning a Listed race at Deauville, but couldn't land a blow in a messy Longchamp Group 2.

140 Mukhadram *(below left)*

5 b h Shamardal - Magic Tree (Timber Country)

William Haggas   Hamdan Al Maktoum

PLACINGS: 11425/12315-   RPR 123+

Starts	1st	2nd	3rd	4th	Win & Pl
10	4	2	1	1	£297,621
7/13	York	1m2¹/²f Cls1 Gp2 gd-fm			£56,710
5/13	Sand	1m2f Cls1 Gp3 gd-sft			£34,026
5/12	NmkR	1m Cls5 Mdn 3yo gd-fm			£3,235
4/12	NmkR	1m Cls4 3yo gd-sft			£5,175

Had won only a maiden prior to last season but

quickly developed into a genuine Group 1 performer as well as winning both races below that level; pushed Al Kazeem close in Prince of Wales's Stakes and would also have been second in Coral-Eclipse but for interference.

141 Mushir

3 b c Oasis Dream - Shimah (Storm Cat)

Roger Varian   Hamdan Al Maktoum

PLACINGS: 11-   RPR 103+

Starts	1st	2nd	3rd	4th	Win & Pl
2	2				£28,107
10/13	York	6f Cls1 List 2yo good			£25,520
9/13	Kemp	6f Cls5 Mdn 2yo stand			£2,588

Won in photo-finishes on both starts last season but had far more in hand when successfully stepping up to Listed company at York, showing a fine turn of foot to storm home having been stuck behind horses; likely to stick to sprint trips on breeding and could go far.

142 Mustajeeb

3 ch c Nayef - Rifqah (Elusive Quality)

Dermot Weld (Ir)   Hamdan Al Maktoum

PLACINGS: 412-   RPR 107

Starts	1st	2nd	3rd	4th	Win & Pl
3	1	1		1	£25,272
7/13	Gway	7f Mdn 2yo yield			£9,256

Impressive winner of a strong Galway maiden last summer and progressed again in Futurity Stakes, failing to cope with War Command but staying on well to take second; may well have found that trip

ONE TO FOLLOW

Tweed Did not see the racecourse until mid-October and scored decisively at Newcastle over 1m4f. A half-sister to useful the Harris Tweed, William Haggas's filly exploited a favourable handicap mark at Newmarket later in the month beating a useful filly hands down. Although beaten when odds-on at Wolverhampton a few days later, she can make up for lost time.
[Dave Edwards, Topspeed]

too short and should improve when stepped up to middle distances.

143 Mutashaded (USA)

4 b c Raven's Pass - Sortita (Monsun)

Roger Varian — Hamdan Al Maktoum

PLACINGS: 1/13- — RPR 110

Starts	1st	2nd	3rd	4th	Win & Pl
3	2	-	1	-	£29,180
79	5/13	Sand	1m2f Cls3 74-88 3yo Hcap gd-fm		£7,439
	10/12	Yarm	1m Cls5 Mdn 2yo heavy		£2,911

Out of a half-sister to Goodwood Cup winner Schiaparelli; won a Sandown handicap off 79 on return and coped well with sharp rise in class when third in King Edward VII Stakes; missed rest of season but remains a fine prospect who is held in highest regard at home.

144 My Titania (Ire)

3 b f Sea The Stars - Fairy Of The Night (Danehill)

John Oxx (Ir) — Christopher Tsui

PLACINGS: 211- — RPR 105+

Starts	1st	2nd	3rd	4th	Win & Pl
3	2	1	-	-	£43,109
	9/13	Curr	7f Gp3 2yo good		£31,707
	9/13	Leop	7f Mdn 2yo good		£9,256

Smooth winner of a Group 3 at the Curragh last September; did little in front according to her rider so should have a lot more to offer in stronger company; expected to stay well and likely to come to Britain for 1,000 Guineas and Oaks if continuing to progress.

145 Nabucco (Ger)

4 b c Areion - Numero Uno (Lavirco)

John Gosden — Gestut Graditz

PLACINGS: 17/4577315- — RPR 101

Starts	1st	2nd	3rd	4th	Win & Pl
9	2	-	1	1	£59,573
	10/13	Siro	1m Gp3 heavy		£22,764
	9/12	Siro	1m List 2yo good		£15,833

Took a couple of runs to find best form last season but went on to win three of last four races; looked particularly good when winning a Salisbury handicap by six lengths off 100 on penultimate start on heavy ground and followed up in Listed company; seems sure to stay 1m4f.

ONE TO FOLLOW

Free Eagle Not many juveniles clock a ton on their debut but Dermot Weld's colt achieved the feat at Leopardstown in August. Although he had his wings clipped at the same track a month later, he is a May foal and could still be destined for the top. *[Dave Edwards, Topspeed]*

146 Narniyn (Ire)

4 b f Dubawi - Narmina (Alhaarth)

Alain de Royer-Dupre (Fr) — HH Aga Khan

PLACINGS: 24111- — RPR 111+

Starts	1st	2nd	3rd	4th	Win & Pl
5	3	1	-	1	£67,479
	10/13	StCl	1m2¹/₂f Gp3 v soft		£32,520
	10/13	Chan	1m2f List 3yo soft		£22,358
	9/13	Chat	1m2f 3yo gd-sft		£6,504

Made giant strides towards end of last season; romping home in a Listed race at Chantilly and looking equally impressive when stepped up to Group 3 level at Saint-Cloud; imposing filly who should have plenty more to offer at four, especially when stepped up in trip.

147 Night Of Thunder (Ire)

3 ch c Dubawi - Forest Storm (Galileo)

Richard Hannon — Saeed Manana

PLACINGS: 11- — RPR 108+

Starts	1st	2nd	3rd	4th	Win & Pl
2	2	-	-	-	£19,070
	10/13	Donc	6f Cls1 List 2yo soft		£15,836
	10/13	Gdwd	6f Cls5 Mdn Auct 2yo soft		£3,235

Won twice on soft ground last October, bolting up in a Goodwood maiden and easily coping with step up to Listed class when landing a good race at Newbury; rated a 2,000 Guineas prospect by connections and should stay a mile, but has to prove himself on faster ground.

148 No Nay Never (USA) *(right)*

3 b/br c Scat Daddy - Cat's Eye Witness (Elusive Quality)

Wesley Ward (US) — Ice Wine Stable, Sue Magnier Et Al

PLACINGS: 111-2 — RPR 117+

Starts	1st	2nd	3rd	4th	Win & Pl
4	3	1	-	-	£251,198
	8/13	Deau	6f Gp1 2yo gd-sft		£162,593
	6/13	Asct	5f Cls1 Gp2 2yo gd-fm		£45,368
	4/13	Keen	4¹/₂f 2yo fast		£19,141

Made a huge impression on two trips to Europe last season, winning at Royal Ascot and producing an even better performance to rout a top-class field in Prix Morny; yet to race beyond 6f but has top mile races on his agenda such as 2,000 Guineas and St James's Palace Stakes.

149 Noozhoh Canarias (Spa)

3 b c Caradak - Noozhah (Singspiel)

E Leon Penate (Sp) — Grupo Bolanos Gran Canarias S L

PLACINGS: 1112- — RPR 115

Starts	1st	2nd	3rd	4th	Win & Pl
4	3	1	-	-	£106,105
	8/13	Buch	6f List 2yo good		£22,358
	6/13	La Z	6f 2yo good		£12,195
	5/13	La Z	4f 2yo good		£6,504

Exciting prospect for Spain; gained biggest win last season in a Listed race at Bordeaux before just being outstayed by Karakontie when stepped up to 7f in Prix Jean Luc Lagardere at Longchamp; had raced too keenly in front that day and should do better if learning to settle.

150 Ocovango
4 br c Monsun - Crystal Maze (Gone West)

Andre Fabre (Fr)   Prince A A Faisal

PLACINGS: **1/115330-7**   RPR **117+**

Starts	1st	2nd	3rd	4th	Win & Pl
8	3	-	2	-	£196,563
	5/13	StCl	1m2f Gp2 3yo gd-sft...................................£60,244		
	3/13	StCl	1m2½f List 3yo v soft...................................£22,358		
	11/12	StCl	1m 2yo heavy...................................£10,000		

Big hope for last season's Derby but lost unbeaten record when managing only fifth behind Ruler Of The World; again came up short in three subsequent top races over 1m4f, apparently struggling to stay when twice faced with soft ground; still a smart middle-distance horse.

151 Oklahoma City
3 b c Oasis Dream - Galaxy Highflyer (Galileo)

Aidan O'Brien (Ir)

Derrick Smith, Mrs John Magnier & Michael Tabor

PLACINGS: **612212-**   RPR **106**

Starts	1st	2nd	3rd	4th	Win & Pl
6	2	3	-	-	£311,999
	10/13	NmkR	7f Cls2 2yo gd-fm...................................£270,550		
	7/13	Naas	6f Mdn 2yo gd-fm...................................£8,134		

Unlucky not to win a Pattern race last season, finishing second three times, but earned a big payday when winning Tattersalls Millions at Newmarket; eligible for some big sales prizes again and capable of winning good races on form of second to Kingston Hill in Autumn Stakes.

152 Olympic Glory (Ire)

4 b c Choisir - Acidanthera (Alzao)

Richard Hannon HE Sheikh Joaan Bin Hamad Al Thani

PLACINGS: 12111/102219- RPR **127**

Starts	1st	2nd	3rd	4th	Win & Pl
11	3	-	-		£1,086,518
10/13	Asct	1m Cls1 Gp1 soft			£601,126
4/13	Newb	7f Cls1 Gp3 3yo gd-sft			£34,026
10/12	Lonc	7f Gp1 2yo heavy			£166,658
8/12	Gdwd	7f Cls1 Gp2 2yo good			£34,026
7/12	NmkJ	7f Cls1 Gp2 2yo heavy			£34,026
6/12	Gdwd	6f Cls5 Mdn 2yo gd-sft			£3,235

Mixed record last season, disappointing twice at Longchamp despite having won a Group 1 there as a juvenile, but went close in Prix Jacques le Marois and easily won Queen Elizabeth II Stakes; saw out trip really well in desperate ground that day so should stay 1m2f.

153 Our Obsession (Ire)

4 ch f Shamardal - Hidden Hope (Daylami)

William Haggas A E Oppenheimer

PLACINGS: 61/11- RPR **108**

Starts	1st	2nd	3rd	4th	Win & Pl
4	3	-	-		£49,702
8/13	York	1m4f Cls1 List gd-fm			£28,355
84	7/13	York	1m2¹/₂f Cls3 76-85 Hcap gd-fm		£16,173
10/12	NmkR	1m Cls4 Mdn 2yo soft			£5,175

Regarded as an Oaks filly after impressive maiden win as a juvenile but held up by injury last season; returned to win both races at York, most notably in a Listed race when stepped up to 1m4f; not sure to be as effective on soft ground; has scope to improve again at four.

154 Outstrip

3 rg c Exceed And Excel - Asi Siempre (El Prado)

Charlie Appleby Godolphin

PLACINGS: 12131- RPR **116**

Starts	1st	2nd	3rd	4th	Win & Pl
5	3	1	1	-	£452,024
11/13	SnAt	1m Gd1 2yo firm			£337,423
9/13	Donc	7f Cls1 Gp2 2yo gd-sft			£50,585
6/13	NmkJ	7f Cls4 Mdn 2yo good			£4,528

Showed a stunning turn of foot to beat Giovanni Boldini in Breeders' Cup Juvenile Turf last season, relishing chance to race on fast ground for first time; had previously won Champagne Stakes and pushed Toormore close, but disappointed in Dewhurst Stakes.

155 Pale Mimosa (Ire)

5 b m Singspiel - Katch Me Katie (Danehill)

Dermot Weld (Ir) Dr R Lambe

PLACINGS: 4/115/174- RPR **110**

Starts	1st	2nd	3rd	4th	Win & Pl
7	3	-	-	2	£73,630
6/13	Leop	1m6f List gd-fm			£25,102
8/12	York	1m4f Cls1 List good			£22,684
8/12	Gway	1m4f Mdn 3yo heavy			£8,913

Lightly raced mare who has won Listed races in each of last two seasons, landing Saval Beg Stakes when stepped up to 1m6f on reappearance to add to Galtres Stakes at York in 2012; disappointed in Irish St Leger but close fourth in Long Distance Cup, proving she stays well.

156 Parbold (Ire)

3 b c Dandy Man - Gala Style (Elnadim)

Richard Fahey D W Armstrong & Cheveley Park Stud

PLACINGS: 1233- RPR **109**

Starts	1st	2nd	3rd	4th	Win & Pl
4	1	1	2	-	£65,093
5/13	York	6f Cls3 Mdn-2yo soft			£9,704

Placed three times at Group 2 level last season over 6f and 7f, finishing behind four subsequent Group 1 winners, so should be capable of winning in a similar grade; looks a sprinter on breeding but finishes his races strongly and may be better over further.

157 Pearl Secret

5 ch h Compton Place - Our Little Secret (Rossini)

David Barron Qatar Racing Limited

PLACINGS: 1/1119/3- RPR **114**

Starts	1st	2nd	3rd	4th	Win & Pl
6	4	-	1	-	£82,573
6/12	Sand	5f Cls1 List 3yo soft			£18,714
5/12	York	5f Cls2 3yo good			£12,938
85	4/12	Donc	5f Cls3 76-87 3yo Hcap heavy		£6,792
10/11	York	5¹/₂f Cls3 Mdn 2yo good			£6,469

Ran a superb race on return last season when third in King's Stand Stakes but missed rest of year after fracturing a splint bone; had progressed well in 2012, suffering only defeat in Nunthorpe Stakes, and should continue to improve if fully recovered after just six career outings.

158 Penglai Pavilion (USA)

4 br c Monsun - Maiden Tower (Groom Dancer)

Charlie Appleby Godolphin

PLACINGS: 1/6121215- RPR **118**

Starts	1st	2nd	3rd	4th	Win & Pl
8	4	2	-	-	£210,065
9/13	StCl	1m4f List 3yo heavy			£22,358
7/13	Deau	1m4¹/₂f 3yo gd-sft			£13,821
6/13	Pari	1m 3yo good			£10,976
10/12	StCl	1m 2yo heavy			£10,000

Allowed to progress quietly by Andre Fabre last

season before coping well with sharp step up in class to finish a terrific fifth in Prix de l'Arc de Triomphe; yet to win above Listed level but had also been beaten by just a head in a Group 2 previously; interesting prospect for Godolphin.

159 Pether's Moon (Ire)
4 b c Dylan Thomas - Softly Tread (Tirol)

Richard Hannon				John Manley
PLACINGS: 72/1202131-				RPR 112aw

Starts	1st	2nd	3rd	4th	Win & Pl
9	3	3	1	-	£65,130
	11/13	Kemp	1m4f Cls1 List stand £20,983		
95	8/13	Gdwd	1m4f Cls2 82-99 3yo Hcap good £31,125		
	4/13	Kemp	1m Cls5 Mdn 3yo stand £3,881		

Very progressive last season and had excuses for all defeats, even when 11th at Royal Ascot having been snatched up twice; went on to win well at Goodwood and Lingfield (stepping up to Listed level); failed to stay 1m6f on penultimate start and could even drop in trip.

160 Pinzolo
3 b c Monsun - Pongee (Barathea)

Charlie Appleby				Godolphin
PLACINGS: 110-				RPR 97+

Starts	1st	2nd	3rd	4th	Win & Pl
3	2	-	-	-	£14,488
	9/13	Newb	1m Cls2 2yo soft £9,960		
	8/13	Nmkj	1m Cls4 Mdn 2yo good £4,528		

From a good middle-distance family (cost 400,000gns as a yearling) and won twice in fair contests last season before disappointing in Racing Post Trophy; clearly held in high regard having been supplemented into that race and has plenty of scope to put that right in time.

161 Pomology (USA)
4 b/br f Arch - Sharp Apple (Diesis)

John Gosden				HRH Princess Haya Of Jordan
PLACINGS: 111-				RPR 108+

Starts	1st	2nd	3rd	4th	Win & Pl
3	3	-	-	-	£39,797
	8/13	Deau	1m4½f Gp3 3yo good £32,520		
80	7/13	Kemp	1m3f Cls4 68-80 3yo Hcap stand £4,690		
	6/13	Wind	1m2f Cls5 Mdn good £2,588		

Unbeaten in three starts last season; stepped up steadily in trip and took sharp rise to Group 3 class

in smooth fashion (handicap victory had come off just 80) when winning over 1m4½f at Deauville; full brother won over 2m so should stay further again.

162 Prince Gibraltar (Fr)
3 ch c Rock Of Gibraltar - Princess Sofia (Pennekamp)

Jean-Claude Rouget (Fr)				Jean-Francois Gribomont
PLACINGS: 311-				RPR 115

Starts	1st	2nd	3rd	4th	Win & Pl
3	2	-	1	-	£128,821
	11/13	StCl	1m2f Gp1 2yo heavy £116,138		
	9/13	Msnl	1m 2yo good £9,756		

Runaway winner of Group 1 Criterium de Saint-Cloud International in November on first start for current yard having been trained previously by Henri-Alex Pantall; may have benefited from racing away from main group but clearly a good prospect for top middle-distance races.

163 Princess Noor (Ire)
3 b f Holy Roman Emperor - Gentle Night (Zafonic)

Roger Varian				Saleh Al Homaizi & Imad Al Sagar
PLACINGS: 19512-				RPR 110

Starts	1st	2nd	3rd	4th	Win & Pl
5	2	1	-	-	£72,827
	7/13	Asct	6f Cls1 Gp3 2yo gd-fm £28,355		
	5/13	Kemp	6f Cls5 Mdn 2yo stand £2,911		

Surprise winner of Princess Margaret Stakes (wore first-time blinkers) having twice been found wanting at a similar level but proved that was no fluke when an excellent second to Vorda in Cheveley Park Stakes; likely to be trained for 1,000 Guineas but yet to race beyond 6f.

164 Producer
5 ch h Dutch Art - River Saint (Irish River)

Richard Hannon				J Palmer-Brown
PLACINGS: 14/31541204/2014101-				RPR 114

Starts	1st	2nd	3rd	4th	Win & Pl
20	8	2	1	4	£375,919
	9/13	Veli	1m Gp2 good £219,512		
	6/13	Nmkj	7f Cls1 Gp3 good £34,026		
	4/13	Leic	7f Cls1 List gd-fm £25,520		
	8/12	Gdwd	7f Cls1 Gp3 gd-sft £31,191		
	6/12	Epsm	7f Cls1 List 3yo good £18,714		
82	9/11	Epsm	7f Cls4 62-85 2yo Hcap good £5,175		
72	8/11	Epsm	7f Cls5 58-75 2yo Hcap good £3,235		
	7/11	Epsm	7f Cls5 Mdn 2yo good £3,881		

Very smart 7f specialist who has won two Group 3

races and two Listed contests at the trip over last two seasons; failed to stay 1m½f when fourth in Diomed Stakes at Epsom but won over a mile for first time in Topkapi Trophy in Turkey under exaggerated waiting tactics.

165 Professor *(below, second left)*
4 ch c Byron - Jubilee (Selkirk)

Richard Hannon				Mrs P Good
PLACINGS: 1451/4111733-				RPR **114+**
Starts	1st	2nd	3rd	4th	Win & Pl
11	5	-	2	2	£84,629

	6/13	Sals	6f Cls1 List gd-fm	£23,818
	6/13	Hayd	6f Cls1 List 3yo gd-fm	£20,983
98	5/13	Asct	7f Cls2 86-98 3yo Hcap gd-fm	£12,938
90	9/12	Newb	6f Cls3 74-90 2yo Hcap gd-fm	£7,159
	7/12	Hayd	6f Cls5 Mdn 2yo gd-sft	£3,235

Won three times on good to firm early last season, landing a handicap over 7f before a pair of Listed races over 6f; seemed less effective on softer ground later in campaign, though still went close when beaten less than a length in third in a Group 3 at Goodwood.

166 Queen Catrine (Ire)
3 b f Acclamation - Kahira (King's Best)

Charles Hills		Qrl, Sheikh Suhaim Al Thani & M Al Kubaisi
PLACINGS: 313223-		RPR **106**
Starts	1st	2nd	3rd	4th	Win & Pl
6	1	2	3	-	£84,687
	6/13	Ayr	6f Cls4 Mdn 2yo gd-fm	£4,528

Placed in four Group races last season, twice running well behind Lucky Kristale and doing even

better when faced with a far stiffer test of stamina (stepping up to a mile on soft ground) to finish third in Prix Marcel Boussac; could return to Longchamp for French Guineas.

167 Radiator
3 b f Dubawi - Heat Haze (Green Desert)

Sir Michael Stoute				K Abdullah
PLACINGS: 514-				RPR **99+**
Starts	1st	2nd	3rd	4th	Win & Pl
3				1	£5,211
	9/13	Ling	7f Cls5 Mdn 2yo gd-fm	£3,068

Superbly bred, being by Dubawi out of Dansili's dam, and looked to have inherited her family's talent when romping home by 15 lengths in a Lingfield maiden; bitterly disappointing next time when a ten-length fourth in Oh So Sharp Stakes but well worth another chance.

168 Red Cadeaux
8 ch g Cadeaux Genereux - Artisia (Peintre Celebre)

Ed Dunlop				The Hon R J Arculli
PLACINGS: /21233881/238962424-				RPR **119**
Starts	1st	2nd	3rd	4th	Win & Pl
42	7	11	6	4	£3,952,923
	12/12	ShTn	1m4f Gp1 good	£710,723
	5/12	York	1m6f Cls1 Gp2 good	£79,394
	6/11	Curr	1m6f Gp3 yld-sft	£32,328
103	5/11	Haml	1m4f Cls1 List 95-109 Hcap good	£26,667
90	4/10	Ling	1m4f Cls2 84-103 Hcap stand	£10,362
84	8/09	Donc	1m4f Cls4 72-85 3yo Hcap soft	£4,857
72	6/09	Wolv	1m4f Cls4 61-79 3yo Hcap stand	£5,181

Likely to be given another globetrotting campaign having finished second in two Melbourne Cups and

a Dubai World Cup in recent years; without a win in Britain and Ireland in seven races since 2012 Yorkshire Cup victory, but finished good second in Geoffrey Freer Stakes last season.

169 Remote

4 b c Dansili - Zenda (Zamindar)

John Gosden					K Abdullah
PLACINGS: 3111-					RPR 116+

Starts	1st	2nd	3rd	4th	Win & Pl
4	3	-	1	-	£62,516
	6/13	Asct	1m2f Cls1 Gp3 3yo gd-fm		£42,533
89	6/13	Donc	1m Cls2 85-103 3yo Hcap good		£12,938
	5/13	Newb	1m2f Cls4 Mdn 3yo gd-fm		£6,469

Won three out of four starts early last season, landing a Doncaster handicap over a mile by six lengths before stepping back up in trip to win a strong Tercentenary Stakes at Royal Ascot; best over 1m2f according to trainer; could be a Group 1 horse at around that trip.

170 Renew (Ire)

4 b c Dansili - Hold Me Love Me (Sadler's Wells)

Marco Botti					O T I Racing
PLACINGS: 64/121231-8					RPR 108

Starts	1st	2nd	3rd	4th	Win & Pl
9	3	2	1	1	£43,425
	9/13	NmkR	1m4f Cls1 List gd-fm		£20,983
85	7/13	Donc	1m4f Cls4 73-85 Hcap gd-fm		£4,690
	5/13	Thsk	1m4f Cls5 Mdn gd-fm		£3,235

Won on first run at Listed level on final start last season at Newmarket over 1m4f; had looked promising in handicaps, losing by a short-head and

then finding ground too soft when stepped up to 1m6f in two runs at Haydock following Doncaster win; may well progress again.

171 Retirement Plan

4 b/br c Monsun - Passage Of Time (Dansili)

Lady Cecil					K Abdullah
PLACINGS: 011-					RPR 103+

Starts	1st	2nd	3rd	4th	Win & Pl
3	2	-	-	-	£14,512
88	8/13	Gdwd	1m3f Cls3 71-89 3yo Hcap good		£9,338
	6/13	Donc	1m4f Cls4 Mdn gd-fm		£5,175

Hugely impressive winner of competitive three-year-old handicap at Glorious Goodwood over 1m4f last season, following up maiden victory at Doncaster; looks type to improve again at four and could stay further; may well be Pattern class.

172 Rex Imperator

5 b g Royal Applause - Elidore (Danetime)

William Haggas					George Turner
PLACINGS: 1205/514050/0262120-					RPR 116

Starts	1st	2nd	3rd	4th	Win & Pl
18	3	5	-	1	£111,814
104	8/13	Gdwd	6f Cls2 95-112 Hcap good		£62,250
98	6/12	Wind	6f Cls3 89-102 Hcap good		£18,675
	8/11	Nott	6f Cls5 Mdn 2yo gd-fm		£3,235

Remarkably easy winner of Stewards' Cup last season on just fourth start for new trainer; had looked smart earlier in career but lost his way in 2012 for Roger Charlton before unsuccessful trip to Dubai; unsuited by softer ground next twice but still second in a 7f Listed race.

173 Rizeena (Ire)

3 b f Iffraaj - Serena's Storm (Statue Of Liberty)

Clive Brittain   Sheikh Rashid Dalmook Al Maktoum

PLACINGS: 51112312-   RPR **113**

Starts	1st	2nd	3rd	4th	Win & Pl
8	4	2	1	-	£271,577
	9/13	Curr	7f Gp1 2yo gd-fm		£106,098
	6/13	Asct	5f Cls1 Gp2 2yo gd-fm		£56,710
	5/13	Sand	5f Cls1 List 2yo gd-sft		£14,461
	5/13	Asct	5f Cls4 Mdn 2yo gd-fm		£5,175

Ran several fine races in top company last season; showed class by winning Queen Mary Stakes despite needing much further, as she showed by following up in Moyglare Stud Stakes and finishing second in Fillies' Mile; should be a strong contender for top fillies' races over a mile.

174 Royal Diamond (Ire)

8 b g King's Best - Irresistible Jewel (Danehill)

Johnny Murtagh (Ir)   Andrew Tinkler

PLACINGS: 38/312321/773212151-   RPR **115**

Starts	1st	2nd	3rd	4th	Win & Pl
31	9	5	4	1	£395,974
	10/13	Asct	2m Cls1 Gp3 soft		£113,420
	8/13	Curr	1m6f Gp3 good		£31,707
	7/13	Leop	1m6f List gd-fm		£21,138
	9/12	Curr	1m6f Gp1 yield		£96,667
80	4/12	Leop	1m6f 71-94 Hcap good		£7,475
85	10/09	Wolv	1m6f Cls4 72-85 3yo Hcap stand		£5,046
80	9/09	Ffos	1m6f Cls2 80-99 3yo Hcap good		£15,578
72	8/09	Yarm	1m6f Cls5 53-72 Hcap good		£2,979
66	7/09	Sand	1m6f Cls4 61-78 3yo Hcap good		£4,857

Surprise winner of Irish St Leger in 2012 after being beaten in previous three runs in handicaps but proved that was no fluke with several fine runs last season, most notably when pipping Harris Tweed in Long Distance Cup at Ascot; should again be a force in top staying races.

175 Royal Empire (Ire)

5 b h Teofilo - Zeiting (Zieten)

Saeed Bin Suroor   Godolphin

PLACINGS: 13162/122011220-   RPR **117**aw

Starts	1st	2nd	3rd	4th	Win & Pl
14	5	5	1	-	£167,925
	8/13	Newb	1m5¹/₂f Cls1 Gp3 good		£34,026
	7/13	Newb	1m2f Cls1 List gd-fm		£20,983
100	1/13	Meyd	1m1¹/₂f 96-104 Hcap stand		£40,491
90	12/12	Kemp	1m Cls3 76-90 Hcap stand		£6,663
	7/12	Ling	1m Cls5 Mdn 3-4yo stand		£2,386

Developed into a smart middle-distance performer

last season, gaining second successive win at Newbury when stepped up in trip for Geoffrey Freer Stakes; finished second in two more Group 3 races under a penalty, although failed to fire when well down field in Melbourne Cup.

176 Royalmania

3 ch f Elusive Quality - Safari Queen (Lode)

Freddy Head (Fr)   Wertheimer & Frere

PLACINGS: 114-   RPR **105+**

Starts	1st	2nd	3rd	4th	Win & Pl
3	2	-	-	1	£37,504
	9/13	Chan	1m 2yo soft		£13,821
	8/13	Deau	7¹/₂f 2yo good		£9,756

Sent off second favourite for Prix Marcel Boussac after impressive wins at Chantilly and Deauville but never threatened in the big race, running on well into fourth having been detached in last; nervous and fragile according to her trainer but certainly capable of better.

177 Ruler Of The World (Ire)

4 ch c Galileo - Love Me True (Kingmambo)

Aidan O'Brien (Ir)
Mrs John Magnier, Michael Tabor & Derrick Smith

PLACINGS: 1115273-   RPR **125**

Starts	1st	2nd	3rd	4th	Win & Pl
7	3	1	1	-	£1,008,492
	6/13	Epsm	1m4f Cls1 Gp1 3yo good		£782,314
	5/13	Ches	1m4¹/₂f Cls1 Gp3 3yo good		£34,026
	4/13	Curr	1m2f Mdn 3yo good		£8,695

Did remarkably well to win Derby on only third ever run (had been unraced as a juvenile) and proved underrated despite failing to win in four subsequent starts, running another stormer when just touched off in Champion Stakes; failed to cope with quicker ground in Irish Derby.

178 Saayerr

3 b c Acclamation - Adorn (Kyllachy)

William Haggas   Sheikh Ahmed Al Maktoum

PLACINGS: 11816-   RPR **108**

Starts	1st	2nd	3rd	4th	Win & Pl
5	3	-	-	-	£52,348
	8/13	Gdwd	6f Cls1 Gp2 2yo good		£42,533
	6/13	Wind	5f Cls3 2yo gd-fm		£2,911
	5/13	Sals	5f Cls4 Mdn 2yo good		£4,205

Slightly patchy record last season, but proved

himself a smart colt when winning Richmond Stakes; had found 5f too sharp at Royal Ascot and struggled to act on soft ground when disappointing in Gimcrack Stakes; likely to be kept to quicker surfaces in future.

179 Saddler's Rock (Ire)
6 b h Sadler's Wells - Grecian Bride (Groom Dancer)

John Oxx (Ir)   Michael O'Flynn

PLACINGS: 131/2319546/578035-0   RPR **112**

Starts	1st	2nd	3rd	4th	Win & Pl
20	4	4	3	1	£218,745
	8/12	Gdwd	2m Cls1 Gp2 good		£56,710
	9/11	Donc	2m2f Cls1 Gp2 good		£56,710
87	7/11	Leop	1m6f 70-89 Hcap gd-fm		£7,733
	6/11	Tipp	1m4½f Mdn gd-yld		£5,948

Looked a top-class stayer in summer of 2012 when following up close third in Ascot Gold Cup with victory in Goodwood Cup; lost his way subsequently, but produced best efforts since then when third in Irish St Leger and beaten just two lengths in fifth in Long Distance Cup.

180 Sandiva (Ire)
3 ch f Footstepsinthesand - Miss Corinne (Mark Of Esteem)

Richard Fahey   HE Sheikh Joaan Bin Hamad Al Thani

PLACINGS: 11217-   RPR **108+**

Starts	1st	2nd	3rd	4th	Win & Pl
5	3	1	-	-	£81,191
	8/13	Deau	7f Gp3 2yo good		£32,520
	6/13	Naas	6f List 2yo gd-fm		£30,386
	5/13	Nott	5f Cls5 Mdn Auct 2yo gd-fm		£3,235

Showed consistently strong form last season until

failing to stay a mile on soft ground in Prix Marcel Boussac (looked set to be placed until final furlong); had finished second in Albany Stakes and won a good Group 3 at Chantilly; worth another chance over a mile this year.

181 Scintillula (Ire)
4 b f Galileo - Scribonia (Danehill)

Jim Bolger (Ir)   Miss K Rausing & Mrs J S Bolger

PLACINGS: 727/4124134463-   RPR **113+**

Starts	1st	2nd	3rd	4th	Win & Pl
13	2	2	2	4	£123,202
	7/13	Leop	1m1f Gp3 good		£31,707
	6/13	Leop	1m Mdn gd-fm		£8,695

Very busy through middle of last season, running nine times in just over three months, and gradually lost form having peaked with Group 3 win at Leopardstown over 1m1f; had proved equally effective over 1m4f when close fourth in Irish Oaks; should have benefited from a break.

182 Seagull Star
3 b c Sea The Stars - Dash To The Top (Montjeu)

William Haggas   Tony Bloom

PLACINGS: 1-   RPR **79+**

Starts	1st	2nd	3rd	4th	Win & Pl
1	1	-	-	-	£4,528
	10/13	NmkR	1m Cls4 Mdn 2yo gd-fm		£4,528

Fantastic middle-distance pedigree being out of Yorkshire Oaks runner-up Dash To The Top; surprised connections with impressive win in only start in a decent 7f maiden at Newmarket in

October; needs fast ground according to trainer; should have plenty more to offer.

183 Seal Of Approval *(below)*

5 b m Authorized - Hannda (Dr Devious)

James Fanshawe					T R G Vestey
PLACINGS: 21/11F1-					**RPR 118**

Starts	1st	2nd	3rd	4th	Win & Pl
6	4	1	-	-	£334,009
	10/13	Asct	1m4f Cls1 Gp1 soft		£300,563
	8/13	Newb	1m4f Cls1 List good		£22,684
88	7/13	Kemp	1m4f Cls3 78-93 Hcap stand		£7,439
	8/12	Kemp	1m3f Cls5 Mdn stand		£2,264

Unbeaten in four completed starts since debut with only defeat last season coming when falling in Park Hill Stakes at Doncaster (was only fourth but staying on well); proved class when bouncing back to win Champion Fillies and Mares Stakes at Ascot; may progress again.

184 Secret Gesture

4 b f Galileo - Shastye (Danehill)

Ralph Beckett			Qatar Racing Ltd & Newsells Park Stud		
PLACINGS: 21/12239-					**RPR 110**

Starts	1st	2nd	3rd	4th	Win & Pl
7	2	3	1	-	£231,304
	5/13	Ling	1m3¹/₂f Cls1 List 3yo gd-sft		£22,684
	10/12	Newb	1m Cls4 Mdn 2yo heavy		£4,399

Nearly horse last season when placed in Epsom, German and Yorkshire Oaks; looked capable of better (raced too close to strong pace at Epsom and found trouble in running at York), although disappointed on final start in Prix de l'Opera when expected to be suited by drop to 1m2f.

185 Secret Number

4 b c Raven's Pass - Mysterial (Alleged)

Saeed Bin Suroor					Godolphin
PLACINGS: 1/13645361-					**RPR 115**

Starts	1st	2nd	3rd	4th	Win & Pl
9	3	-	2	1	£283,963
	10/13	Asct	1m4f Cls1 Gp3 gd-sft		£34,026
	3/13	Meyd	1m1¹/₂f Cls1 3yo stand		£92,025
	10/12	Kemp	1m Cls5 Mdn 2yo stand		£2,911

Gained first two victories on artificial surfaces but produced a string of solid efforts on turf through the summer and thoroughly deserved excellent victory in Cumberland Lodge Stakes at Ascot; didn't quite stay 1m6f despite not being beaten far when sixth in St Leger.

186 Seussical (Ire)

4 b/br c Galileo - Danehill Music (Danehill Dancer)

Luca Cumani					O T I Racing
PLACINGS: 655/1131-					**RPR 116**

Starts	1st	2nd	3rd	4th	Win & Pl
7	3	-	1	-	£32,431
103	10/13	York	1m2¹/₂f Cls2 91-110 Hcap good		£19,407
87	5/13	Gowr	1m1¹/₂f 69-87 3yo Hcap gd-fm		£5,610
72	3/13	Dund	1m 50-72 3yo Hcap stand		£4,488

Proved well ahead of the handicapper when romping home by six lengths at York off 103 on first start following switch from David Wachman last time; had finished third when stepped up to Listed class on final start in Ireland but looks ready to return to at least that level.

ONE TO FOLLOW

Plutocracy Improved markedly on BHB ratings last season and might not yet have reached the peak of his capabilities. David Lanigan's lightly raced four-year-old goes well fresh, has a willing attitude and is the type to progress even further this year and prove most effective at around 1m4f on decent ground. *[Dave Edwards, Topspeed]*

187 Sharestan (Ire)

6 b g Shamardal - Sharesha (Ashkalani)

Saeed Bin Suroor   **Godolphin**

PLACINGS: 13/12311/13791-   RPR **111**

Starts		1st	2nd	3rd	4th	Win & Pl
12		6	1	3	-	£189,544
	9/13	Ayr	1m2f Cls1 List gd-sft			£34,026
	1/13	Meyd	1m1f good			£46,012
	6/12	Curr	1m List sft-hvy			£24,375
	6/12	Curr	1m2f List soft			£22,750
97	3/12	Curr	1m 83-105 Hcap yield			£30,000
	6/11	Curr	1m Mdn yield			£7,435

Dual Listed winner for John Oxx in 2012 to prompt move to Godolphin and won first start in Britain last year (had been successful in Dubai previously) when quickening up best off slow pace to win another Listed race at Ayr; should be well up to winning at Pattern level.

188 Shea Shea (SAF)

7 b g National Emblem - Yankee Clipper (Jallad)

Mike de Kock (SA)   **Mssrs Brian Joffe & Myron C Berzack**

PLACINGS: /12613136/11/711242-   RPR **123+**

Starts		1st	2nd	3rd	4th	Win & Pl
22		10	4	3	1	£730,941
	3/13	Meyd	5f Gp1 good			£368,098
	3/13	Meyd	5f List good			£64,417
	4/12	Turf	5f Gd1 good			£49,761
	3/12	Vaal	5¹/₂f good			£4,727
	5/11	Scot	6f Gd1 good			£33,309
	3/11	Turf	5¹/₂f Gd3 soft			£12,112
	1/11	Turf	6f yield			£5,390
	12/10	Turf	7f List good			£7,061
	9/10	Turf	7f good			£4,289
	7/10	Turf	7f Mdn 2yo good			£4,185

Arrived in Britain last season as a triple Group 1 winner over 5f and 6f in South Africa and Dubai and unlucky not to add to tally when second in King's Stand and Nunthorpe Stakes, not helped by draw on both occasions; seemed less effective over extra furlong when fourth in July Cup.

189 Shifting Power

3 ch c Compton Place - Profit Alert (Alzao)

Richard Hannon   **Ms Elaine Chivers & Potensis Ltd**

PLACINGS: 11-   RPR **104+**

Starts		1st	2nd	3rd	4th	Win & Pl
2		2	-	-	-	£7,762
	8/13	Nmkl	7f Cls4 2yo good			£4,528
	7/13	Sand	7f Cls5 Mdn Auct 2yo gd-fm			£3,235

Held in high regard and justified strong market support to win both starts this season, with second victory coming by eased-down six lengths from subsequent Acomb winner Treaty Of Paris in novice stakes at Newmarket; strapping colt with plenty of scope for improvement.

190 Shining Emerald

3 b c Clodovil - Janayen (Zafonic)

Paul Deegan (Ir)   **Jaber Abdullah**

PLACINGS: 23113-   RPR **107+**

Starts		1st	2nd	3rd	4th	Win & Pl
5		2	1	2	-	£37,589
	9/13	Curr	6f List 2yo good			£21,138
	9/13	List	7f Mdn 2yo heavy			£8,976

Made a huge impression when winning by 16 lengths at Listowel on heavy ground and proved much more than a mudlark when dropping in trip

on good ground to run away with a strong Listed race at the Curragh; possibly below best when third in Killavullan Stakes next time.

191 Short Squeeze (Ire)

4 b g Cape Cross - Sunsetter (Diesis)

Hugo Palmer   W Duff Gordon, R Smith, B Mathieson

PLACINGS: 092/52531115-   RPR 111

Starts	1st	2nd	3rd	4th	Win & Pl
11	3	2	1	-	£44,803
94	9/13	Hayd	1m Cls2 89-105 Hcap good		£16,173
82	8/13	York	1m Cls2 82-100 3yo Hcap gd-sft		£19,407
75	7/13	Sand	1m Cls4 75-83 Hcap gd-fm		£5,175

Improved rapidly to land a hat-trick of handicap wins last season, hacking up by four and a half lengths on third occasion despite climbing 19lb to 94; came up short at Group 3 level but well worth another chance; has Toorak Handicap at Caulfield in October as long-term aim.

192 Simenon (Ire)

7 b g Marju - Epistoliere (Alzao)

Willie Mullins (Ir)   Wicklow Bloodstock Limited

PLACINGS: /350/11655/4223405-5   RPR 116

Starts	1st	2nd	3rd	4th	Win & Pl
28	4	3	5	5	£458,543
	6/12	Asct	2m5¹/₂f Cls2 gd-sft		£34,238
95	6/12	Asct	2m4f Cls2 84-95 Hcap gd-sft		£34,238
	9/09	Ayr	1m Cls4 2yo gd-sft		£5,828
	7/09	NmkJ	7f Cls4 Mdn 2yo good		£5,181

Has mixed Flat racing with hurdling in recent seasons and went from strength to strength last year when close second in Ascot Gold Cup and Lonsdale Cup; campaigned abroad towards end of year, mainly over inadequate trips, and did so with great distinction, especially when fourth in Melbourne Cup.

193 Sky Hunter

4 b c Motivator - Pearl Kite (Silver Hawk)

Saeed Bin Suroor   Godolphin

PLACINGS: 1/1131-   RPR 117

Starts	1st	2nd	3rd	4th	Win & Pl
5	4	-	1	-	£197,357
	7/13	Vich	1m4f List 3yo gd-sft		£22,358
	5/13	MsnL	1m2¹/₂f 3yo good		£13,821
	4/13	Lonc	1m2f 3yo good		£11,789
	11/12	MsnL	1m2f 2yo heavy		£10,000

Won three out of four starts for Andre Fabre last season, suffering only defeat when third in Prix du Jockey-Club; won a Listed race over 1m4f next

time; by Motivator out of a mare who was second over 1m6f and has had three Listed winners up to that trip so may well flourish over further.

194 Sky Lantern (Ire)

4 gr f Red Clubs - Shawanni (Shareef Dancer)

Richard Hannon   B Keswick

PLACINGS: 112218/2112510-   RPR 120+

Starts	1st	2nd	3rd	4th	Win & Pl
13	4	4	-	-	£791,866
	9/13	NmkR	1m Cls1 Gp1 good-fm		£110,131
	6/13	Asct	1m Cls1 Gp1 3yo gd-fm		£216,349
	5/13	NmkR	1m Cls1 Gp1 3yo gd-fm		£241,585
	9/12	Curr	7f Gp1 2yo good		£108,750
	6/12	Naas	6f List 2yo gd-yld		£36,563
	5/12	Gdwd	6f Cls5 Mdn 2yo good		£3,235

Four-time Group 1 winner who dominated three-year-old fillies' division over a mile before claiming older scalps for first time in Sun Chariot Stakes; also beaten four times but carried across track in Falmouth Stakes and again unlucky in running on only try at 1m2f in Nassau Stakes.

195 Slade Power (Ire)

5 b h Dutch Art - Girl Power (Key Of Luck)

Eddie Lynam (Ir)   Mrs S Power

PLACINGS: 21/12118/371310210-   RPR 119

Starts	1st	2nd	3rd	4th	Win & Pl
16	7	3	2	-	£445,604
	10/13	Asct	6f Cls1 Gp2 soft		£207,856
	8/13	Curr	6f Gp3 good		£31,707
	6/13	Curr	5f Gp3 good		£30,488
	7/12	Fair	6f List soft		£21,667
	6/12	Hayd	6f Cls1 List 3yo gd-fm		£18,714
92	4/12	Cork	6f 75-96 3yo Hcap good		£10,833
	12/11	Dund	6f Mdn 2yo stand		£7,733

Hugely consistent in top sprints last season, finishing out of first three on just three occasions (undone by poor draw in Diamond Jubilee Stakes and dwelt at start at York and Hong Kong); gained deserved win in Champions Sprint at Ascot on soft ground but equally effective on quicker.

196 Snow Sky

3 b c Nayef - Winter Silence (Dansili)

Sir Michael Stoute   K Abdullah

PLACINGS: 3418-   RPR 93

Starts	1st	2nd	3rd	4th	Win & Pl
4	1	-	1	1	£4,998
	10/13	Sals	1m Cls4 Mdn 2yo heavy		£4,205

Twice beaten for speed on good to firm but broke his maiden at third attempt on heavy ground at

Salisbury, storming home by 11 lengths; only eighth in Racing Post Trophy but kept on again in final furlong and should flourish over much longer trip (dam won over 1m6f).

197 Soft Falling Rain (SAF)

5 b h National Assembly - Gardener's Delight (Giant's Causeway)

Mike de Kock (SA)   Hamdan Al Maktoum

PLACINGS: 1111/111210-   RPR **125+**

Starts	1st	2nd	3rd	4th	Win & Pl
10	8	1	-	-	£590,626
9/13	NmkR	1m Cls1 Gp2 gd-fm			£51,039
3/13	Meyd	1m Gp2 stand			£368,098
2/13	Meyd	1m Gp3 3yo stand			£92,025
1/13	Meyd	7f 3yo stand			£18,405
4/12	Turf	6f Gd1 2yo good			£24,881
3/12	Turf	5f List 2yo good			£6,718
2/12	Turf	5f 2yo good			£4,230
1/12	Turf	5f Mdn 2yo good			£3,732

Won just one out of three starts in Britain last summer having been unbeaten in South Africa and Dubai; still enhanced reputation with impressive win over Montiridge in Joel Stakes having needed first run over inadequate 7f; unsuited by soft ground in Queen Elizabeth II Stakes.

198 Sole Power

7 br g Kyllachy - Demerger (Distant View)

Eddie Lynam (Ir)   Mrs S Power

PLACINGS: 9/2223715/241415362-   RPR **120**

Starts	1st	2nd	3rd	4th	Win & Pl
37	7	7	6	4	£1,120,631
6/13	Asct	5f Cls1 Gp1 good			£198,485
5/13	NmkR	5f Cls1 Gp3 gd-fm			£34,026
9/12	Donc	5f Cls1 List good			£23,680
5/11	Hayd	5f Cls1 Gp2 good			£45,416
8/10	York	5f Cls1 Gp1 gd-fm			£136,248
4/10	Dund	5f stand			£10,075
11/09	Dund	5f Mdn 2yo stand			£9,057

Top-class Irish sprinter who won King's Stand Stakes in June three years after other Group 1 win in 2010 Nunthorpe Stakes; has run many fine races otherwise and seemed stronger last season, finishing unlucky fifth in July Cup and second in Hong Kong Sprint on rare attempts at 6f; prefers quick ground.

199 Somewhat (USA)

3 b c Dynaformer - Sometime (Royal Academy)

Mark Johnston   Sheikh Majid Bin Mohammed Al Maktoum

PLACINGS: 142129-   RPR **111+**

Starts	1st	2nd	3rd	4th	Win & Pl
6	2	2	-	1	£60,581
8/13	Newb	7f Cls1 List 2yo good			£14,461
6/13	Muss	7f Cls5 Mdn 2yo gd-fm			£4,205

Progressive juvenile last season and pushed Berkshire close in Royal Lodge Stakes having won impressively at Newbury before that; was expected to enjoy softer ground (has a high knee action) but ran no sort of race in Racing Post Trophy; still a good middle-distance prospect.

200 Sound Reflection (USA)

3 b f Street Cry - Echoes In Eternity (Spinning World)

Charlie Appleby   Godolphin

PLACINGS: 116-   RPR **100**

Starts	1st	2nd	3rd	4th	Win & Pl
3	2	-	-	-	£16,340
9/13	Kemp	7f Cls3 2yo stand			£9,338
8/13	NmkJ	7f Cls4 Mdn 2yo good			£4,528

Impressive winner at Newmarket and Kempton before being found out by lack of early pace in Fillies' Mile, pulling hard and leaving little in the tank for closing stages when fading into sixth; always expected to improve significantly at three and could make up into an Oaks filly.

201 Statutory (Ire)

4 b g Authorized - Mialuna (Zafonic)

Saeed Bin Suroor   Sheikh Hamdan Bin Mohammed Al Maktoum

PLACINGS: 215341421-00   RPR **107+**

Starts	1st	2nd	3rd	4th	Win & Pl
11	3	2	1	2	£32,143
10/13	Pont	2m2f Cls3 good			£7,763
90 8/13	Ches	2m Cls3 76-90 Hcap good			£7,763
7/13	Haml	1m3f Cls5 Mdn gd-fm			£3,235

Made great progress in just four months of racing for Mark Johnston last season having made debut only in July; took big leap forward when stepped up to 2m for first time, winning a Chester handicap by nine lengths, and also won over 2m2f in a conditions race at Pontefract; promising stayer.

202 Steeler (Ire)

4 ch c Raven's Pass - Discreet Brief (Darshaan)

Charlie Appleby   Sheikh Hamdan Bin Mohammed Al Maktoum

PLACINGS: 212113/450   RPR **111**

Starts	1st	2nd	3rd	4th	Win & Pl
9	3	2	1	1	£129,285
9/12	NmkR	1m Cls1 Gp2 2yo good			£56,710
9/12	Gdwd	7f Cls1 List 2yo good			£14,178
8/12	Gdwd	7f Cls2 Mdn 2yo good			£11,321

Missed last season having been banned for a positive drugs test but returned in Dubai in January; had been a smart and progressive two-year-old in 2011, gaining biggest victory in Royal Lodge Stakes at Newmarket before a fine third to Kingsbarns in Racing Post Trophy.

203 Stencive

5 b h Dansili - Madeira Mist (Grand Lodge)

William Haggas   B Kantor & M Jooste

PLACINGS: 3/42122/622-   RPR **110+**

Starts	1st	2nd	3rd	4th	Win & Pl
9	1	5	1	1	£87,291
7/12	NmkJ	1m4f Cls5 Mdn 3yo gd-fm			£3,235

Second in two top handicaps last season and looked unlucky not to win John Smith's Cup over

1m2f at York when finishing fast but losing out by a neck; would have been better suited by further and was set to run in Ebor before setback; should progress into Pattern races.

204 Sudden Wonder (Ire)

3 ch c New Approach - Dubai Surprise (King's Best)

Charlie Appleby   Godolphin

PLACINGS: 421-   RPR **96+**

Starts	1st	2nd	3rd	4th	Win & Pl
3	1	1	-	1	£10,399
	10/13	NmkR	1m Cls2 2yo soft £8,715		

Half-brother to several useful winners who could be even better judged on steady progress made in maidens last season, culminating in runaway eight-length win at Newmarket on soft ground; had run well behind Pinzolo and Outstrip previously; could be a Derby horse.

205 Sudirman (USA)

3 b c Henrythenavigator - Shermeen (Desert Style)

David Wachman (Ir)   Mrs Fitri Hay

PLACINGS: 5311125-   RPR **115**

Starts	1st	2nd	3rd	4th	Win & Pl
7	3	1	1	-	£189,882
	8/13	Curr	6f Gp1 2yo good £94,309		
	6/13	Curr	6f Gp2 2yo good £48,780		
	6/13	Leop	6f Mdn 2yo gd-fm £9,256		

Won Phoenix Stakes at the Curragh last season, repeating previous narrow win over Big Time with War Command well below best in third; unable to confirm strength of that form when well beaten by Toormore over extra furlong in National Stakes and struggling on softer ground in Middle Park.

206 Sun Central (Ire)

5 ch h Galileo - Bordighera (Alysheba)

William Haggas   Lael Stable

PLACINGS: 7/31210/1211-   RPR **117**

Starts	1st	2nd	3rd	4th	Win & Pl
10	5	2	1	-	£84,826
108	8/13	Ches	1m5¹/₂f Cls1 List 94-108 Hcap good £20,983		
100	7/13	York	1m6f Cls1 List 96-109 Hcap gd-fm £22,684		
92	5/13	Sals	1m6f Cls3 76-93 Hcap gd-fm £13,695		
85	8/12	Asct	1m4f Cls3 85-95 3yo Hcap gd-fm £14,754		
	6/12	Ches	1m2¹/₂f Cls4 Mdn good £5,175		

Won three out of four last season, starting with win off 92 and finishing with impressive victory in Listed handicap at Chester off 108; suffered sole defeat when just outstayed on only attempt at 2m; best on fast ground and missed subsequent targets in much softer conditions.

ONE TO FOLLOW

Adelaide looked a Group winner in waiting when impressing on his debut late last year on testing ground. *[Simon Turner, Racing Post Ratings]*

207 Supplicant

3 b c Kyllachy - Pious (Bishop Of Cashel)

Richard Fahey   Cheveley Park Stud

PLACINGS: 13251116-   RPR **111**

Starts	1st	2nd	3rd	4th	Win & Pl
8	4	1	1	-	£85,211
	9/13	Newb	6f Cls1 Gp2 2yo soft £36,862		
	8/13	Ripn	6f Cls1 List 2yo good £17,013		
	8/13	Ripn	6f Cls3 2yo good £9,452		
	5/13	Bevl	5f Cls5 Mdn 2yo gd-fm £3,409		

Consistent performer who gained biggest win on soft ground when outstaying fair field in Mill Reef Stakes; had also won on good to firm on debut as well as twice more on good; came up short at top level when moderate sixth in Middle Park Stakes.

208 Surcingle (USA)

3 b f Empire Maker - Promising Lead (Danehill)

Sir Michael Stoute   K Abdullah

PLACINGS: 17-   RPR **78+**

Starts	1st	2nd	3rd	4th	Win & Pl
2	1	-	-	-	£4,851
	9/13	Leic	1m¹/₂f Cls4 Mdn 2yo gd-fm..............£4,852		

Big and imposing filly who won really won on her debut (stormed clear by four lengths having looked very green early) only to disappoint on much softer ground in Listed company next time; Group 1-winning dam got better with age and remains a smart middle-distance prospect.

209 Tac De Boistron (Fr)

7 gr g Take Risks - Pondiki (Sicyos)

Marco Botti   Australian Thoroughbred Bloodstock

PLACINGS: 142441/5352160/3121-   RPR **119+**

Starts	1st	2nd	3rd	4th	Win & Pl
32	7	3	3	6	£405,723
	10/13	Lonc	1m7¹/₂f Gp1 v soft......................£116,138		
	9/13	Ches	1m4¹/₂f Cls1 List soft..................£21,904		
	7/12	Lonc	1m6f Gp2 soft......................£61,750		
	11/11	StCl	1m7¹/₂f List heavy..................£22,414		
	7/11	Vich	1m7f 4yo Hcap v soft..................£20,259		
0	4/11	StCl	1m2¹/₂f 4yo Hcap heavy..................£20,259		
	6/10	Stra	1m2¹/₂f 3yo soft......................£7,080		

Progressive stayer who excelled for new yard last season having previously been trained mainly in France; easy winner of Prix Royal-Oak over 2m at Longchamp having shown speed to win a Listed race at Chester over 1m4f; didn't quite stay 2m4f when second in Prix du Cadran.

210 Taghrooda

3 b f Sea The Stars - Ezima (Sadler's Wells)

John Gosden   Hamdan Al Maktoum

PLACINGS: 1-   RPR **85+**

Starts	1st	2nd	3rd	4th	Win & Pl
1	1	-	-	-	£4,528
	9/13	NmkR	1m Cls4 Mdn 2yo good..................£4,528		

Out of a triple Listed winner at up to 1m6f and did

very well to make a winning debut at 20-1 in a traditionally strong fillies' maiden at Newmarket won recently by Light Shift and Midday; looks an exciting prospect over middle distances.

211 Talent

4 ch f New Approach - Prowess (Peintre Celebre)

Ralph Beckett   J L Rowsell & M H Dixon

PLACINGS: 31/11723-   RPR **115**

Starts	1st	2nd	3rd	4th	Win & Pl
7	3	1	2	-	£456,714
	5/13	Epsm	1m4f Cls1 Gp1 3yo gd-sft		£241,726
	5/13	NmkR	1m2f Cls1 List 3yo gd-fm		£22,684
	9/12	Kemp	7f Cls3 2yo stand		£5,603

Stormed through late to easily win last season's Oaks, following up a Listed win at Newmarket; flopped in Irish Oaks (may have found ground too quick) but proved class with terrific second in St Leger; fair third in Champion Fillies and Mares Stakes at Ascot last time.

212 Tapestry (Ire)

3 b f Galileo - Rumplestiltskin (Danehill)

Aidan O'Brien (Ir)
Mrs J Magnier, M Tabor, D Smith & Flaxman Stable

PLACINGS: 112-   RPR **111**

Starts	1st	2nd	3rd	4th	Win & Pl
3	2	1	-	-	£97,699
	8/13	Curr	7f Gp2 2yo good		£52,846
	7/13	Curr	6f Mdn 2yo gd-fm		£10,098

Among last season's leading juvenile fillies and arguably unlucky to lose unbeaten record in Moyglare Stud Stakes when promoted to second having been cut up; looks likely to flourish over middle distances, including the Oaks, but could start off in 1,000 Guineas first.

213 Tarfasha (Ire)

3 ch f Teofilo - Grecian Bride (Groom Dancer)

Dermot Weld (Ir)   Hamdan Al Maktoum

PLACINGS: 213-   RPR **97+**

Starts	1st	2nd	3rd	4th	Win & Pl
3	1	1	1	-	£15,792
	7/13	Gway	7f Mdn 2yo yield		£9,256

Showed very strong form in maidens last season, pushing Geoffrey Chaucer close before thrashing a subsequent Listed runner-up at Galway; disappointing third when stepped up to Pattern

company behind My Titania; may well do better over middle distances.

214 Tasaday (USA)

4 gr f Nayef - Tashelka (Mujahid)

Saeed Bin Suroor   Godolphin

PLACINGS: 111/2341132-91   RPR **116+**

Starts	1st	2nd	3rd	4th	Win & Pl
12	6	2	2	1	£428,583
	2/14	Meyd	1m2f List good		£72,289
	8/13	Deau	1m2f Gp2 3yo good		£60,244
	7/13	Deau	1m2f Gp3 3yo gd-sft		£32,520
	10/12	Deau	1m Gp3 2yo v soft		£33,333
	10/12	Chan	1m 2yo v soft		£12,083
	9/12	Chan	1m 2yo soft		£10,000

Admirably tough and durable filly for Andre Fabre when kept on the go throughout last season; finished in the first four at Group 1 level four times (including when beaten a nose in Prix de l'Opera) as well as twice winning in lesser Group races; should continue to do well.

215 Tawhid

4 gr c Invincible Spirit - Snowdrops (Gulch)

Saeed Bin Suroor   Godolphin

PLACINGS: 0211/4332341-   RPR **114**

Starts	1st	2nd	3rd	4th	Win & Pl
11	3	2	3	2	£95,191
	9/13	Newb	7f Cls1 List soft		£20,983
	10/12	Newb	7f Cls1 Gp3 2yo heavy		£20,983
	10/12	Nott	1m⅟₂f Cls5 Mdn 2yo soft		£3,235

Very smart performer on soft ground; ran away with Horris Hill Stakes on heavy as a juvenile and gained first win since then when easily landing a Listed race on soft at Newbury; had run well on quicker in between, most notably when second to Montiridge at Goodwood.

216 Telescope (Ire)

4 b c Galileo - Velouette (Darshaan)

Sir Michael Stoute
Highclere Thoroughbred Racing -Wavertree

PLACINGS: 21/121-   RPR **116+**

Starts	1st	2nd	3rd	4th	Win & Pl
5	3	2			£111,594
	8/13	York	1m4f Cls1 Gp2 3yo-fm		£85,065
	7/13	Leic	1m2f Cls3 3yo gd-fm		£7,561
	9/12	NmkR	1m Cls4 Mdn 2yo good		£4,528

One-time Derby hope who took longer than

expected to come to hand, but showed potential later in campaign, most notably when winning Great Voltigeur Stakes from St Leger fifth and sixth; missed end of season with leg injury that required surgery; likely to ply his trade in top races over 1m4f.

217 Terrific (Ire)

3 b f Galileo - Shadow Song (Pennekamp)

Aidan O'Brien (Ir)				Derrick Smith
PLACINGS: 011-				RPR 95

Starts	1st	2nd	3rd	4th	Win & Pl
3	2	-	-	-	£25,109
	8/13	Curr	7f 2yo good.. £15,854
	8/13	Curr	1m Mdn 2yo gd-fm.. £9,256

Half-sister to two Group 1 winners from same yard who progressed well last season when fitted with blinkers to win twice at the Curragh, making virtually all both times; yet to step up in grade but looks capable of winning good races at around a mile and possibly further.

218 Tested

3 b f Selkirk - Prove (Danehill)

Dermot Weld (Ir)				K Abdullah
PLACINGS: 1-				RPR 91+

Starts	1st	2nd	3rd	4th	Win & Pl
1	1	-	-	-	£9,256
	9/13	Curr	7f Mdn 2yo good... £9,256

Described by her trainer as immature last season and put away after her only start at the Curragh in September; still managed to beat smart rival Sparrow in a 7f maiden on soft ground, finishing strongly having looked green when first asked to quicken; should step up on that.

219 The Fugue

5 b/br m Dansili - Twyla Tharp (Sadler's Wells)

John Gosden				Lord Lloyd-Webber
PLACINGS: 1/4132123/371122-				RPR 123+

Starts	1st	2nd	3rd	4th	Win & Pl
14	5	4	3	1	£1,630,757
	9/13	Leop	1m2f Gp1 good.. £353,252
	8/13	York	1m4f Cls1 Gp1 gd-fm....................................... £200,895
	8/12	Gdwd	1m2f Cls1 Gp1 good... £104,914
	5/12	York	1m2¹/₂f Cls1 Gp3 3yo good.............................. £36,862
	10/11	NmkR	7f Cls4 Mdn 2yo good...................................... £4,399

Hugely consistent performer in Group 1 middle-

distances races over last two seasons, winning three times and getting placed in six others; dominated younger rivals in Yorkshire Oaks last season before enjoying breakthrough victory against colts in Irish Champion Stakes.

220 The Grey Gatsby (Ire)

3 gr c Mastercraftsman - Marie Vison (Entrepreneur)

Kevin Ryan				F Gillespie
PLACINGS: 1227-				RPR 107

Starts	1st	2nd	3rd	4th	Win & Pl
4	1	2	-	-	£39,517
	7/13	York	6f Cls3 Auct Mdn 2yo gd-fm........................... £7,439

Looked best horse in last season's Acomb Stakes, finishing strongly in second having been caught too far back off slow pace, and built on that when chasing home Outstrip in Campagne Stakes; failed to stay a mile on soft ground in Racing Post Trophy; capable of better.

221 The Lark

4 ch f Pivotal - Gull Wing (In The Wings)

Michael Bell				Lady Bamford
PLACINGS: 41/33517-				RPR 108

Starts	1st	2nd	3rd	4th	Win & Pl
7	2	-	2	1	£110,521
	9/13	Donc	1m6¹/₂f Cls1 Gp2 gd-sft................................... £51,039
	10/12	Donc	1m Cls5 Mdn 2yo soft...................................... £3,299

Among last season's leading three-year-old fillies over middle distances, finishing a fine third in Oaks at Epsom before winning Park Hill Stakes at Doncaster when stepped up to 1m6f; disappointed twice in France, getting too far back both times; could stay further.

222 Thistle Bird

6 b m Selkirk - Dolma (Marchand De Sable)

Roger Charlton				Lady Rothschild
PLACINGS: 414135/11212/319263-				RPR 115

Starts	1st	2nd	3rd	4th	Win & Pl
17	6	3	3	2	£218,395
	5/13	Epsm	1m¹/₂f Cls3 Gp3 gd-sft..................................... £34,026
	9/12	Hayd	1m Cls5 List firm... £18,714
	7/12	Asct	1m Cls5 List firm... £18,714
	6/12	Wind	1m¹/₂f Cls1 List good.. £18,714
	84	8/11	Wind	1m¹/₂f Cls4 66-84 Hcap gd-fm........................ £4,075
	5/11	Nott	1m¹/₂f Cls5 Mdn 3yo gd-fm.............................. £4,209

Was expected to retire at end of last season but

has been given another chance to claim elusive Group 1 success; twice beaten less than half a length at that level when placed in Nassau Stakes and Prix de l'Opera; gained biggest win in Princess Elizabeth Stakes at Epsom and continues to improve.

223 Tiger Cliff (Ire)

5 b g Tiger Hill - Verbania (In The Wings)

Alan King   W H Ponsonby

PLACINGS: 2132/1218-   RPR **107**

Starts	1st	2nd	3rd	4th	Win & Pl
8	3	3	1	-	£190,249
98	8/13	York	1m6f Cls2 93-107 Hcap soft.........................£155,625
88	5/13	NmkR	1m6f Cls2 82-101 Hcap gd-fm...................£18,675
	8/12	Kemp	1m3f Cls5 Auct Mdn 3-5yo stand...............£2,264

Progressed well for Lady Cecil last year and won the Ebor following near miss at Royal Ascot; raced too keenly when favourite for Cesarewitch; switched yards to go hurdling this winter but had those plans put off for another year with more big staying races on his agenda for now.

224 Times Up

8 b g Olden Times - Princess Genista (Ile De Bourbon)

Ed Dunlop   Mrs I H Stewart-Brown & M J Meacock

PLACINGS: 112315/44711/603138-   RPR **115**

Starts	1st	2nd	3rd	4th	Win & Pl
34	10	5	6	5	£443,106
	9/13	Donc	2m2f Cls1 Gp2 gd-sft.........................£56,710
	9/12	Donc	2m2f Cls1 Gp2 good..........................£56,710
	8/12	York	2m¹/₂f Cls1 Gp2 gd-sft......................£79,394
	9/11	NmkR	2m Cls1 List gd-fm...........................£17,013
	5/11	York	1m6f Cls1 List good.........................£19,870
102	5/11	NmkR	1m4f Cls2 87-102 Hcap gd-fm...........£24,924
97	11/10	Donc	1m4f Cls2 87-108 Hcap gd-sft..........£62,310
89	7/10	NmkJ	1m4f Cls3 80-93 Hcap gd-fm...............£9,714
84	8/09	NmkJ	1m4f Cls4 66-84 Hcap gd-fm................£5,181
	7/09	Pont	1m4f Cls5 Mdn gd-fm..........................£3,238

Won second successive Doncaster Cup last season, confirming liking for left-handed tracks having also done well in Lonsdale Cup at York (first and third in last two seasons); seems less effective going right-handed having run below par several times at Ascot and Sandown.

225 Toormore (Ire)

3 b c Arakan - Danetime Out (Danetime)

Richard Hannon   Middleham Park Racing IX & James Pak

PLACINGS: 111-   RPR **122+**

Starts	1st	2nd	3rd	4th	Win & Pl
3	3	-	-	-	£141,046
	9/13	Curr	7f Gp1 2yo good.............................£94,309
	7/13	Gdwd	7f Cls1 Gp2 2yo gd-sft.....................£42,533
	5/13	Leic	6f Cls4 Mdn 2yo good......................£4,205

Arguably last season's leading juvenile colt when winning all three starts; just pipped Outstrip to win Vintage Stakes and followed up with easy defeat of Group 1 winner Sudirman in National Stakes; missed Racing Post Trophy due to soft ground; major 2,000 Guineas contender.

226 Top Notch Tonto (Ire)

4 ch g Thousand Words - Elite Hope (Moment Of Hope)

Brian Ellison   Keith Brown

PLACINGS: 13033613/4654312112-   RPR **120**

Starts	1st	2nd	3rd	4th	Win & Pl
19	5	2	5	3	£322,810
	10/13	Rdcr	7f Cls1 List gd-fm...........................£22,684
	9/13	Hayd	1m Cls1 Gp3 gd-sft..........................£34,026
87	7/13	NmkJ	1m Cls3 77-89 3yo Hcap gd-fm.........£9,338
92	9/12	Ayr	1m Cls2 72-92 2yo Hcap heavy..........£9,338
	5/12	Bevl	5f Cls5 Mdn 2yo good.......................£2,420

Big improver in second half of last season, culminating with second in Queen Elizabeth II Stakes having won a Newmarket handicap off 87 just four runs earlier; relished soft ground in QEII (regarded as imperative by trainer) yet had also won a Listed race impressively on good to firm.

227 Top Trip

5 b h Dubai Destination - Topka (Kahyasi)

Francois Doumen (Fr)   J Vasicek

PLACINGS: 2/11215546/6235-   RPR **114**

Starts	1st	2nd	3rd	4th	Win & Pl
13	3	3	1	1	£228,464
	5/12	Lonc	1m3f Gp2 3yo gd-sft..........................£61,750
	3/12	StCl	1m2f 3yo heavy.................................£12,083
	1/12	Deau	1m1¹/₂f 3yo stand.............................£10,000

Produced a mighty effort when finishing a close third in Ascot Gold Cup last season despite never having run beyond 2m previously; had been beaten just a nose in Yorkshire Cup prior to that and should be a threat in similar races as he remains unexposed over staying trips.

228 Toronado (Ire)

4 b c High Chaparral - Wana Doo (Grand Slam)

Richard Hannon   HE Sheikh Joaan Bin Hamad Al Thani

PLACINGS: 111/14216-   RPR **129**

Starts	1st	2nd	3rd	4th	Win & Pl
8	5	1	-	1	£374,001
	7/13	Gdwd	1m Cls1 Gp1 gd-sft..........................£170,130
	4/13	NmkR	1m Cls1 Gp3 3yo gd-fm......................£34,026
	9/12	Donc	7f Cls1 Gp2 2yo good.......................£46,559
	7/12	Asct	7f Cls1 List 2yo good........................£13,043
	6/12	Newb	6'¹/₂f Cls4 Mdn 2yo gd-sft...................£3,429

Troubled by breathing problems last season (such as when flopping in 2,000 Guineas and Juddmonte International) but confirmed brilliance with near miss in St James's Palace Stakes and revenge victory over Dawn Approach in Sussex Stakes; sets strong standard over a mile.

ONE TO FOLLOW

Australia This potential Classic contender already boasts quality form. He's won two of his three races, including a Group 3 on his final start, but is likely to do significantly better this season. *[Simon Turner, Racing Post Ratings]*

229 Trade Storm *(below, winning)*

6 b h Trade Fair - Frisson (Slip Anchor)

David Simcock   Qatar Racing Limited

PLACINGS: 4/70213/011454433-02   RPR **118**

Starts	1st	2nd	3rd	4th	Win & Pl
29	3	3	3	8	£523,746
	3/13	Meyd	1m Gp2 good		.....£92,025
104	2/13	Meyd	1m1f 100-115 Hcap good		.....£64,417
98	8/12	York	1m Cls2 83-107 Hcap gd-fm		.....£46,688
	4/11	Donc	7f Cls3 3yo gd-fm		.....£5,608
	6/10	Newb	6¹/₂f Cls4 Mdn 2yo gd-fm		.....£4,533

Progressed well in Dubai last season but subsequently held back by Group 2 penalty incurred there, running best races in that grade when third in Celebration Mile at Goodwood and close fourth in Summer Mile at Ascot; came up short at Group 1 level but fair third in Woodbine Mile.

230 Trading Leather (Ire)

4 b c Teofilo - Night Visit (Sinndar)

Jim Bolger (Ir)   Mrs J S Bolger

PLACINGS: 2115/2311223-   RPR **121**

Starts	1st	2nd	3rd	4th	Win & Pl
11	4	4	2	-	£1,152,826
	6/13	Curr	1m4f Gp1 3yo gd-fm		.....£589,431
	6/13	Curr	1m2f List gd-fm		.....£22,195
	10/12	NmkR	1m Cls1 Gp3 2yo gd-sft		.....£22,684
	9/12	Gowr	1m Mdn 2yo good		.....£7,475

Consistent performer in top middle-distance races last season, winning Irish Derby and doing well against older horses when placed three more times at Group 1 level; slightly below best on only two runs on going slower than good to firm and missed Champion Stakes due to soft ground.

231 Treve (Fr) 🏇

4 b f Motivator - Trevise (Anabaa)

Criquette Head-Maarek (Fr)

HE Sheikh Joaan Bin Hamad Al Thani

PLACINGS: 1/1111-   RPR **131+**

Starts	1st	2nd	3rd	4th	Win & Pl
5	5	-	-	-	£2,880,821
	10/13	Lonc	1m4f Gp1 soft		.....£2,229,854
	9/13	Lonc	1m4f Gp1 good		.....£162,593
	6/13	Chan	1m2¹/₂f Gp1 3yo good		.....£464,553
	5/13	StCl	1m 3yo good		.....£13,821
	9/12	Lonc	1m 2yo gd-sft		.....£10,000

Magnificent unbeaten filly who took winning run to five races with breathtaking five-length victory in a seemingly red-hot Prix de l'Arc de Triomphe last season; has Arc as main objective again with top middle-distance races along the way including Prince of Wales's Stakes.

232 Tropics (USA)

6 ch g Speightstown - Taj Aire (Taj Alriyadh)

Dean Ivory   Dean Ivory

PLACINGS: 2213/712116101-   RPR **117**

Starts	1st	2nd	3rd	4th	Win & Pl
13	6	3	3	1	£124,634
	10/13	Asct	6f Cls1 Gp3 gd-sft		.....£39,697
	8/13	NmkJ	6f Cls1 List gd-sft		.....£22,684
100	7/13	York	6f Cls2 80-100 Hcap gd-fm		.....£31,125
94	6/13	Wind	6f Cls2 88-105 Hcap good		.....£18,675
84	5/13	Wind	6f Cls4 72-85 Hcap good		.....£4,852
	10/12	Kemp	7f Cls5 Mdn stand		.....£2,264

Hugely progressive sprinter last season having started from mark of 84 to win three handicaps, most notably Sky Bet Dash at York off 100; beaten favourite in Stewards' Cup (drawn wrong side) and Ayr Gold Cup, but proved up to Pattern level when winning Group 3 over 6f at Ascot.

233 Trumpet Major (Ire)

5 b h Arakan - Ashford Cross (Cape Cross)

Richard Hannon   John Manley

PLACINGS: 021415/140150/10066-   RPR **117+**

Starts	1st	2nd	3rd	4th	Win & Pl
19	6	1	1	2	£199,712
	4/13	Sand	1m Cls1 Gp2 good		.....£51,039
	8/12	Gdwd	1m Cls1 Gp3 3yo good		.....£21,508
	4/12	NmkR	1m Cls1 Gp3 3yo gd-sft		.....£31,191
	9/11	Donc	7f Cls1 Gp2 2yo gd-fm		.....£42,533
	8/11	NmkJ	7f Cls2 2yo gd-fm		.....£7,763
	5/11	Gdwd	6f Cls4 Mdn 2yo gd-fm		.....£4,533

Has an excellent record when fresh and enjoyed biggest win on return last season when landing bet365 Mile at Sandown; lost way subsequently (had followed similar pattern in 2012 until mid-season break) but again failed to fire when returned from layoff, perhaps finding 7f too sharp.

234 Valirann (Fr)

4 b c Nayef - Valima (Linamix)

Alain de Royer-Dupre (Fr)   HH Aga Khan

PLACINGS: 21111-   RPR **111+**

Starts	1st	2nd	3rd	4th	Win & Pl
5	4	1	-	-	£149,593
	10/13	Lonc	1m7f Gp2 3yo sft		.....£92,683
	9/13	Lonc	1m7f Gp3 3yo good		.....£32,520
	8/13	Deau	1m5¹/₂f 3yo good		.....£11,789
	7/13	Vich	1m4f 3yo good		.....£8,537

Won final four races last season (none by more than a length) as he gradually stepped up in trip, culminating with gutsy victory in Group 2 Prix Chaudenay over 1m7f when proving he could cope with soft ground; likely contender for top-class staying contests.

ONE TO FOLLOW

Stars Over The Sea Won an Ayr maiden and followed up in good nursery at Newcastle in August. Likely to progress further this year for Mark Johnston. *[Simon Turner, Racing Post Ratings]*

235 Vancouverite

4 b c Dansili - Villarrica (Selkirk)

Charlie Appleby   **Godolphin**

PLACINGS: **611119-**   RPR **118+**

Starts	1st	2nd	3rd	4th	Win & Pl
6	4	-	-	-	£228,048

8/13	Deau	1m2f Gp2 3yo good	£185,366
7/13	Comp	1m2f List 3yo gd-sft	£22,358
7/13	Lonc	1m2f 3yo good	£13,821
4/13	Chat	1m2f 3yo soft	£6,504

Completed a four-timer for Andre Fabre when impressively winning a 1m2f Group 2 at Deauville in August; expected to improve for step up in trip but disappointed when only ninth in Prix Niel, failing to quicken off slow pace (may have been unsuited by soft ground); should have more to offer.

236 Venus De Milo (Ire)

4 br f Duke Of Marmalade - Inchmahome (Galileo)

Aidan O'Brien (Ir)
      Mrs John Magnier, Michael Tabor & Derrick Smith

PLACINGS: **112128-**   RPR **115**

Starts	1st	2nd	3rd	4th	Win & Pl
6	3	2	-	-	£210,940

8/13	Cork	1m4f Gp3 good	£40,955
6/13	Naas	1m2f List 3yo gd-fm	£26,423
6/13	Fair	1m4f Mdn yld-sft	£5,610

Made rapid strides last season in just over three months of racing having made debut in June; won three times and produced best performances when second in Irish Oaks and Yorkshire Oaks, both on good to firm ground; unsuited by soft going when eighth in Prix Vermeille.

237 Verrazano (USA)

4 b c More Than Ready - Enchanted Rock (Giant's Causeway)

Aidan O'Brien (Ir)   Let's Go Stable, Michael B Tabor Et Al

PLACINGS: **1111011743-**   RPR **124aw**

Starts	1st	2nd	3rd	4th	Win & Pl
10	6	-	1	1	£1,022,269

7/13	Monm	1m1f Gd1 3yo fast	£368,098
6/13	Monm	1m¹/₂f Gd3 3yo fast	£55,215
4/13	Aqud	1m1f Gd1 3yo fast	£368,098
3/13	Tamp	1m¹/₂f Gd2 3yo fast	£128,834
2/13	Gulf	1m 3yo fast	£16,012
1/13	Gulf	6¹/₂f 3yo fast	£15,460

Group 1 winner in the United States last year and switched to new yard in bid to boost profile with top-level victory in Europe; won five of first six races last year but only fourth when favourite for Breeders' Cup Dirt Mile; likely to be aimed at Queen Anne Stakes.

238 Viztoria (Ire)

4 b f Oratorio - Viz (Darshaan)

Eddie Lynam (Ir)   **Mrs K Lavery**

PLACINGS: **112/16163-**   RPR **114+**

Starts	1st	2nd	3rd	4th	Win & Pl
8	4	1	1	-	£204,178

9/13	Donc	7f Cls1 Gp2 gd-sft	£56,710
5/13	Curr	7f Gp3 yield	£38,313
9/12	Curr	6f List 2yo heavy	£21,396
7/12	Naas	6f Mdn 2yo heavy	£8,338

Dual winner over 6f on heavy ground as a juvenile but tried over further last season until failing to see out trip in Prix de la Foret, subsequently finishing third in Champions Sprint at Ascot; still won twice over 7f on ground quicker than ideal and could do better in soft-ground sprints.

239 Vorda (Fr)

3 b f Orpen - Velda (Observatory)

Philippe Sogorb (Fr)
H H Sheikh Mohammed Bin Khalifa Al Thani

PLACINGS: 111217- RPR 113+

Starts	1st	2nd	3rd	4th	Win & Pl
6	4	1	-	-	£265,420
9/13	NmkR	6f Cls1 Gp1 2yo gd-fm			£103,949
7/13	MsnL	5½f Gp2 2yo good			£60,244
6/13	MsnL	5f List 2yo good			£22,358
4/13	Chan	5f 2yo good			£13,821

Had an outstanding campaign in Europe last season, suffering only defeat to No Nay Never in Prix Morny and winning Cheveley Park Stakes; looks a dubious stayer over a mile on pedigree and failed to dispel doubts when disappointing seventh in Breeders' Cup Juvenile Fillies Turf.

240 Waila

4 ch f Notnowcato - Crystal Cavern (Be My Guest)

Sir Michael Stoute Sir Evelyn De Rothschild

PLACINGS: 7/1517- RPR 110

Starts	1st	2nd	3rd	4th	Win & Pl
5	2	-	-	-	£33,188
7/13	NmkJ	1m4f Cls1 List 2yo gd-fm			£22,684
4/13	Sand	1m2f Cls4 Mdn 3yo good			£6,469

Ran better than fifth place suggests in Ribblesdale Stakes (had beaten winner in a Sandown maiden on previous start) and proved point with brilliant ten-length win in a Listed race at Newmarket on good to firm; well below form on soft ground when stepped up to Group 1 level next time.

241 War Command (USA)

3 b c War Front - Wandering Star (Red Ransom)

Aidan O'Brien (Ir) J Allen, Mrs J Magnier, M Tabor & D Smith

PLACINGS: 11311- RPR 118

Starts	1st	2nd	3rd	4th	Win & Pl
5	4	-	1	-	£369,264
10/13	NmkR	7f Cls1 Gp1 2yo gd-ft			£228,541
8/13	Curr	7f Gp2 2yo good			£48,780
6/13	Asct	6f Cls1 Gp2 2yo good			£68,052
6/13	Leop	7f Mdn 2yo gd-fm			£9,256

Breathtaking six-length winner of Coventry Stakes at Royal Ascot last season; disappointingly beaten next time as that race failed to work out but still bounced back to grind out victory in Dewhurst Stakes; may yet prove capable of better when returned to a much faster surface.

242 Washaar (Ire)

3 b c Kodiac - Dabtiyra (Dr Devious)

Richard Hannon Hamdan Al Maktoum

PLACINGS: 13114- RPR 108

Starts	1st	2nd	3rd	4th	Win & Pl
5	3	-	1	1	£46,611
8/13	Sals	1m Cls1 List 2yo gd-fm			£15,595
7/13	Asct	7f Cls1 List 2yo gd-fm			£14,461
6/13	Hayd	7f Cls5 Mdn 2yo gd-sft			£2,588

Dual Listed winner last season and did well to defy a penalty at Salisbury when stepped up to a mile having raced too keenly; again seemed to do too much early when close fourth in Royal Lodge Stakes behind Berkshire; may well prove capable of better.

243 Wentworth (Ire)

4 b c Acclamation - Miss Corinne (Mark Of Esteem)

Richard Hannon Mrs John Magnier, Michael Tabor & Derrick Smith

PLACINGS: 611/34315- RPR 110+

Starts	1st	2nd	3rd	4th	Win & Pl
8	3	-	2	1	£121,876
8/13	Gdwd	1m Cls2 91-107 Hcap good			£80,925
9/12	Newb	1m Cls2 2yo gd-fm			£9,338
8/12	York	7f Cls2 Mdn 2yo good			£16,173

Had little go right last season but confirmed potential when winning Betfred Mile at Goodwood on good ground; had struggled on quicker ground on previous two runs (including when good fourth in Britannia Stakes) but failed to act on heavy when favourite in Listed company last time.

244 Willing Foe (USA)

7 b/br g Dynaformer - Thunder Kitten (Storm Cat)

Saeed Bin Suroor Godolphin

PLACINGS: 6/1110/42/31338/1- RPR 116

Starts	1st	2nd	3rd	4th	Win & Pl
13	5	1	3	1	£215,179
5/13	Newb	1m5½f Cls1 List gd-fm			£20,983
8/12	York	1m6f Cls2 96-109 Hcap gd-sft			£140,063
10/10	NmkR	1m4f Cls2 87-105 Hcap good			£9,970
9/10	Donc	1m2½f Cls3 good			£9,347
7/10	Donc	1m2½f Cls5 Mdn 3-4yo good			£2,590

Suffered abbreviated campaign last season but looked an improved performer when thrashing Harris Tweed by six lengths in Aston Park Stakes at Newbury; trainer had Ascot Gold Cup in mind following that victory and may yet manage to make mark in top staying contests.

245 Winning Express (Ire)
4 gr f Camacho - Lady Fabiola (Open Forum)

Ed McMahon   Milton Express Limited

PLACINGS: 112/341232-   RPR **108**

Starts	1st	2nd	3rd	4th	Win & Pl
9	3	3	2		£136,154

6/13	Wwck	7f Cls1 List 3yo gd-fm £22,684
9/12	Sals	6f Cls1 List 2yo good £17,580
8/12	Sand	5f Cls5 Mdn 2yo good £3,235

Finished second in Cheveley Park Stakes as a juvenile and was a fine second over same course and distance on final start last season when running over 6f for first time since; won a Listed race over 7f in between but seemingly less effective over longer trips; could be a top sprinter.

246 Wonderfully (Ire)
3 b f Galileo - Massarra (Danehill)

Aidan O'Brien (Ir)

Michael Tabor, Derrick Smith & Mrs John Magnier

PLACINGS: 171646-   RPR **105**

Starts	1st	2nd	3rd	4th	Win & Pl
6	2	-	-	1	£50,373

7/13	Leop	7f Gp3 2yo gd-fm £31,707
6/13	Fair	6f Mdn 2yo gd-fm £7,012

Appeared to be crying out for further throughout last season but still managed to win a Group 3 at the Curragh and finish fourth in Fillies' Mile (would also have been much closer in Moyglare Stud Stakes but for being badly hampered); should come into her own over middle distances.

247 York Glory (USA)
6 rg h Five Star Day - Minicolony (Pleasant Colony)

Kevin Ryan   Salman Rashed & Mohamed Khalifa

PLACINGS: 744011/245614210822-   RPR **114**

Starts	1st	2nd	3rd	4th	Win & Pl
29	8	8	1	4	£185,466

100	6/13	Asct	6f Cls2 95-108 Hcap gd-fm £93,375
94	4/13	Pont	6f Cls2 86-100 Hcap good...............£12,450
98	11/12	Wolv	5f Cls3 80-98 Hcap stand...............£6,792
92	11/12	Ling	6f Cls3 85-95 Hcap stand...............£6,663
88	8/11	York	5f Cls2 81-94 3yo Hcap good...........£12,938
83	8/11	Thsk	5f Cls4 71 83 3yo Hcap gd-sft...........£4,075
	6/11	Pont	6f Cls5 3yo gd-fm £2,267
	5/11	Sthl	7f Cls6 Auct Mdn 3-4yo stand...........£1,706

Has been a frustrating horse to follow, often finding trouble in running due to need to come late off strong gallop, but proved quality when running away with last season's Wokingham off mark of

100; second in Group 3 and Listed races and capable of winning at that level.

248 Zibelina (Ire)
4 b f Dansili - Zaeema (Zafonic)

Charlie Appleby   Godolphin

PLACINGS: 1114-   RPR **109**

Starts	1st	2nd	3rd	4th	Win & Pl
4	3	-	-	1	£61,007

8/13	Deau	1m Gp3 3yo good £32,520
7/13	Asct	1m Cls1 List good £22,684
6/13	Newc	7f Cls5 Mdn gd-sft £2,588

Won first three starts last season, defying lack of experience to beat older horses in a Listed race at Ascot and following up in a Group 3 at Deauville; better than she showed at Sandown next time when keen early and failing to get home.

249 Zoustar (Aus)
4 b c Northern Meteor - Zouzou (Redoute's Choice)

Chris Waller (Aus)   Iskander Com, Ms J L Leslie Et Al

PLACINGS: 124111-   RPR **117+**

Starts	1st	2nd	3rd	4th	Win & Pl
6	4	1	-	1	£832,596

11/13	Flem	6f Gp1 3yo good £193,910
10/13	Rand	6f Gp2 3yo good £68,397
9/13	Rose	7f Gp1 3yo good £398,333
5/13	Doom	7f Gp2 2yo good £103,846

Latest sprinting sensation from Australia who is likely to compete at Royal Ascot before going on to July Cup; won last three starts in 2013, including two at Group 1 level over 6f and 7f, having been running over further previously.

250 Zurigha (Ire)
4 b f Cape Cross - Noyelles (Docksider)

Richard Hannon   Saeed H Al Tayer

PLACINGS: 16/14061-   RPR **108** RPR

Starts	1st	2nd	3rd	4th	Win & Pl
7	3	-	-	1	£58,367

9/13	NmkR	1m Cls1 List gd-fm £20,983
4/13	Kemp	1m Cls2 3yo stand £12,450
9/12	Kemp	7f Cls5 Mdn 2yo stand £3,235

Made good progress early last season, winning at Kempton and finishing fourth in Poule D'Essai des Pouliches; broke blood vessels when flopping at Royal Ascot and found ground too soft at Doncaster next time, but bounced back to form when winning a Listed race at Ascot on final start.

TEN TO FOLLOW HORSES LISTED BY TRAINER

Ralf Rohne
1144 Nabucco (Ger)

Charlie Appleby
1040 Cat O'Mountain (USA)
1043 Certify (USA)
1065 Encke (USA)
1117 Libertarian
1121 Long John (Aus)
1128 Maputo
1153 Outstrip
1157 Penglai Pavilion (USA)
1159 Pinzolo
1199 Sound Reflection (USA)
1201 Steeler (Ire)
1203 Sudden Wonder (Ire)
1234 Vancouverite
1247 Zibelina (Ire)

Andrew Balding
1039 Casual Smile
1094 Highland Colori (Ire)

Corine Barande-Barbe
1047 Cirrus Des Aigles (Fr)

David Barron
1156 Pearl Secret

Ralph Beckett
1118 Lightning Spear
1183 Secret Gesture
1210 Talent

Michael Bell
1220 The Lark

Jim Bolger
1180 Scintillula (Ire)
1229 Trading Leather (Ire)

Marco Botti
1002 Al Thakhira
1088 Guest Of Honour (Ire)
1114 Lat Hawill (Ire)
1134 Moohaajim (Ire)
1136 Mount Athos (Ire)
1169 Renew (Ire)
1208 Tac De Boistron (Fr)

Clive Brittain
1172 Rizeena (Ire)

Henry Candy
1036 Cape Peron

Lady Cecil
1105 Joyeuse
1170 Retirement Plan

Roger Charlton
1221 Thistle Bird

Paul Cole
1022 Berkshire (Ire)

Robert Cowell
1111 Kingsgate Native (Ire)

Luca Cumani
1000 Afsare
1053 Danadana (Ire)
1091 Havana Cooler (Ire)
1185 Seussical (Ire)

Tom Dascombe
1028 Brown Panther

Mike Kock
1187 Shea Shea (Saf)
1196 Soft Falling Rain (Saf)

Alain de Royer-Dupre
1125 Mandour (USA)
1127 Manndawi (Fr)
1145 Narniyn (Ire)
1233 Valirann (Fr)

Paul Deegan
1016 Avenue Gabriel
1189 Shining Emerald

Mikel Delzangles
1074 Flotilla (Fr)
1138 Mshawish (USA)

Francois Doumen
1226 Top Trip

Ed Dunlop
1008 Amazing Maria (Ire)
1167 Red Cadeaux
1223 Times Up

Brian Ellison
1225 Top Notch Tonto (Ire)

Andre Fabre
1059 Earnshaw (USA)
1064 Elliptique (Ire)
1067 Esoterique (Ire)
1073 Flintshire
1078 Galiway
1132 Miss France (Ire)
1149 Ocovango

Richard Fahey
1079 Garswood
1092 Heaven's Guest (Ire)
1155 Parbold (Ire)
1179 Sandiva (Ire)
1206 Supplicant

James Fanshawe
1182 Seal Of Approval

C Ferland
1100 Indonesienne (Ire)

Jim Goldie
1103 Jack Dexter

John Gosden
1034 Camborne
1075 Flying Officer (USA)
1086 Gregorian (Ire)
1109 Kingman
1160 Pomology (USA)
1168 Remote
1209 Taghrooda
1218 The Fugue

William Haggas
1051 Conduct (Ire)
1084 Graphic (Ire)
1089 Harris Tweed
1093 Heeraat (Ire)
1139 Mukhadram
1152 Our Obsession (Ire)
1171 Rex Imperator
1177 Saayerr
1181 Seagull Star
1202 Stencive
1205 Sun Central (Ire)

Richard Hannon
1010 Anjaal
1018 Baltic Knight (Ire)
1019 Barley Mow (Ire)
1029 Brown Sugar (Ire)
1030 Bunker (Ire)
1046 Chief Barker (Ire)

1133 Montiridge (Ire)
1146 Night Of Thunder (Ire)
1151 Olympic Glory (Ire)
1158 Pether's Moon (Ire)
1163 Producer
1164 Professor
1188 Shifting Power
1193 Sky Lantern (Ire)
1224 Toormore (Ire)
1227 Toronado (Ire)
1232 Trumpet Major (Ire)
1241 Washaar (Ire)
1242 Wentworth (Ire)
1249 Zurigha (Ire)

Freddy Head
1044 Charm Spirit (Ire)
1175 Royalmania

Criquette Head-Maarek
1230 Treve (Fr)

Charles Hills
1032 Cable Bay (Ire)
1035 Cambridge
1106 Just The Judge (Ire)
1113 Kiyoshi
1165 Queen Catrine (Ire)

Tom Hogan
1082 Gordon Lord Byron (Ire)

Dean Ivory
1231 Tropics (USA)

Mark Johnston
1090 Hartnell
1198 Somewhat (USA)

Alan King
1222 Tiger Cliff (Ire)

Barry Lalor
1123 Maarek

David Lanigan
1024 Biographer

Elie Lellouche
1060 Ectot

Eddie Lynam
1194 Slade Power (Ire)
1197 Sole Power
1237 Viztoria (Ire)

Ger Lyons
1027 Brendan Brackan (Ire)

George Margarson
1122 Lucky Kristale

Tony Martin
1055 Dark Crusader (Ire)

Willie McCreery
1072 Fiesolana (Ire)

Ed McMahon
1244 Winning Express (Ire)

Brian Meehan
1102 Intibaah

Ismail Mohammed
1061 Educate

Gary Moore
1058 Dutch Masterpiece

Willie Mullins
1191 Simenon (Ire)

John Joseph Murphy
1023 Big Time (Ire)

Johnny Murtagh
1007 Altruistic (Ire)
1021 Belle De Crecy (Ire)
1173 Royal Diamond (Ire)

Jeremy Noseda
1083 Grandeur (Ire)

Aidan O'Brien
1015 Australia
1026 Bracelet (Ire)
1031 Buonarroti (Ire)
1042 Century (Ire)
1045 Chicquita (Ire)
1048 Coach House (Ire)
1052 Cristoforo Colombo (USA)
1056 Darwin (USA)
1057 Dazzling (Ire)
1066 Ernest Hemingway (Ire)
1070 Eye Of The Storm (Ire)
1071 Festive Cheer (Fr)
1076 Francis Of Assisi (Ire)
1080 Geoffrey Chaucer (USA)
1081 Giovanni Boldini (USA)
1085 Great White Eagle (USA)
1087 Guerre (Ire)
1099 Indian Maharaja (Ire)
1104 Johann Strauss (Ire)
1110 Kingsbarns (Ire)
1115 Leading Light (Ire)
1124 Magician (Ire)
1129 Marvellous (Ire)
1130 Mekong River (Ire)

Ger Lyons
1150 Oklahoma City
1176 Ruler Of The World (Ire)
1211 Tapestry (Ire)
1216 Terrific (Ire)
1235 Venus De Milo (Ire)
1240 War Command (USA)
1245 Wonderfully (Ire)

John Oxx
1143 My Titania (Ire)
1178 Saddler's Rock (Ire)

Hugo Palmer
1012 Ascription (Ire)
1190 Short Squeeze (Ire)

H-A Pantall
1108 Kenhope (Fr)

Jonthan Pease
1107 Karakontie (Jpn)

E Leon Penate
1148 Noozhoh Canarias (Spa)

Todd Pletcher
1236 Verrazano (USA)

Johnny Portman
1011 Annecdote

Jean-Claude Rouget
1116 Lesstalk In Paris (Ire)
1161 Prince Gibraltar (Fr)

Kevin Ryan
1013 Astaire (Ire)
1096 Hot Streak (Ire)
1219 The Grey Gatsby (Ire)
1246 York Glory (USA)

David Simcock
1033 Cafe Society (Fr)
1038 Caspar Netscher
1228 Trade Storm

Bryan Smart
1137 Moviesta (USA)

Philippe Sogorb
1041 Catcall (Fr)
1238 Vorda (Fr)

Olly Stevens
1119 Lightning Thunder

Sir Michael Stoute
1014 Astonishing (Ire)
1025 Bold Sniper
1054 Dank
1063 Elik (Ire)
1068 Estimate (Ire)
1095 Hillstar
1101 Integral

1126 Mango Diva
1166 Radiator
1195 Snow Sky
1207 Surcingle (USA)
1215 Telescope (Ire)
1239 Waila

Saeed Bin Suroor
1001 Ahzeemah (Ire)
1003 Albasharah (USA)
1020 Be Ready (Ire)
1049 Code Of Honor
1069 Excellent Result (Ire)
1097 Hunter's Light (Ire)
1098 Ihtimal (Ire)
1120 Lockwood
1174 Royal Empire (Ire)
1184 Secret Number
1186 Sharestan (Ire)
1192 Sky Hunter
1200 Statutory (Ire)
1213 Tasaday (USA)
1214 Tawhid
1243 Willing Foe (USA)

Mark Usher
1131 Miracle Of Medinah

Roger Varian
1004 Aljamaaheer (Ire)
1009 Ambivalent (Ire)
1062 Ektihaam (Ire)
1112 Kingston Hill
1135 Morawij
1140 Mushir
1142 Mutashaded (USA)
1162 Princess Noor (Ire)

David Wachman
1050 Come To Heel (Ire)
1204 Sudirman (USA)

Chris Waller
1248 Zoustar (Aus)

Wesley Ward
1147 No Nay Never (USA)

Dermot Weld
1005 Along Came Casey (Ire)
1017 Balansiya (Ire)
1037 Carla Bianca (Ire)
1077 Free Eagle (Ire)
1141 Mustajeeb
1154 Pale Mimosa (Ire)
1212 Tarfasha (Ire)
1217 Tested

Andreas Wohler
1006 Altano (Ger)

LEADING BRITISH FLAT TRAINERS: 2013

Trainer	Wins-runs	Wins (%)	2nd	3rd	4th	Win prize	Total prize	Profit/loss (£)
Richard Hannon Snr	187–1130	17	146	139	128	£2,923,741	£4,233,900	-276.75
Aidan O'Brien	13–80	16	11	9	9	£2,700,650	£3,819,986	-9.06
Saeed Bin Suroor	80–430	19	68	54	43	£1,802,479	£2,492,082	-77.91
Mark Johnston	166–1176	14	140	129	122	£1,619,887	£2,406,327	-278.13
Richard Fahey	147–1110	13	142	126	127	£1,527,548	£2,344,899	-131.91
John Gosden	69–355	19	60	47	38	£1,133,475	£1,817,076	-6.94
William Haggas	88–408	22	69	60	45	£1,045,040	£1,775,610	-3.19
Sir Michael Stoute	68–326	21	45	56	31	£1,112,280	£1,612,949	-70.35
Kevin Ryan	74–611	12	52	62	56	£1,018,988	£1,500,222	-14.73
Andrew Balding	72–511	14	60	71	54	£780,208	£1,200,157	+20.15
Roger Varian	66–301	22	44	38	27	£796,347	£1,182,139	+32.95
Charlie Hills	53–439	12	66	54	59	£532,886	£1,171,545	-43.86
Roger Charlton	36–190	19	24	27	20	£782,628	£1,073,759	-25.73
David O'Meara	105–701	15	58	80	68	£693,826	£1,032,967	-57.45
Jim Bolger	2–19	11	4	0	3	£425,325	£995,906	-14.38
Ralph Beckett	46–286	16	40	33	30	£545,621	£982,807	+11.33
Clive Cox	27–264	10	31	32	35	£792,554	£971,457	-62.84
Luca Cumani	52–266	20	51	32	30	£525,082	£937,366	-63.07
Charlie Appleby	38–209	18	29	22	27	£587,527	£836,319	-23.11
James Fanshawe	26–130	20	13	23	14	£502,037	£799,711	+37.46
Lady Cecil	29–128	23	27	13	14	£581,316	£781,903	+32.30
Mick Channon	60–739	8	98	99	93	£325,926	£752,219	-349.43
Tim Easterby	59–794	7	67	68	79	£450,285	£748,955	-354.13
David Simcock	51–299	17	39	41	33	£404,079	£744,559	+55.78
Brian Ellison	43–383	11	47	42	33	£275,783	£708,819	-27.44
Eddie Lynam	4–14	29	1	3	1	£497,077	£696,811	+12.00
Marco Botti	33–270	12	38	38	29	£345,702	£656,610	-73.26
Elaine Burke	29–205	14	34	31	24	£213,960	£644,864	-53.03
Ed Dunlop	35–256	14	41	21	28	£325,943	£641,305	-40.44
David Barron	55–300	18	38	26	20	£368,919	£626,037	+31.51
Andreas Wohler	1–6	17	0	1	0	£603,962	£624,137	+1.50
Michael Bell	32–349	9	46	42	39	£191,300	£484,296	-163.06
Jim Goldie	34–350	10	31	45	45	£210,353	£444,211	-86.41
Tom Dascombe	34–263	13	33	38	27	£245,171	£386,144	-109.44
Brian Meehan	29–258	11	31	32	30	£179,247	£381,614	-74.15
Robert Cowell	7–154	5	15	13	20	£261,333	£381,531	-47.80
Clive Brittain	15–158	9	17	20	18	£186,377	£370,456	-13.05
Michael Dods	39–345	11	40	32	41	£208,258	£365,465	-10.97
David Wachman	1–10	10	0	5	1	£77,375	£343,410	-5.67
Corine Barande-Barbe	0–2	0	1	0	1	£0	£336,584	-2.00
David Nicholls	38–419	9	51	37	37	£168,632	£331,009	-128.88
Jeremy Noseda	29–156	19	25	17	15	£197,364	£328,855	+0.76
Ian Williams	29–195	15	22	22	24	£180,246	£315,142	+38.67
Henry Candy	20–171	12	20	20	27	£133,300	£311,256	-37.92
Michael Easterby	36–371	10	33	25	22	£181,165	£310,380	-66.88
Mike de Kock	3–18	17	5	0	3	£87,900	£291,714	-4.50
Bryan Smart	20–232	9	26	22	28	£165,792	£277,356	-98.2
Sir Henry Cecil	15–70	21	14	8	9	£181,118	£275,558	+13.81
Ed McMahon	14–139	10	18	18	20	£153,825	£275,344	-20.22
David Elsworth	17–113	15	16	19	6	£157,233	£271,796	-2.41

Statistics for March 22 – November 9, 2013

LEADING BRITISH FLAT JOCKEYS: 2013

Jockey	Wins-runs	Wins (%)	2nd	3rd	4th	Win prize	Total prize	Profit/loss (£)
Richard Hughes	203–995	20	169	130	90	£3,104,247	£4,106,563	-168.32
Ryan Moore	186–879	21	133	132	100	£2,938,246	£4,476,063	-100.86
Silvestre de Sousa	153–789	19	105	80	74	£2,115,791	£2,686,877	+74.33
William Buick	115–647	18	94	73	60	£1,407,236	£2,544,817	-53.93
Luke Morris	109–925	12	101	108	110	£437,249	£746,840	-274.95
Joe Fanning	109–852	13	113	104	90	£896,864	£1,406,303	-242.68
Paul Hanagan	107–719	15	91	81	86	£970,237	£1,866,071	-131.78
Neil Callan	105–647	16	83	84	62	£884,948	£1,212,208	-43.02
Graham Lee	99–896	11	94	103	105	£719,562	£1,293,093	-280.69
Jim Crowley	99–673	15	85	72	56	£625,088	£1,226,068	-24.13
Adam Kirby	88–644	14	79	91	75	£1,001,490	£1,302,298	-25.97
Andrea Atzeni	86–624	14	92	68	79	£920,021	£1,375,221	+23.66
Jamie Spencer	84–561	15	83	69	62	£806,521	£1,922,296	-158.75
Danny Tudhope	84–498	17	50	70	56	£483,080	£787,152	-52.58
James Doyle	82–602	14	79	78	69	£1,201,137	£1,761,236	-106.40
Dane O'Neill	76–515	15	62	65	68	£401,239	£685,275	-35.11
George Baker	74–489	15	66	49	52	£660,617	£891,634	-14.25
Mickael Barzalona	74–358	21	55	47	34	£638,506	£1,146,170	-22.49
Tom Queally	72–637	11	62	73	75	£967,321	£1,402,555	-165.90
Graham Gibbons	71–509	14	62	49	42	£429,197	£662,748	-73.16
Franny Norton	70–466	15	66	58	63	£452,021	£702,214	-42.33
Martin Harley	68–604	11	80	80	67	£448,507	£855,551	-157.42
Paul Mulrennan	65–524	12	63	56	57	£496,274	£721,368	-14.83
Kieren Fallon	61–537	11	73	56	60	£564,351	£1,163,293	-131.99
P J McDonald	59–542	11	65	59	52	£231,202	£363,111	-39.32
Robert Winston	59–510	12	58	48	68	£480,591	£709,661	-128.47
Shane Kelly	55–456	12	48	55	50	£197,775	£418,730	-40.49
Seb Sanders	54–416	13	53	57	38	£304,033	£467,351	-40.52
Richard Kingscote	54–401	13	52	51	52	£484,653	£741,813	-106.18
Tom Eaves	53–764	7	86	71	73	£269,667	£483,599	-268.88
Tony Hamilton	52–461	11	55	64	50	£447,543	£697,299	-144.64
David Probert	51–417	12	55	51	41	£298,155	£585,597	+40.40
Jason Hart	51–369	14	44	33	44	£194,610	£308,134	+30.94
Freddie Tylicki	50–441	11	36	62	42	£219,807	£363,304	-58.65
Liam Keniry	47–579	8	50	66	61	£351,152	£506,811	-204.04
Pat Dobbs	47–424	11	50	32	60	£282,438	£455,593	-171.75
Sean Levey	44–410	11	49	41	40	£189,812	£382,835	-98.37
Martin Lane	42–429	10	43	39	46	£375,330	£518,247	-75.43
Cathy Gannon	41–499	8	47	58	60	£153,414	£295,951	-181.17
Hayley Turner	41–304	13	43	35	33	£216,621	£326,614	-77.86
Ted Durcan	40–399	10	39	42	55	£161,143	£301,449	-157.11
Thomas Brown	40–240	17	26	25	33	£177,126	£244,046	-2.97
Jimmy Quinn	39–445	9	27	38	48	£150,847	£272,387	+0.00
Pat Cosgrave	39–360	11	38	30	39	£144,438	£280,855	+15.44
Robert Havlin	39–357	11	50	49	39	£303,340	£440,756	-145.62
Oisin Murphy	38–226	17	22	28	21	£304,385	£376,309	+38.67
Liam Jones	37–331	11	37	39	40	£329,455	£451,864	-109.54
Martin Dwyer	35–422	8	43	40	49	£183,598	£327,243	-152.92
Andrew Mullen	35–389	9	34	42	42	£170,621	£246,286	-40.27
Robert Tart	35–343	10	43	52	33	£183,534	£306,941	-86.68

Statistics for March 22 – November 9, 2013

RACING POST RATINGS: LAST SEASON'S LEADING TWO-YEAR-OLDS

KEY: Horse name, best RPR figure, finishing position when
earning figure, (details of race where figure was earned)

Aeolus 99 2 (6f, Donc, Sft, Oct 26)
Al Thakhira 110 1 (7f, Newm, GS, Oct 12)
All Set To Go (IRE) 98 4 (1m, Curr, Gd, Sep 29)
Along Again (IRE) 98 3 (6f, Asco, GF, Jul 27)
Altruistic (IRE) 104 3 (1m, Donc, Sft, Oct 26)
Alutiq (IRE) 99 5 (6f, York, GF, Aug 22)
Amazing Maria (IRE) 106 1 (7f, Good, Gd, Aug 24)
Ambiance (IRE) 102 3 (5f, Good, GS, Jul 30)
American Hope (USA) 96 2 (6f, Linw, SD, Feb 28)
Andhesontherun (IRE) 95 8 (6f, Good, Gd, Aug 1)
Anjaal 110 4 (7f, Newm, GS, Oct 12)
Anticipated (IRE) 106 2 (5f, Good, GS, Jul 30)
Aqlaam Vision 95 1 (7f, Newb, Hvy, Oct 26)
Astaire (IRE) 116 1 (6f, Newm, GS, Oct 12)
Australia 118 1 (1m, Leop, Gd, Sep 7)
Autumn Lily (USA) 99 1 (7f, Newm, GF, Sep 28)
Avenue Gabriel 104 5 (1m, Newm, GF, Sep 27)
Azagal (IRE) 98 6 (6f, York, GF, Aug 22)
Bahamian Heights 97 1 (6f, York, GF, Aug 21)
Ballybacka Queen (IRE) 97 2 (1m, Curr, Gd, Sep 15)
Barley Mow (IRE) 100 2 (7f, Donc, GS, Sep 13)
Be Ready (IRE) 108 1 (7f, Donc, GS, Sep 13)
Ben Hall (IRE) 98 6 (6f, Good, Gd, Aug 1)
Berkshire (IRE) 111 1 (1m, Newm, GF, Sep 28)
Big Time (IRE) 113 2 (6f, Curr, Gd, Aug 11)
Blockade (IRE) 99 2 (7f, Newm, GS, Oct 12)
Bon Voyage 95 3 (7f, Newm, GF, Oct 5)
Boom The Groom (IRE) 96 3 (5f, Curr, Gd, Aug 24)
Bow Creek (IRE) 100 1 (7f, Newb, Sft, Sep 21)
Brave Boy (IRE) 99 1 (6f 15y, Nott, Gd, Aug 13)
Brazos (IRE) 96 4 (7f, Newm, Gd, Sep 26)
Brown Sugar (IRE) 110 1 (6f, Kemw, SD, Sep 7)
Bunker (IRE) 98 2 (7f, Asco, GF, Jun 22)
Buonarroti (IRE) 102 5 (1m, Donc, Sft, Oct 26)
Bye Bye Birdie (IRE) 105 1 (6f, Curr, GF, Jun 30)
Cable Bay (IRE) 115 2 (7f, Newm, GS, Oct 12)
Carla Bianca (IRE) 102 4 (7f, Curr, GF, Sep 1)
Chicago Girl (IRE) 104 2 (7f, Curr, Gd, Sep 29)
Chief Barker (IRE) 101 1 (1m, Hayd, GS, Sep 7)
Chriselliam (IRE) 114 1 (1m, Newm, GF, Sep 27)
Club Wexford (IRE) 95 2 (5f, Curr, GF, May 25)
Coach House (IRE) 104 2 (5f, Asco, GF, Jun 20)
Come To Heel (IRE) 105 4 (6f, Newm, GF, Sep 28)
Complicit (IRE) 95 2 (6f, Sali, Hvy, Oct 2)
Coral Mist 98 1 (6f, Ayr, GS, Sep 21)
Cordite (IRE) 94 4 (7f, Newb, Hvy, Oct 26)
Coulsty (IRE) 98 2 (6f, York, GF, Aug 21)
Craftsman (IRE) 105 1 (7f, Leop, Sft, Oct 26)
Day Of Conquest 98 3 (7f, Newb, Hvy, Oct 26)
Dazzling (IRE) 96 3 (1m, Curr, Gd, Oct 13)
Dolce N Karama (IRE) 103 4 (1m, Donc, Sft, Oct 26)
Dorothy B (IRE) 104 5 (6f, Newm, GF, Sep 28)
Dutch Romance 94 3 (7f, Newb, Hvy, Oct 26)
Emirates Flyer 104 2 (6f, Redc, GF, Oct 5)
Excel's Beauty 98 2 (5f 34y, Newb, Gd, Aug 16)
Exogenesis (IRE) 107 3 (7f, Curr, GF, Aug 24)
Expedition (IRE) 97 3 (6f, Curr, GF, Sep 1)
Expert (IRE) 101 3 (6f, Donc, GS, Sep 11)
Extortionist (IRE) 102 3 (5f, Donc, GS, Sep 13)
Fast (IRE) 96 4 (5f, Donc, GS, Sep 13)
Fig Roll 99 4 (6f, Newj, GF, Jul 12)
Figure Of Speech (IRE) 107 4 (6f 8y, Newb, Sft, Sep 21)
Flying Jib 104 1 (1m, Curr, Gd, Oct 13)
Fountain Of Youth (IRE) 98 4 (5f, Asco, Gd, Jun 18)
Free Eagle (IRE) 104 2 (1m, Leop, Gd, Sep 7)
Friendship (IRE) 104 1 (7f 100y, Tipp, Gd, Aug 22)
Galiway 100 2 (7f, Newb, Hvy, Oct 26)
Gamesome (FR) 95 1 (6f 15y, Nott, GS, Aug 16)
Geoffrey Chaucer (USA) 108 1 (1m, Curr, Gd, Sep 29)

Giovanni Boldini (USA) 115 1 (7f, Dunw, SD, Oct 11)
God Willing 102 4 (1m, Newm, GS, Oct 12)
Gold Peregrine 94 2 (6f, Naas, Yld, Aug 5)
Good Old Boy Lukey 104 1 (7f, Newj, GF, Jul 13)
Great White Eagle (USA) 107 1 (6f, Curr, GF, Sep 1)
Green Door (IRE) 108 1 (5f, Donc, GS, Sep 13)
Guerre (USA) 98 2 (6f, Curr, Gd, Sep 29)
Haikbidiac (IRE) 101 1 (6f, York, GF, Aug 22)
Hartnell 101 1 (1m 2f, Newm, Sft, Nov 2)
Harwoods Volante (IRE) 94 2 (7f, Linw, SD, Mar 5)
Hay Chewed (IRE) 94 1 (5f, Thir, Gd, Aug 2)
Heart Focus (IRE) 99 4 (6f, Asco, GF, Jun 21)
Hidden Oasis (IRE) 104 1 (7f, Naas, Sft, Oct 20)
Hoku (IRE) 98 2 (6f, Ayr, GS, Sep 21)
Home School (IRE) 104 2 (7f, Leop, Gd, Jul 25)
Hot Streak (IRE) 115 2 (6f, Newm, GS, Oct 12)
Hunters Creek (IRE) 94 4 (7f, Newm, GF, Oct 5)
Hurryupharriet (IRE) 98 1 (5f, Ayr, Sft, Sep 20)
Ihtimal (IRE) 107 3 (1m, Newm, GF, Sep 27)
Il Paparazzi 100 3 (7f, York, GF, Aug 21)
Indian Maharaja (IRE) 102 1 (7f 100y, Tipp, Gd, Aug 9)
Invincible Strike (IRE) 97 2 (5f 216y, Wolw, SD, Nov 16)
J Wonder (USA) 97 7 (6f, York, GF, Aug 22)
Jallota 107 3 (6f, Newj, GF, Jul 11)
Johann Strauss 110 2 (1m, Donc, Sft, Oct 26)
Joyeuse 105 1 (6f, Sali, GF, Sep 5)
Justice Day (IRE) 110 3 (6f, Newm, GS, Oct 12)
Kaiulani (IRE) 94 8 (6f, York, GF, Aug 22)
Kingfisher (IRE) 102 5 (1m, Newm, GF, Sep 28)
Kingman 112 1 (7f 16y, Sand, GF, Aug 31)
Kingston Hill 119 1 (1m, Donc, Sft, Oct 26)
Kiyoshi 111 2 (7f, Curr, GF, Sep 1)
Lady Heidi 97 1 (1m 4y, Pont, Hvy, Oct 21)
Lady Lara (IRE) 94 3 (1m, Donc, GS, Sep 13)
Langavat (IRE) 97 2 (5f 6y, Sand, GF, Jul 5)
Lightning Thunder 109 2 (7f, Newm, GF, Sep 27)
Lone Warrior (IRE) 97 3 (7f, Asco, GF, Jul 27)
Lucky Kristale 110 1 (6f, York, GF, Aug 22)
Lyn Valley 97 1 (7f, Good, GF, Sep 3)
Majeyda (USA) 101 1 (1m, Newm, Sft, Nov 2)
Mandatario 102 2 (7f, Dunw, SD, Oct 11)
Mansion House (IRE) 105 3 (6f 63y, Curr, GF, Jul 20)
Mecca's Angel (IRE) 97 1 (5f, Souw, SD, Jul 9)
Mekong River (IRE) 104 1 (1m 1f, Leop, Sft, Nov 3)
Meritocracy (IRE) 95 1 (5f 16y, Chep, GF, Jul 12)
Merletta 100 4 (6f, York, GF, Aug 22)
Michaelmas (USA) 102 2 (7f, Leop, Gd, Jul 25)
Midnite Angel (IRE) 97 2 (7f, Newj, GF, Aug 10)
Minorette (USA) 96 3 (1m, Curr, Gd, Sep 15)
Miracle Of Medinah 105 1 (7f, Newm, Gd, Sep 26)
Miss France (IRE) 112 1 (7f, Newm, GF, Sep 27)
Morning Post 103 3 (6f, Redc, GF, Oct 5)
Mushir 103 1 (6f, York, Gd, Oct 12)
Music Theory (IRE) 103 3 (7f 16y, Sand, GF, Aug 31)
Musical Comedy 105 1 (6f 8y, Newb, Sft, Oct 25)
Mustajeeb 107 2 (7f, Curr, Gd, Aug 24)
My Catch (IRE) 97 5 (5f, Asco, Gd, Jun 18)
My Titania (IRE) 105 1 (7f, Curr, Gd, Sep 29)
Nezar (IRE) 97 3 (7f, Newm, Gd, Sep 26)
Night Of Thunder (IRE) 108 1 (6f, Donc, Sft, Oct 26)
No Leaf Clover (IRE) 103 2 (6f, York, Gd, Oct 12)
No Nay Never (USA) 109 1 (5f, Asco, GF, Jun 20)
Oklahoma City 106 2 (1m, Newm, GS, Oct 12)
One Chance (IRE) 95 3 (5f, Asco, GF, Jun 19)
Outstrip 115 1 (7f, Donc, GS, Sep 14)
Parbold (IRE) 109 3 (6f, York, Sft, Aug 24)
Peniaphobia (IRE) 100 1 (5f 34y, Newb, GF, Jul 20)
Perhaps (IRE) 105 2 (7f, Curr, Gd, Aug 11)
Pinzolo 97 1 (1m, Newb, Sft, Sep 20)
Piping Rock 107 1 (7f, Newb, Hvy, Oct 26)
Pleasant Bay (IRE) 95 4 (5f, Curr, Gd, Aug 24)
Postponed (IRE) 96 2 (7f, Newm, GF, Oct 5)

Princess Noor (IRE) 110 2 (6f, Newm, GF, Sep 28)
Qawaasem (IRE) 100 2 (7f, Good, Gd, Aug 24)
Queen Catrine (IRE) 102 2 (6f, York, GF, Aug 22)
Radiator 99 1 (7f, Ling, GF, Sep 4)
Remember You (IRE) 95 5 (6f, Ayr, GS, Sep 21)
Rizeena (IRE) 113 1 (7f, Curr, GF, Sep 1)
Rosso Corsa 97 4 (7f, Good, GS, Jul 31)
Rufford (IRE) 109 2 (6f 8y, Newb, Sft, Sep 21)
Saayerr 108 1 (6f, Good, Gd, Aug 1)
Sacha Park (IRE) 95 2 (6f, Naas, GF, Jun 3)
Safety Check (IRE) 100 1 (1m, Newm, Gd, Sep 26)
Salford Red Devil 97 7 (6f, Good, Gd, Aug 1)
Sandiva (IRE) 105 1 (6f, Naas, GF, Jun 3)
Scotland (GER) 95 1 (1m 114y, Epso, Gd, Sep 29)
Shamshon (IRE) 105 5 (6f 8y, Newb, Sft, Sep 21)
Shifting Power 104 1 (7f, Newj, Gd, Aug 2)
Shining Emerald 107 1 (6f, Curr, Gd, Sep 29)
Sign From Heaven (IRE) 96 2 (5f, Dunw, SD, Sep 27)
Simple Love (USA) 96 5 (7f, Leop, GF, Jul 18)
Sir Jack Layden 109 3 (1m, Newm, GF, Sep 28)
Sir John Hawkins (USA) 104 4 (6f, Newj, GF, Jul 11)
Sleeper King (IRE) 101 4 (5f, Good, GS, Jul 30)
Sniper 95 1 (7f, Naas, Sft, Oct 20)
Somewhat (USA) 111 1 (7f, Newb, Gd, Aug 17)
Sound Reflection (USA) 100 6 (1m, Newm, GF, Sep 27)
Speedfiend 106 4 (6f, Newm, GS, Oct 12)
Steventon Star 98 3 (7f, Linw, SD, Mar 5)
Stormardal (IRE) 100 5 (7f, Newm, GS, Oct 12)
Strategical (USA) 100 1 (5f 6y, Sand, Gd, Aug 30)
Stubbs (IRE) 101 3 (6f, Donc, Sft, Oct 26)

Sudden Wonder (IRE) 96 1 (1m, Newm, Sft, Oct 23)
Sudirman (IRE) 115 2 (7f, Curr, Gd, Sep 15)
Supplicant 111 1 (6f 8y, Newb, Sft, Sep 21)
Sweet Acclaim (IRE) 96 3 (7f, Newm, GF, Sep 27)
Sweet Emma Rose (USA) 99 2 (5f, Asco, GF, Jun 19)
Tapestry (IRE) 111 3 (7f, Curr, GF, Sep 1)
Tarfasha (IRE) 97 1 (7f, Galw, Yld, Jul 30)
Terrific (IRE) 95 1 (7f, Curr, Gd, Aug 24)
The Grey Gatsby (IRE) 107 2 (7f, Donc, GS, Sep 14)
Thewandaofu (IRE) 96 5 (7f, Newm, GS, Oct 12)
Thunder Strike 100 2 (6f, York, GF, Aug 22)
Toast Of New York (USA) 99 1 (6f 32y, Wolw, SD, Nov 1)
Toofi (IRE) 97 1 (6f, Newm, Gd, Sep 21)
Toormore (IRE) 122 1 (7f, Curr, Gd, Sep 15)
Trading Profit 103 1 (7f 9y, Leic, Sft, Oct 15)
Treaty Of Paris (IRE) 104 1 (7f, York, GF, Aug 21)
Truth Or Dare 104 3 (1m, Newm, GS, Oct 12)
Umneyati 95 3 (5f, Ayr, Sft, Sep 20)
Valonia 97 3 (7f, Newm, GS, Oct 12)
Ventura Mist 97 3 (6f, Ayr, GS, Sep 21)
Viva Verglas (IRE) 97 1 (5f 20y, Wolw, SD, Oct 26)
Vorda (FR) 113 1 (6f, Newm, GF, Sep 28)
War Command (USA) 118 1 (7f, Newm, GS, Oct 12)
Washaar (IRE) 108 4 (1m, Newm, GF, Sep 28)
Wedding Ring (IRE) 96 3 (7f, Newj, GF, Aug 10)
Whaleweigh Station 101 5 (6f, Newj, GF, Jul 11)
Wilshire Boulevard (IRE) 110 2 (6f, York, Sft, Aug 24)
Wind Fire (USA) 102 3 (6f, York, GF, Aug 22)
Wonderfully (IRE) 105 4 (1m, Newm, GF, Sep 27)

RACING POST RATINGS: LAST SEASON'S TOP PERFORMERS 3YO+

A Boy Named Suzi 103 4 (1m 6f, York, Sft, May 17)
Abstraction (IRE) 108 5 (5f, Curr, Gd, Aug 24)
Addictive Dream (IRE) 103 2 (5f, Linw, SD, Dec 4)
Address Unknown 104 1 (2m 2f 147y, Ches, GF, May 8)
Afonso De Sousa (USA) 106 3 (1m 2f 150y, Dunw, SD, Oct 18)
Afsare 121 1 (1m, Sali, Gd, Aug 15)
Agent Allison 103 2 (7f, Newb, GS, Apr 20)
Ahtoug 104 1 (5f, Asco, Gd, Aug 10)
Ahzeemah (IRE) 117 1 (2m 88y, York, GS, Aug 23)
Aiken 106 6 (1m 5f 61y, Newb, Gd, Aug 17)
Ajjaadd (USA) 104 1 (5f, Epso, Gd, Apr 24)
Al Kazeem 126 1 (1m 2f 7y, Sand, GF, Jul 6)
Al Waab (IRE) 111 2 (1m 2f 7y, Wind, Sft, Aug 24)
Albasharah (USA) 114 5 (1m 2f, Asco, GF, Jun 19)
Alben Star (IRE) 104 3 (5f 216y, Wolw, SD, Dec 20)
Alhebayeb (IRE) 109 4 (1m, Hayd, Fm, May 25)
Aljamaaheer (IRE) 119 1 (1m, Asco, GF, Jul 13)
Along Came Casey (IRE) 111 1 (1m 1f 100y, Gowr, Gd, Aug 14)
Aloof (IRE) 105 2 (1m 1f, Curr, GF, Sep 1)
Alta Lilea (IRE) 103 3 (1m 6f, Good, Gd, Aug 1)
Altano (GER) 112 3 (2m, Good, Gd, Aug 1)
Amarillo (IRE) 114 2 (7f, Newm, GS, Oct 12)
Ambivalent (IRE) 111 1 (1m 2f, Curr, GF, Jun 30)
An Saighdiur (IRE) 104 3 (6f, Ayr, GS, Sep 21)
Anaconda (FR) 105 1 (1m, Linw, SD, Nov 16)
Ancient Cross 106 1 (6f, Ayr, GS, Sep 21)
Angels Will Fall (IRE) 106 1 (5f 140y, Donc, GS, Sep 14)
Annecdote 107 1 (7f, Good, Gd, Aug 2)
Annunciation 103 1 (6f, Asco, Gd, Aug 10)
Ansgar (IRE) 109 2 (1m, Curr, Gd, Sep 15)
Arctic (IRE) 105 6 (6f, Curr, GF, May 25)
Area Fifty One 108 2 (1m 2f 88y, York, Gd, Oct 12)
Arnold Lane (IRE) 111 4 (7f, Asco, GS, Oct 5)
Arsaadi (IRE) 105 3 (1m, Asco, GF, Jun 19)
Artistic Jewel (IRE) 110 1 (6f, Pont, GF, Aug 18)
Ascription (IRE) 113 1 (1m, Donc, GS, Sep 14)
Ashdan 109 2 (1m, Newj, GF, Jul 11)
Askar Tau (FR) 103 (2m, Good, Gd, Aug 1)
Astonishing (IRE) 110 1 (1m 4f, Newm, Gd, Sep 26)
Baccarat (IRE) 105 1 (6f, Ripo, Gd, Aug 17)
Ballesteros 108 5 (5f 34y, Newb, Sft, Sep 21)

Ballista (IRE) 113 1 (5f 16y, Ches, GF, May 8)
Balmont Mast (IRE) 108 1 (6f, Curr, Gd, Oct 13)
Baltic Knight (IRE) 113 2 (1m, Donc, Gd, Jun 1)
Bana Wu 106 3 (1m 2f, Asco, GF, Jun 21)
Bancnuanaheireann (IRE) 103 2 (1m 2f, Linw, SD, Nov 16)
Banna Boirche (IRE) 113 1 (7f, Fair, Gd, Jun 12)
Banoffee (IRE) 105 5 (1m 3f 200y, Hayd, GF, Jul 6)
Barbican 108 4 (1m 4f, Asco, GF, Jul 28)
Barnet Fair 103 1 (5f, Asco, GF, Jul 28)
Battle Of Marengo (IRE) 118 4 (1m 4f 10y, Epso, Gd, Jun 1)
Beatrice Aurore (IRE) 109 4 (1m, Asco, GF, Jun 19)
Belgian Bill 107 1 (1m, Asco, GF, Jun 19)
Belle De Crecy (IRE) 112 2 (1m 4f, Asco, Sft, Oct 19)
Bertiewhittle 108 2 (7f, Asco, GS, Oct 5)
Big Break 107 2 (7f 100y, Tipp, Yld, Oct 6)
Big Johnny D (IRE) 103 1 (7f, Hayd, Sft, Sep 6)
Biographer 112 6 (2m, Asco, Sft, Oct 19)
Black Spirit (USA) 107 4 (1m 2f 60y, Donc, GS, Sep 12)
Body And Soul (IRE) 107 1 (6f, York, GF, Jun 15)
Bogart 109 1 (5f 89y, York, GF, Aug 21)
Bold Sniper 105 1 (1m 4f, Asco, GF, Jul 13)
Bold Thady Quill (IRE) 108 4 (7f, Leop, Yld, Jun 13)
Bonfire 106 3 (1m 1f, Newm, GF, Apr 18)
Boom And Bust (IRE) 111 2 (7f, Good, Gd, Aug 25)
Boomerang Bob (IRE) 105 1 (6f, Wind, GF, Jun 3)
Boomshackerlacker (IRE) 108 2 (1m 14y, Sand, Hvy, Sep 18)
Borderlescott 105 3 (5f, Beve, GF, Aug 31)
Brae Hill (IRE) 104 3 (1m, Donc, Sft, Mar 30)
Brendan Brackan (IRE) 114 1 (1m 100y, Galw, Yld, Jul 30)
Breton Rock (IRE) 108 1 (7f, Asco, GF, Jun 19)
Bronze Prince 104 1 (7f, Kemw, SD, Mar 30)
Brown Panther 117 1 (2m, Good, Gd, Aug 1)
Buckland (IRE) 106 4 (2m, Asco, Gd, May 3)
Burano (IRE) 105 4 (1m 2f 7y, Sand, Gd, Apr 27)
Burke's Rock 103 1 (1m, Good, Gd, May 4)
Cai Shen (IRE) 105 3 (1m 2f, Linw, SD, Mar 16)
Camborne 116 1 (1m 3f 5y, Newb, Sft, Sep 21)
Camelot 120 2 (1m 2f 110y, Curr, GF, Aug 31)
Cameron Highland (IRE) 108 1 (1m 3f 135y, Wind, Sft, Aug 24)
Cap O'Rushes 113 4 (1m 4f, Curr, GF, Jun 29)
Cape Classic (IRE) 106 3 (7f, Asco, GF, May 11)

Cape Of Approval (IRE) 110 1 (5f, Cork, Sft, Jun 16)
Cape Peron 110 2 (1m, Good, Gd, Aug 2)
Caponata (USA) 111 2 (1m 2f, Curr, GF, Aug 11)
Captain Cat (IRE) 104 2 (1m, Kemw, SD, Dec 12)
Captain Joy (IRE) 109 3 (1m, Curr, GF, Jun 29)
Captain Ramius (IRE) 109 2 (6f, Donc, Sft, Mar 30)
Caravan Rolls On 104 2 (1m 6f, Asco, GF, Jul 12)
Caspar Netscher 112 2 (7f, Good, GS, Jul 30)
Cat O'Mountain (USA) 108 1 (1m 3f, Kemw, SD, Sep 25)
Caucus 113 1 (2m 78y, Sand, GF, Jul 6)
Cavalryman 109 6 (2m, Good, Gd, Aug 1)
Chancery (USA) 103 4 (1m 4f, Newm, GF, Sep 27)
Chapter Seven 111 3 (1m 1f, Newm, GS, Oct 12)
Chiberta King 108 4 (2m 2f, Newm, GS, Oct 12)
Chicquita (IRE) 114 1 (1m 4f, Curr, GF, Jul 20)
Chigun 114 1 (1m, Curr, GF, May 25)
Chil The Kite 111 3 (1m 14y, Sand, Gd, Apr 26)
Chilworth Icon 103 3 (6f, Newm, GF, May 18)
Chookie Royale 106 2 (1m, Kemw, SD, Oct 31)
Chopin (GER) 116 7 (1m 4f 10y, Epso, Gd, Jun 1)
Cirrus Des Aigles (FR) 126 2 (1m 2f, Asco, Sft, Oct 19)
City Girl (IRE) 103 1 (6f, Newj, Gd, Jun 28)
City Style (USA) 114 1 (1m 208y, York, GS, Aug 23)
Clon Brulee (IRE) 105 3 (1m 2f, Ayr, GS, Sep 21)
Code Of Honor 112 2 (1m 1f, Newm, GF, Sep 28)
Colonel Mak 104 1 (6f, Pont, GS, Jul 28)
Colour Vision (FR) 112 4 (2m 4f, Asco, GF, Jun 20)
Commissioned (IRE) 104 1 (1m 6f, Muss, GF, Oct 14)
Conduct (IRE) 111 1 (1m 4f, Donc, Sft, Nov 9)
Confessional 105 1 (5f, Hayd, GS, Sep 7)
Contributer (IRE) 107 4 (1m 4f, Asco, GF, Jun 21)
Correspondent 106 1 (7f 122y, Ches, GS, Aug 17)
Count Of Limonade (IRE) 110 1 (1m, Curr, GF, Jun 29)
Crazy Buddies (IRE) 113 1 (1m, Naas, GF, Jul 24)
Cristoforo Colombo (USA) 107 5 (1m, Newm, GF, May 4)
Cubanita 109 1 (1m 4f 5y, Newb, Hvy, Oct 26)
Cushion 103 2 (1m 2f, Newm, GF, Oct 5)
Custom Cut (IRE) 111 2 (1m, Leop, Yld, May 12)
Dabadiyan (IRE) 107 2 (1m 2f 150y, Dunw, SD, Sep 27)
Daddy Long Legs (USA) 105 5 (1m, Newm, Sft, Nov 2)
Dalkala (USA) 111 1 (1m 2f 88y, York, Gd, May 16)
Danadana (IRE) 117 2 (1m 208y, York, GS, Aug 23)
Dance And Dance (IRE) 103 8 (1m, York, Gd, May 16)
Danchai 104 1 (1m 2f 88y, York, GF, Jul 13)
Dandino 117 2 (1m 4f, Asco, GF, Jun 22)
Dandy Boy (ITY) 103 (6f, Curr, Gd, Sep 14)
Dank 114 1 (1m 1f, Curr, GF, Jul 21)
Darwin (USA) 114 1 (7f, Curr, GF, Jul 20)
Dashing Star 104 2 (1m 6f, York, Sft, Aug 24)
David Livingston (IRE) 115 1 (1m 2f 95y, Hayd, GF, Aug 10)
Dawn Approach (IRE) 128 2 (1m, Good, GS, Jul 31)
Declaration Of War (USA) 124 1 (1m 2f 88y, York, GF, Aug 21)
Demora 103 1 (5f, Hayd, Gd, Sep 28)
Dick Doughtywylie (USA) 108 6 (1m 2f 7y, Sand, GF, Jul 5)
Diescentric (USA) 111 1 (7f, Newc, GS, Jun 29)
Dinkum Diamond (IRE) 108 3 (5f, Epso, Gd, Jun 1)
Directorship 105 1 (1m, Newm, Gd, May 4)
Disclaimer 108 1 (1m 3f, Good, Gd, May 24)
Doc Hay (USA) 109 1 (6f, Ripo, Gd, Sep 28)
Don't Call Me (IRE) 111 4 (1m, Asco, GF, Jun 19)
Dubai Hills 107 1 (7f, Souw, SD, Dec 10)
Duke Of Firenze 105 1 (5f, Epso, Gd, Jun 1)
Dunaden (FR) 121 2 (1m 4f 10y, Epso, Gd, Jun 1)
Dundonnell (USA) 116 1 (7f, Newm, GF, May 18)
Dungannon 106 1 (5f, Donc, Sft, Oct 26)
Duntle (IRE) 111 3 (1m, Newm, GF, Sep 28)
Dutch Masterpiece 113 1 (5f, Curr, Gd, Aug 24)
Dutch Rose (IRE) 104 2 (7f 200y, Carl, Sft, Sep 11)
Educate 117 1 (1m 1f, Newm, GF, Sep 28)
Ehtedaam (USA) 107 1 (1m, Kemw, SD, Aug 28)
Ektihaam (IRE) 121 1 (1m 4f, Asco, GF, May 11)
El Salvador (IRE) 109 6 (2m 4f, Asco, GF, Jun 20)
Elik (IRE) 105 2 (1m 6f, Good, Gd, Aug 1)
Elkaayed (USA) 111 5 (1m 2f, Asco, GF, Jun 20)
Elleval (IRE) 106 2 (1m 2f, Leop, Gd, Sep 7)
Elusive Kate (USA) 117 1 (1m, Newj, GF, Jul 12)

Elusivity (IRE) 111 4 (5f, York, Gd, May 25)
Emell 106 2 (1m 67y, Wind, Gd, Jun 29)
Emerald Wilderness (IRE) 104 1 (1m, Linw, SD, Feb 2)
Emirates Queen 111 1 (1m 3f 200y, Hayd, GF, Jul 6)
Energia Davos (BRZ) 105 4 (1m 2f, Linw, SD, Dec 21)
Ernest Hemingway (IRE) 116 1 (1m 4f, Leop, GF, Aug 8)
Es Que Love (IRE) 110 3 (1m, Newj, GF, Jul 20)
Eshtibaak (IRE) 109 2 (1m 2f, Redc, GF, May 27)
Estimate (IRE) 113 1 (2m 4f, Asco, GF, Jun 20)
Eton Forever (IRE) 115 1 (7f, Hayd, GS, May 11)
Eton Rifles (IRE) 111 2 (5f, Asco, GS, Oct 5)
Euphrasia (IRE) 108 1 (1m 2f, Leop, Hvy, Oct 26)
Excelette (IRE) 106 3 (5f, York, GF, Jul 13)
Excellent Guest 104 1 (7f, Asco, GF, May 11)
Excess Knowledge 112 3 (1m 2f 7y, Sand, GF, Jul 5)
Eye Of The Storm (IRE) 114 3 (2m, Asco, Sft, Oct 19)
Face The Problem (IRE) 106 3 (5f 89y, York, GF, Aug 21)
Farhh 127 1 (1m 2f, Asco, Sft, Oct 19)
Farmleigh House (IRE) 111 1 (6f, Dunw, SD, Aug 18)
Farraaj (IRE) 107 1 (1m 2f, Linw, SD, Mar 16)
Fattsota 107 5 (1m 3f 5y, Newb, Sft, Sep 21)
Fencing (USA) 115 1 (1m, Asco, Gd, May 1)
Festive Cheer (FR) 115 3 (1m 4f, Curr, GF, Jun 29)
Field Of Dream 109 1 (7f, Newj, GF, Jul 13)
Fiesolana (IRE) 116 1 (7f, Newm, GS, Oct 12)
Fire Ship 110 1 (1m 4y, Pont, GS, Jul 28)
First Mohican 113 1 (1m 2f 88y, York, GS, May 15)
Flying Officer (USA) 105 1 (1m 2f 7y, Wind, GF, Jun 30)
Flying The Flag (IRE) 112 1 (1m 2f, Curr, GF, Jun 28)
Forest Edge (IRE) 108 1 (5f, Linw, SD, Dec 4)
Forgotten Voice (IRE) 114 1 (1m 4f, Good, Gd, Aug 2)
Fort Knox 107 1 (1m, Leop, Sft, Apr 14)
Foundry (IRE) 113 5 (1m 6f 132y, Donc, GS, Sep 14)
Francis Of Assisi (IRE) 109 1 (7f, Leop, Sft, Nov 3)
Free Zone 109 4 (5f, Asco, GS, Oct 5)
French Navy 114 2 (1m, Newm, Sft, Nov 2)
Fulbright 104 3 (1m, Donc, Fm, Jul 18)
Gabrial (IRE) 113 1 (1m, Donc, Gd, Apr 13)
Gabriel's Lad (IRE) 108 2 (7f, Asco, Gd, Sep 7)
Gale Force Ten 115 1 (7f, Asco, GF, Jun 19)
Galician 106 1 (1m, Linw, SD, Dec 28)
Galileo Rock (IRE) 118 3 (1m 4f 10y, Epso, Gd, Jun 1)
Gallipot 104 7 (1m 3f 200y, Hayd, GF, Jul 6)
Garswood 113 1 (7f, Newm, Gd, Apr 17)
Gatewood 109 2 (1m 2f 60y, Donc, GS, Sep 11)
Genzy (FR) 108 4 (1m 5f 61y, Newb, Gd, Aug 17)
George Vancouver (USA) 104 7 (1m, Asco, Gd, Jun 18)
Ghurair (USA) 108 4 (1m 2f 88y, York, Gd, May 16)
Gifted Girl (IRE) 110 2 (1m 3f 5y, Newb, Sft, Sep 21)
Giofra 111 3 (1m, Newj, GF, Jul 12)
Glass Office 110 2 (6f, Hayd, GF, Jun 8)
Glen Moss (IRE) 105 1 (7f, Newb, Gd, Aug 17)
Glen's Diamond 114 1 (1m 6f, York, Sft, May 17)
Global Village (IRE) 104 4 (1m, Newb, GS, Apr 20)
Gloomy Sunday (FR) 110 1 (2m 78y, Sand, GS, May 30)
Glory Awaits (IRE) 115 2 (1m, Newm, GF, May 4)
Good Choice 107 1 (1m, Newm, Gd, May 4)
Gordon Lord Byron (IRE) 121 1 (6f, Hayd, GS, Sep 7)
Gospel Choir 106 5 (1m 4f, Asco, GS, Oct 5)
Gracia Directa (GER) 105 2 (6f, York, GF, Jul 12)
Grandeur (IRE) 118 2 (1m 2f 88y, York, GF, Jul 27)
Graphic (IRE) 112 1 (1m 75y, Nott, Sft, Nov 6)
Greatwood 110 2 (1m 4f, Donc, GS, Sep 14)
Greek War (IRE) 104 1 (1m 2f, Newj, GS, Aug 24)
Gregorian (IRE) 118 1 (7f, Newb, Gd, Aug 17)
Grey Mirage 105 1 (7f, Kemw, SD, Nov 13)
Guarantee 105 4 (1m 6f, Good, Gd, Aug 1)
Guest Of Honour (IRE) 116 3 (1m, Asco, GF, Jul 13)
Haafaguinea 106 1 (1m 2f 6y, Newb, Sft, Sep 21)
Hallelujah 107 3 (6f, York, Gd, Jul 12)
Hamish McGonagall 114 4 (5f, York, GS, Aug 23)
Hamza (IRE) 113 1 (6f, Newm, GF, May 5)
Handsome Man (IRE) 104 2 (1m 4f, Newj, GF, Jun 8)
Harasiya (IRE) 108 4 (1m 2f, Curr, GF, Jun 30)
Harris Tweed 118 1 (1m 6f, Good, GS, Jul 30)
Harrison George (IRE) 105 3 (5f, Donc, Sft, Oct 26)

Hasopop (IRE) 109 3 (7f, Asco, Gd, Sep 7)
Havana Gold (IRE) 111 2 (1m, Newm, GF, Apr 18)
Hawkeyethenoo (IRE) 114 2 (5f, Donc, Sft, Oct 26)
Hay Dude 108 2 (1m, Hayd, GS, Sep 7)
Heaven's Guest (IRE) 109 1 (7f, Asco, GS, Oct 5)
Heavy Metal 104 9 (6f, Newj, GF, Jun 8)
Heeraat (IRE) 116 1 (6f 8y, Newb, GF, Jul 20)
Heirloom 104 1 (1m 4f, Curr, Gd, Oct 13)
Helene Super Star (USA) 110 2 (1m 2f, Curr, GF, Jun 9)
Hi There (IRE) 104 1 (1m 2f 6y, Newb, Hvy, Oct 26)
High Jinx (IRE) 113 2 (2m 2f, Donc, GS, Sep 13)
Highland Colori (IRE) 116 1 (7f, Donc, Sft, Oct 26)
Highland Knight (IRE) 114 2 (1m 14y, Sand, Gd, Apr 26)
Hillstar 119 3 (1m 4f, Asco, GF, Jul 27)
Hippy Hippy Shake 107 2 (1m 1f 198y, Sali, GF, Aug 14)
Hitchens (IRE) 113 1 (6f 18y, Ches, Gd, Aug 4)
Hoof It 108 5 (6f, Linw, SD, Dec 18)
Hot Bed (IRE) 107 3 (1m, York, GF, Aug 22)
Hot Snap 113 1 (7f, Newm, Gd, Apr 17)
Hoyam 105 2 (6f 15y, Nott, Gd, May 11)
Humidor (IRE) 108 2 (5f 13y, Nott, Gd, Apr 10)
Hunter's Light (IRE) 114 4 (1m 2f, Asco, Sft, Oct 19)
I'm Your Man (FR) 114 2 (1m 4f, Newj, Gd, Jun 29)
Ighraa (IRE) 107 4 (1m 114y, Epso, GS, May 31)
Igugu (AUS) 106 2 (1m, Newm, GF, Sep 27)
Indian Chief (IRE) 110 3 (1m 2f 88y, York, Gd, May 16)
Inis Meain (USA) 107 2 (1m 4f, List, Hvy, Sep 18)
Instance 106 3 (7f, Good, Gd, Aug 2)
Integral 116 2 (1m, Newm, GF, Sep 28)
Intello (GER) 111 1 (1m 1f, Newm, Gd, Apr 17)
Intense Pink 107 3 (7f, Ling, Sft, May 11)
Intibaah 113 1 (6f, Asco, Sft, Oct 4)
Intransigent 109 1 (7f, Hayd, GF, Sep 5)
Ithoughtitwasover (IRE) 104 3 (1m 4f, York, GF, Jul 12)
Jack Dexter 119 1 (6f, Donc, Sft, Nov 9)
Jathabah (IRE) 104 3 (1m 4f, York, GF, Aug 22)
Jimmy Styles 111 2 (6f, Newm, GF, Apr 18)
Jiroft (ITY) 106 5 (5f, Epso, Gd, Jun 1)
Joshua Tree (IRE) 109 3 (1m 4f 10y, Epso, Gd, Jun 1)
Judge 'N Jury 105 3 (5f, York, Gd, May 16)
Just Pretending (USA) 112 3 (1m 4f, Curr, GF, Jul 20)
Just The Judge (IRE) 111 1 (1m, Curr, GF, May 26)
Justineo 110 3 (5f, Good, Gd, Aug 2)
Jwala 115 1 (5f, York, GS, Aug 23)
Kassiano (GER) 107 6 (1m 3f 5y, Newb, Sft, Sep 21)
Kendam (FR) 108 2 (7f, Ling, Sft, May 11)
Kenhope (FR) 110 2 (1m, Asco, GF, Jun 21)
Khione 104 1 (1m 4f, Good, Gd, May 4)
Khubala (IRE) 105 1 (6f, Wind, Gd, Jun 3)
King George River (IRE) 105 3 (1m, York, GS, Aug 23)
King's Warrior (FR) 104 4 (1m 2f 18y, Epso, Gd, Apr 24)
Kingsbarns (IRE) 118 3 (1m, Asco, Sft, Oct 19)
Kingsdesire (IRE) 106 2 (1m 2f 6y, Pont, GS, Apr 9)
Kingsgate Choice (IRE) 113 1 (5f, Muss, GF, Jun 15)
Kingsgate Native (IRE) 117 1 (5f, Hayd, Fm, May 25)
Kitten On The Run (USA) 106 4 (1m 2f 6y, Newb, GF, May 18)
Krypton Factor 111 3 (6f, Asco, GF, Jun 22)
La Collina (IRE) 111 1 (1m, Leop, Gd, Sep 7)
Labarinto 107 3 (1m 1f 192y, Good, GS, Jul 30)
Ladies Are Forever 111 2 (6f, York, Gd, Sep 8)
Ladys First 110 2 (1m, Asco, GF, Jun 19)
Ladyship 105 1 (6f, Newm, Gd, Sep 26)
Lahaag 106 1 (1m 4f, York, Gd, Oct 11)
Lancelot Du Lac (ITY) 109 1 (6f, Kemw, SD, Nov 27)
Last Train 104 (2m 4f, Asco, GF, Jun 20)
Law Enforcement (IRE) 110 1 (1m, Newj, GF, Jul 13)
Leading Light 118 1 (1m 6f 132y, Donc, GS, Sep 14)
Leitir Mor (IRE) 109 3 (1m, Leop, Gd, Aug 15)
Lethal Force (IRE) 124 1 (6f, Newj, GF, Jul 13)
Levitate 110 1 (7f, Donc, Sft, Nov 9)
Libertarian 118 2 (1m 4f 10y, Epso, Gd, Jun 1)
Libranno 113 4 (7f, Hayd, GF, Jun 8)
Lightning Cloud (IRE) 106 1 (7f, Asco, GF, Jun 21)
Lily's Angel (IRE) 110 2 (1m, Leop, Gd, Sep 7)
Little White Cloud (IRE) 106 2 (1m 2f, Curr, GF, May 26)
Loch Garman (IRE) 112 2 (1m 2f, Leop, Yld, May 12)

Lockwood 116 2 (7f, Donc, GS, Sep 14)
Lost In The Moment (IRE) 113 2 (1m 4f, Good, Gd, Aug 2)
Loving Spirit 106 3 (7f, Asco, GS, Oct 5)
Lucky Beggar (IRE) 108 1 (6f, Newj, GF, Jul 27)
Maarek 118 1 (5f, Naas, Sft, Apr 20)
Magic City (IRE) 107 1 (7f, Good, Gd, Aug 24)
Magical Dream (IRE) 106 3 (1m 2f, Curr, Gd, Sep 14)
Magical Macey (USA) 107 1 (5f, Newc, GS, Jun 28)
Magician (IRE) 123 1 (1m, Curr, GF, May 25)
Main Sequence (USA) 113 3 (1m 3f 5y, Newb, Sft, Sep 21)
Majestic Myles (IRE) 109 7 (1m, Donc, Sft, Mar 30)
Making Eyes (IRE) 104 1 (1m 2f 32y, Newc, GS, Jun 28)
Manalapan (IRE) 107 2 (1m 2f 150y, Dunw, SD, Oct 18)
Mandour (USA) 114 1 (1m 2f 7y, Sand, GF, Jul 5)
Mango Diva 104 1 (1m 1f 198y, Sali, GF, Aug 14)
Maputo 116 1 (1m 2f, Curr, GF, Aug 11)
Mars (IRE) 121 3 (1m, Asco, Gd, Jun 18)
Marshgate Lane (USA) 109 1 (1m 1f 103y, Wolw, SD, Dec 14)
Masamah (IRE) 111 1 (5f, Asco, GF, Jul 13)
Mass Rally (IRE) 113 1 (6f, York, Gd, Oct 12)
Master Of War 106 3 (6f, Newj, GS, Aug 24)
Maureen (IRE) 107 1 (7f, Newb, GS, Apr 20)
Maxios 112 6 (1m 2f, Asco, GF, Jun 19)
Medicean Man 113 3 (5f, Asco, GS, Oct 5)
Mezzotint (IRE) 104 2 (7f, Newm, GF, Sep 28)
Miblish 113 5 (1m 2f, Asco, Gd, Jun 19)
Midnight Soprano (IRE) 104 6 (1m 3f 200y, Hayd, GF, Jul 6)
Mijhaar 113 1 (1m 4f 17y, Hami, GS, May 17)
Mince 110 1 (6f, Newm, GF, Oct 5)
Mirsaale 109 9 (1m 4f 10y, Epso, Gd, Jun 1)
Missunited (IRE) 105 1 (1m 4f, Galw, Gd, Sep 9)
Mister Impatience 105 3 (1m 6f 132y, Donc, Sft, Oct 25)
Mister Music 105 3 (1m, Newm, GF, Oct 5)
Mizzava (IRE) 104 5 (1m, Asco, GF, Jun 21)
Mobaco (FR) 106 5 (1m 1f 192y, Good, GS, May 25)
Mocenigo (IRE) 104 3 (1m, Hayd, Fm, May 25)
Model Pupil 109 7 (2m 4f, Asco, GF, Jun 20)
Moment In Time (IRE) 110 2 (1m 3f 200y, Hayd, GF, Jul 6)
Monsieur Chevalier (IRE) 108 5 (7f, Good, GS, Jul 30)
Mont Ras (IRE) 107 1 (1m, York, GF, Aug 22)
Montaser (IRE) 107 4 (1m 4f, Good, Gd, Aug 2)
Montiridge (IRE) 117 2 (1m, Newm, GF, Sep 27)
Moohaajim (IRE) 104 3 (7f, Newb, GS, Apr 20)
Moonstone Magic 104 1 (1m 75y, Nott, Sft, May 29)
Morache Music 110 1 (6f, Donc, Sft, Oct 25)
Morandi (FR) 111 7 (1m 2f, Asco, Sft, Oct 19)
Morawij 111 1 (5f 6y, Sand, Gd, Jun 15)
Moth (IRE) 108 3 (1m, Newm, GF, May 5)
Mount Athos (IRE) 120 2 (1m 6f, Good, Gd, Aug 24)
Move In Time 107 4 (5f, Curr, Gd, Jun 29)
Moviesta (USA) 115 1 (5f, Good, Gd, Aug 2)
Mshawish (USA) 114 1 (1m, Asco, Gd, Jun 18)
Mukhadram 123 3 (1m 2f 7y, Sand, GF, Jul 6)
Mull Of Killough (IRE) 117 2 (1m, Asco, GF, Jul 13)
Music Master 106 2 (6f, Asco, GS, Oct 5)
Mutashaded (USA) 110 3 (1m 4f, Asco, GF, Jun 21)
My Freedom (IRE) 110 1 (7f 32y, Wolw, SD, Oct 26)
My Propeller (IRE) 106 1 (5f, Ayr, GF, Jun 22)
Nabucco 113 1 (1m 1f 198y, Sali, Hvy, Oct 2)
Nargys (IRE) 110 4 (1m, Asco, GF, Jun 19)
Navajo Chief 110 1 (1m, York, Gd, May 16)
Nazreef 103 2 (7f, Souw, SS, Feb 12)
Nephrite 108 2 (7f, Curr, Yld, Apr 7)
Nevis (IRE) 108 1 (1m 3f 106y, Ling, Sft, May 11)
Nichols Canyon 110 2 (1m 4f 5y, Newb, Hvy, Oct 26)
Ninjago 107 1 (6f, Asco, Gd, May 1)
No Heretic 110 5 (2m, Good, Gd, Aug 1)
Noble Mission 113 3 (1m 4f 5y, Newb, Hvy, Oct 26)
Noble Storm (USA) 104 3 (5f, Hayd, Gd, Sep 28)
Nocturn 107 2 (6f, Newj, GS, Aug 24)
Nocturnal Affair (SAF) 104 9 (6f, Curr, Gd, Sep 14)
Novellist (IRE) 128 1 (1m 4f, Asco, GF, Jul 27)
Number Theory 110 3 (1m 6f, York, Sft, Aug 24)
Nymphea (IRE) 108 2 (1m 3f 200y, Hayd, GF, Jun 8)
Ocean Tempest 109 1 (7f 2y, Ches, Gd, Sep 28)
Ocean War 108 8 (1m 2f, Asco, GF, Jun 21)

Ocovango 117 5 (1m 4f 10y, Epso, Gd, Jun 1)
Olympic Glory (IRE) 127 1 (1m, Asco, Sft, Oct 19)
One Word More (IRE) 104 2 (7f, Donc, GS, Sep 11)
Opinion (IRE) 109 1 (1m 4f, Asco, GF, Jun 22)
Oriental Fox (GER) 111 1 (2m 2f, Newm, Gd, Sep 21)
Ottoman Empire (FR) 107 4 (1m 2f, Asco, GF, Jun 21)
Our Jonathan 106 3 (6f, Donc, Sft, Mar 30)
Our Obsession (IRE) 108 1 (1m 4f, York, GF, Aug 22)
Out Of Bounds (USA) 110 1 (1m 2f 60y, Donc, GS, Sep 11)
Paene Magnus (IRE) 106 1 (1m 2f 150y, Dunw, SD, Oct 18)
Pale Mimosa (IRE) 110 4 (2m, Asco, Sft, Oct 19)
Pallasator 107 3 (1m 6f, Hayd, GS, Sep 7)
Parish Hall (IRE) 112 4 (1m 2f, Leop, Gd, Sep 7)
Pastoral Player 114 2 (7f, Hayd, GF, Jun 8)
Pearl Of Africa (IRE) 104 4 (1m 2f, Curr, Gd, Sep 14)
Pearl Secret 114 3 (5f, Asco, Gd, Jun 18)
Penitent 117 2 (1m 114y, Epso, GS, May 31)
Pether's Moon (IRE) 112 1 (1m 4f, Kemw, SD, Nov 6)
Phiz (GER) 104 2 (1m 6f 132y, Donc, GS, Sep 12)
Pied A Terre (AUS) 105 2 (7f, Donc, GF, Aug 17)
Pintura 110 2 (7f, Galw, Sft, Aug 3)
Piscean (USA) 107 2 (6f, Linw, SD, Feb 9)
Place In My Heart 106 1 (5f 11y, Bath, Gd, Apr 19)
Planteur (IRE) 114 1 (1m 2f 7y, Wind, Sft, Aug 24)
Poole Harbour (IRE) 104 4 (6f, Wind, Gd, Jun 29)
Premio Loco (USA) 117 2 (1m, Asco, GF, Jun 19)
Prince Alzain (USA) 114 1 (1m 1f 103y, Wolw, SD, Nov 7)
Prince Bishop (IRE) 114 1 (1m 4f, Kemw, SD, Sep 7)
Prince Of Johanne (IRE) 110 1 (1m 14y, Sand, GF, Jul 6)
Princess Highway (USA) 105 3 (1m 2f, Naas, Sft, May 15)
Prodigality 107 2 (6f, Good, Gd, May 4)
Producer 114 1 (7f, Newj, Gd, Jun 29)
Professor 114 1 (6f, Sali, GF, Jun 16)
Proud Chieftain 104 2 (1m 2f, Newm, Sft, Nov 2)
Prussian 104 5 (1m 3f 200y, Hayd, GF, Jun 8)
Purr Along 106 4 (1m, Newj, GF, Jul 12)
Queensberry Rules (IRE) 104 6 (1m, York, GF, Aug 22)
Questioning (IRE) 109 3 (1m 75y, Nott, Sft, May 29)
Quick Wit 112 2 (1m, York, GF, Jun 15)
Quiz Mistress 109 2 (1m 4f 5y, Newb, GS, Apr 20)
Racy 105 2 (5f, Hayd, Gd, Sep 28)
Ralston Road (IRE) 109 7 (1m 6f 132y, Donc, GS, Sep 14)
Rawaaq 104 1 (7f, Leop, Sft, Apr 14)
Reckless Abandon 116 3 (5f, Hayd, Fm, May 25)
Reckoning (IRE) 104 2 (1m 2f 32y, Newc, GS, Jun 28)
Red Avenger (USA) 104 2 (1m 2f, Newj, GF, Jul 11)
Red Cadeaux 117 2 (1m 5f 61y, Newb, Gd, Aug 17)
Red Jazz (USA) 112 2 (7f, Newj, Gd, Jun 29)
Redvers (IRE) 105 1 (7f, Asco, Gd, Sep 7)
Rehn's Nest (IRE) 108 2 (1m, Curr, GF, May 26)
Remote 116 1 (1m 2f, Asco, GF, Jun 20)
Renew (IRE) 108 1 (1m 4f, Newm, GF, Sep 27)
Repeater 112 3 (2m 2f, Donc, GS, Sep 13)
Reply (IRE) 112 1 (7f, Naas, GF, Jun 3)

Rewarded 110 1 (1m 1f 192y, Good, GS, May 25)
Rex Imperator 116 1 (6f, Good, Gd, Aug 3)
Rich Coast 109 1 (1m 100y, Cork, Sft, Oct 19)
Riposte 111 5 (1m 4f, Curr, GF, Jul 20)
Robin Hoods Bay 112 1 (1m 2f 95y, Hayd, GF, Aug 10)
Roca Tumu (IRE) 107 1 (1m, Asco, GF, Jun 20)
Rocky Ground (IRE) 104 1 (5f, Beve, GF, Sep 24)
Royal Diamond (IRE) 115 1 (2m, Asco, Sft, Oct 19)
Royal Empire (IRE) 117 2 (1m 4f, Kemw, SD, Sep 7)
Royal Rock 107 1 (6f 3y, Yarm, GS, Sep 17)
Royal Skies (IRE) 104 3 (1m 3f 101y, Yarm, GS, Sep 17)
Ruler Of The World (IRE) 125 3 (1m 2f, Asco, Sft, Oct 19)
Russian Soul (IRE) 110 1 (6f, Curr, Gd, Sep 14)
Saddler's Rock (IRE) 112 5 (2m, Asco, Sft, Oct 19)
Sajjhaa 110 4 (1m 1f 192y, Good, Gd, Aug 3)
Sandagiyr (FR) 112 3 (1m, Good, Gd, Aug 2)
Santefisio 109 4 (7f, Asco, GF, Jun 21)
Saxo Jack (FR) 106 4 (1m 2f 6y, Newb, Sft, Sep 21)
Say (IRE) 109 3 (1m, Leop, Gd, Sep 7)
Scintillula (IRE) 113 1 (1m 1f, Leop, Gd, Jul 25)
Scream Blue Murder (IRE) 106 4 (6f, Curr, Gd, Sep 14)
Sea Siren (AUS) 116 1 (6f, Fair, GF, Jul 14)
Seal Of Approval 118 1 (1m 4f, Asco, Sft, Oct 19)
Secret Asset (IRE) 105 1 (5f, York, GF, Jul 12)
Secret Gesture 110 3 (1m 4f, York, GF, Aug 22)
Secret Number 115 1 (1m 4f, Asco, GS, Oct 5)
Secret Witness 107 3 (5f 140y, Donc, GS, Sep 14)
Seek Again (USA) 109 1 (1m 208y, York, Gd, Oct 12)
Seeking Magic 104 1 (6f, Good, Gd, Aug 3)
Sennockian Star 107 2 (1m 2f 88y, York, Sft, Aug 24)
Sentaril 104 2 (1m, Good, Gd, May 4)
Set The Trend 107 1 (7f, Hayd, GF, Jul 20)
Seussical (IRE) 116 1 (1m 2f 88y, York, Gd, Oct 12)
Shamaal Nibras (USA) 104 3 (7f, Asco, GF, Jun 21)
Shamexpress (NZ) 107 7 (6f, Newj, GF, Jul 13)
Sharestan (IRE) 108 1 (1m 2f, Ayr, GS, Sep 21)
Shea Shea (SAF) 119 2 (5f, Asco, Gd, Jun 18)
Shebebi (USA) 106 1 (7f, Donc, GF, Aug 17)
Sheikhzayedroad 112 3 (1m 4f, Good, Gd, Aug 2)
Shikarpour (IRE) 114 2 (1m 2f, Asco, GF, Jun 20)
Shirocco Star 109 3 (1m 2f, Curr, GF, Jun 30)
Short Squeeze (IRE) 111 1 (1m, Hayd, Gd, Sep 28)
Shropshire (IRE) 107 4 (6f 110y, Donc, GS, Sep 13)
Shuruq (USA) 109 3 (1m 14y, Sand, GF, Aug 31)
Side Glance 110 7 (1m 2f, Asco, GF, Jun 19)
Simenon (IRE) 116 2 (2m 88y, York, GS, Aug 23)
Sir Ector (USA) 107 1 (1m 6f, Leop, Sft, Nov 3)
Sir Graham Wade (IRE) 109 3 (2m, Asco, Gd, May 1)
Sir John Hawkwood (IRE) 113 1 (1m 4f, York, Sft, May 17)
Sir Patrick Moore (FR) 106 2 (7f, Newb, GS, Apr 20)
Sirius Prospect (USA) 112 1 (7f, York, Sft, Aug 24)
Sky Lantern (IRE) 120 1 (1m, Asco, GF, Jun 21)
Slade Power (IRE) 119 1 (6f, Asco, Sft, Oct 19)
Smarty Socks (IRE) 105 2 (7f, York, GF, Jul 27)

Smoothtalkinrascal (IRE) 107 2 (5f; Epso, Gd, Jun 1)
Snow Queen (IRE) 106 5 (1m, Newm, GF, May 5)
Snowboarder (USA) 111 3 (1m, Good, Gd, Aug 2)
Society Rock (IRE) 122 1 (6f, York, GS, May 15)
Soft Falling Rain (SAF) 125 1 (1m, Newm, GF, Sep 27)
Solar Deity (IRE) 115 2 (1m 1f 103y, Wolw, SD, Dec 14)
Sole Power 120 1 (5f, Asco, Gd, Jun 18)
Songcraft (IRE) 111 2 (1m 6f, York, GF, Jul 13)
Soul (AUS) 105 5 (6f, Hayd, GS, Sep 7)
Sound Hearts (USA) 104 1 (1m 2f, Newm, GF, Oct 5)
Souviens Toi 106 2 (1m 4f 8y, Pont, Gd, Jun 23)
Sovereign Debt (IRE) 117 2 (1m, Newb, GF, May 18)
Spillway 110 4 (1m 3f 5y, Newb, Sft, Sep 21)
Spinatrix 112 2 (6f, Donc, Sft, Oct 25)
Spirit Quartz (IRE) 113 1 (5f 13y, Nott, Gd, Apr 10)
Spiritual Star (IRE) 104 3 (7f, Donc, GF, Aug 17)
Sruthan (IRE) 112 1 (7f 100y, Tipp, Yld, Oct 6)
St Jean (IRE) 106 4 (1m 4f, Leop, GF, Aug 8)
St Nicholas Abbey (IRE) 126 1 (1m 4f 10y, Epso, Gd, Jun 1)
Stand My Ground (IRE) 107 3 (1m, Donc, Gd, Apr 13)
Starscope 105 4 (1m 2f 88y, York, Gd, May 16)
Statutory (IRE) 107 1 (2m 1f 216y, Pont, Gd, Oct 7)
Stencive 110 2 (1m 2f 88y, York, GF, Jul 13)
Stepper Point 109 4 (5f 34y, Newb, Sft, Sep 21)
Steps (IRE) 111 1 (5f, Asco, GS, Oct 5)
Steps To Freedom (IRE) 107 2 (1m 2f 150y, Dunw, SD, Aug 18)
Stipulate 114 2 (1m, Good, Gd, Aug 24)
Storm King 104 5 (1m, York, GF, Jun 15)
Strictly Silver (IRE) 108 4 (1m 2f 88y, York, Sft, Aug 24)
String Theory (IRE) 105 1 (1m 1f 103y, Wolw, SD, Dec 26)
Stuccodor (IRE) 106 3 (7f, Galw, Sft, Aug 3)
Sugar Boy (IRE) 111 1 (1m 2f 7y, Sand, Gd, Apr 26)
Sun Central (IRE) 117 1 (1m 5f 89y, Ches, Gd, Aug 31)
Sweet Lightning 112 1 (1m, Curr, Hvy, Mar 24)
Swiss Spirit 116 2 (5f, Hayd, Fm, May 25)
Switcher (IRE) 105 2 (7f, Donc, GS, Sep 12)
Tac De Boistron (FR) 115 1 (1m 4f 66y, Ches, Sft, Sep 14)
Take Cover 107 2 (6f, Linw, SD, Nov 16)
Talent 115 1 (1m 4f 10y, Epso, GS, May 31)
Tales Of Grimm (USA) 113 2 (1m 1f, Newm, GS, Oct 12)
Tamarkuz (USA) 107 1 (1m, Kemw, SD, Oct 10)
Tandem 104 3 (1m 2f, Leop, Gd, Sep 7)
Tangerine Trees 109 3 (5f, Newm, GF, May 4)
Tantshi (IRE) 104 1 (7f, Asco, GS, Oct 5)
Tariq Too 106 2 (7f, Donc, Sft, Nov 9)
Tarooq (USA) 110 1 (6f, Linw, SD, Dec 18)
Tawhid 114 2 (1m, Good, Gd, Aug 2)
Telescope (IRE) 116 1 (1m 4f, York, GF, Aug 21)
Testudo (IRE) 106 3 (1m 4f, Newm, GF, Sep 27)
Tha'ir (IRE) 109 2 (1m 2f 60y, Donc, GS, Sep 12)
The Apache (SAF) 110 4 (1m 2f 88y, York, GF, Jul 27)
The Fugue 123 1 (1m 2f, Leop, Gd, Sep 7)
The Gold Cheongsam (IRE) 105 1 (7f, Newb, GF, Jul 20)
The Lark 108 3 (1m 4f 10y, Epso, GS, May 31)

The United States (IRE) 107 1 (1m 2f, Leop, Gd, Sep 7)
Thistle Bird 115 2 (1m 1f 192y, Good, Gd, Aug 3)
Thomas Chippendale (IRE) 119 1 (1m 4f, Asco, GF, Jun 22)
Thomas Hobson 106 1 (1m 4f, Donc, Sft, Oct 26)
Tickled Pink (IRE) 114 1 (6f, Newm, GF, Apr 18)
Tiger Cliff (IRE) 107 8 (2m 2f, Newm, GS, Oct 12)
Times Up 115 1 (2m 2f, Donc, GS, Sep 13)
Tobann (IRE) 104 1 (7f, Leop, Gd, Aug 15)
Tominator 110 1 (2m 19y, Newc, GS, Jun 29)
Top Notch Tonto (IRE) 120 2 (1m, Asco, Sft, Oct 19)
Top Trip 114 3 (2m 4f, Asco, GF, Jun 20)
Toronado (IRE) 129 1 (1m, Good, GS, Jul 31)
Trade Commissioner (IRE) 109 7 (1m, Asco, GF, Jun 19)
Trade Storm 118 4 (1m, Asco, GF, Jul 13)
Trading Leather (IRE) 121 2 (1m 2f 88y, York, GF, Aug 21)
Travel Brother 113 5 (1m 2f 7y, Sand, GF, Jul 5)
Tropics (USA) 117 1 (6f, Asco, GS, Oct 5)
Trumpet Major (IRE) 117 1 (1m 14y, Sand, Gd, Apr 26)
Tullius (IRE) 111 3 (1m, Newm, Sft, Nov 2)
Two For Two (IRE) 106 4 (1m, York, Gd, May 16)
Ultrasonic (USA) 105 3 (1m 4y, Pont, GF, Jul 9)
Universal (IRE) 117 1 (1m 4f, Newj, GF, Jul 11)
Urban Dance (IRE) 106 2 (1m 4f, Newm, GF, Sep 28)
Valbchek (IRE) 108 1 (6f, Linw, SD, Nov 16)
Validus 107 2 (1m, Newm, GF, Oct 5)
Vasily 105 1 (1m 2f 7y, Sand, GF, Aug 31)
Venus De Milo (IRE) 115 2 (1m 4f, York, GF, Aug 22)
Viztoria (IRE) 114 1 (7f, Donc, GS, Sep 14)
Voleuse De Coeurs (IRE) 118 1 (1m 6f, Curr, Gd, Sep 15)
Waila 110 1 (1m 4f, Newj, GF, Jul 20)
Wannabe Better (IRE) 109 1 (1m, Naas, Sft, Oct 20)
Wannabe Loved 106 4 (1m 3f 200y, Hayd, GF, Jul 6)
Was (IRE) 110 2 (1m 2f, Curr, GF, Jun 30)
We'll Go Walking (IRE) 105 2 (1m 1f 100y, Gowr, Sft, Apr 28)
Well Acquainted (IRE) 107 1 (7f, Epso, GS, May 31)
Well Sharp 107 1 (2m 4f, Asco, Gd, Jun 18)
Wentworth (IRE) 110 1 (1m, Good, Gd, Aug 2)
Whaileyy (IRE) 110 2 (6f, Linw, SD, Jan 5)
Wigmore Hall (IRE) 114 3 (1m 4f, Newm, GF, May 4)
Wild Coco (GER) 109 1 (1m 6f, Good, Gd, Aug 1)
Willie The Whipper 107 2 (1m 2f, Ayr, GS, Sep 21)
Willing Foe (USA) 116 1 (1m 5f 61y, Newb, GF, May 18)
Windhoek 111 2 (1m 1f 207y, Beve, GF, Aug 31)
Winning Express (IRE) 108 2 (6f, Newm, GF, Oct 5)
Winsili 116 1 (1m 1f 192y, Good, Gd, Aug 3)
Winterlude (IRE) 108 1 (1m 4f, Linw, SD, Oct 16)
Woolfall Sovereign (IRE) 105 1 (5f, Linw, SD, Jan 22)
Yellow Rosebud (IRE) 110 1 (7f, Galw, Hvy, Aug 1)
York Glory (USA) 114 1 (6f, Asco, GF, Jun 22)
Zanetto 111 1 (6f 8y, Newb, GF, May 17)
Zibelina (IRE) 109 4 (1m 14y, Sand, GF, Aug 31)
Zurigha (IRE) 108 1 (1m, Newm, GF, Sep 27)

TOPSPEED: LAST SEASON'S LEADING TWO-YEAR-OLDS

KEY: Horse name, best Topspeed figure, finishing position when earning figure, (details of race where figure was earned)

Adhwaa 86 2 (1m, Newm, Sft, Nov 2)
Aeolus 92 1 (6f, York, Gd, Oct 11)
Afternoon Sunlight (IRE) 85 2 (7f, Leop, Gd, Sep 7)
Al Thakhira 94 1 (7f, Newm, GS, Oct 12)
Alutiq (IRE) 85 7 (5f, Asco, GF, Jun 19)
Amazing Maria (IRE) 99 1 (7f, Good, Gd, Aug 24)
Ambiance (IRE) 97 4 (5f, Asco, GF, Jun 20)
Anjaal 93 4 (7f, Newm, GS, Oct 12)
Anticipated (IRE) 95 3 (5f, Asco, Gd, Jun 18)
Art Official (IRE) 83 1 (7f, Good, Gd, Aug 3)
Astaire (IRE) 103 1 (6f, Newm, GS, Oct 12)
Australia 89 1 (1m, Leop, Gd, Sep 7)
Autumn Lily (USA) 85 1 (7f, Newm, GF, Sep 28)
Avenue Gabriel 88 3 (7f, Leop, GF, Jul 18)
Azagal (IRE) 83 6 (6f, York, GF, Aug 22)
Bahamian Heights 90 1 (6f, York, GF, Aug 21)
Barley Mow (IRE) 84 1 (7f, Newb, Gd, Aug 16)
Be Ready (IRE) 83 2 (7f, Newb, Gd, Aug 17)
Beldale Memory (IRE) 83 1 (5f, York, Sft, May 17)
Ben Hall (IRE) 87 7 (5f, Asco, Gd, Jun 18)
Berkshire (IRE) 102 1 (7f, Asco, GF, Jun 22)
Big Time (IRE) 102 2 (6f, Curr, Gd, Aug 11)
Blockade (IRE) 84 2 (7f, Newm, GS, Oct 12)
Bon Voyage 85 3 (7f, Newm, GF, Oct 5)
Boom The Groom (IRE) 86 4 (6f, Curr, GF, Sep 1)
Bow Creek (IRE) 90 1 (7f, Newb, Sft, Sep 21)
Braidley (IRE) 83 1 (7f, Donc, Gd, Sep 11)
Brave Boy (IRE) 85 1 (6f 15y, Nott, GF, Jul 19)
Brown Sugar (IRE) 87 1 (6f, Kemw, SD, Sep 7)
Bunker (IRE) 94 2 (7f, Asco, GF, Jun 22)
Bushcraft (IRE) 86 2 (5f 16y, Ches, GS, Aug 17)
Bye Bye Birdie (IRE) 83 1 (6f, Curr, GF, Jun 30)
Cable Bay (IRE) 99 2 (7f, Newm, GS, Oct 12)
Cape Factor (IRE) 87 1 (6f, Newm, Sft, Nov 1)
Carla Bianca (IRE) 87 4 (7f, Curr, GF, Sep 1)
Charles Molson 85 1 (5f 11y, Bath, Sft, Oct 20)
Cheeky Chappie (IRE) 83 2 (1m, Dunw, SD, Sep 27)
Chicago Girl (IRE) 94 2 (7f, Curr, Gd, Sep 29)
Chief Barker (IRE) 86 1 (1m, Hayd, GS, Sep 7)
Claim The Roses (USA) 83 1 (6f, Kemw, SD, Aug 29)
Coach House (IRE) 103 2 (5f, Asco, GF, Jun 20)
Coral Mist 86 1 (6f, Ayr, GS, Sep 21)
Cordite (IRE) 86 4 (7f, Newb, Hvy, Oct 26)
Coulsty (IRE) 91 2 (6f, York, GF, Aug 21)
Craftsman (IRE) 90 1 (7f, Leop, Sft, Oct 26)
Day Of Conquest 91 3 (7f, Newb, Hvy, Oct 26)
Deeds Not Words (IRE) 88 1 (5f, Hayd, Gd, Sep 27)
Emirates Flyer 96 5 (5f, Asco, GF, Jun 20)
Ertijaal (IRE) 86 2 (5f 218y, Leic, Gd, May 28)
Evason 83 1 (1m, Nava, Sft, Oct 23)
Exogenesis (IRE) 84 1 (7f, Leop, GF, Jul 4)
Expedition (IRE) 88 3 (6f, Curr, GF, Sep 1)
Expert (IRE) 94 2 (6f, Good, GF, Sep 3)
Extortionist (IRE) 97 1 (5f, Asco, Gd, Jun 18)
Extra Noble 85 2 (1m, Donc, GS, Sep 14)
Fast (IRE) 88 4 (5f, Donc, GS, Sep 13)
Fig Roll 90 4 (5f, Asco, GF, Jun 19)
Figure Of Speech (IRE) 86 4 (6f, Good, Gd, Aug 1)
Fine 'n Dandy (IRE) 88 1 (5f 16y, Ches, GS, May 9)
Flippant (IRE) 84 1 (1m, Hayd, Gd, Sep 28)
Fountain Of Youth (IRE) 94 4 (5f, Asco, Gd, Jun 18)
Free Eagle (IRE) 100 1 (1m, Leop, Gd, Aug 15)
Friendship (IRE) 86 1 (7f 100y, Tipp, Gd, Aug 22)
Galiway 93 2 (7f, Newb, Hvy, Oct 26)
Ghaawy 83 1 (1m 3y, Yarm, GS, Sep 17)
Giovanni Boldini (USA) 88 3 (7f, Curr, Gd, Sep 15)
God Willing 83 4 (1m, Newm, GS, Oct 12)

Golden Town (IRE) 91 1 (7f, York, GS, Aug 23)
Good Old Boy Lukey 89 1 (7f, Newj, GF, Jul 13)
Great White Eagle (USA) 98 1 (6f, Curr, GF, Sep 1)
Greed Is Good 88 1 (1m, Ripo, Gd, Sep 28)
Green Door (IRE) 101 1 (5f, Donc, GS, Sep 13)
Haikbidiac (IRE) 94 1 (6f, York, GF, Aug 22)
Hartnell 90 1 (1m, Donc, Sft, Oct 25)
Heart Focus (IRE) 86 4 (7f, Leop, GF, Jul 18)
Hidden Oasis (IRE) 89 2 (1m, List, Sft, Sep 16)
Hoku (IRE) 85 2 (6f, Ayr, GS, Sep 21)
Hors De Combat 83 1 (7f, Newj, GF, Aug 16)
Hot Streak (IRE) 103 1 (5f, Asco, GS, Oct 5)
Hunters Creek (IRE) 84 4 (7f, Newm, GF, Oct 5)
I'm Yours (IRE) 83 2 (1m, Nava, Yld, Oct 9)
Ihtimal (IRE) 95 1 (7f, Newj, GF, Aug 10)
Il Paparazzi 83 3 (7f, York, GF, Aug 21)
Indy (IRE) 85 1 (6f, Donc, Sft, Nov 9)
Invincible Strike (IRE) 90 2 (5f 216y, Wolw, SD, Nov 16)
Island Remede 84 3 (1m, Newm, Sft, Nov 2)
J Wonder (USA) 86 1 (6f, Newj, Gd, Aug 3)
Jallota 86 2 (6f, Newm, Gd, Sep 21)
Jazz (IRE) 83 1 (6f, Donc, Sft, Nov 9)
Justice Day (IRE) 95 3 (6f, Newm, GS, Oct 12)
Kingman 96 1 (7f, Newj, Gd, Jun 29)
Kingston Hill 94 1 (1m, Newm, GS, Oct 12)
Kiyoshi 98 2 (7f, Curr, GF, Sep 1)
Lady Heidi 83 1 (1m 4y, Pont, Hvy, Oct 21)
Langavat (IRE) 87 2 (5f 6y, Sand, GF, Jul 5)
Lat Hawill (IRE) 85 1 (7f, Newc, GF, Oct 2)
Legend Rising (IRE) 84 1 (6f 16y, Chep, GS, Jun 14)
Lightning Thunder 96 2 (7f, Newm, GF, Sep 27)
Lilbourne Lass 83 2 (5f 34y, Newb, GF, Jul 20)
Lily Rules (IRE) 85 2 (7f, Newj, Gd, Aug 17)
Lucky Kristale 97 1 (6f, York, GF, Aug 22)
Lyn Valley 90 1 (7f, Good, GF, Sep 3)
Madeed 85 1 (1m, Good, Gd, Aug 23)
Majeyda (USA) 97 1 (1m, Newm, Sft, Nov 2)
Mansion House (IRE) 85 3 (6f 63y, Curr, GF, Jul 20)
Marvellous (IRE) 86 1 (1m, Nava, Yld, Oct 9)
Master Carpenter (IRE) 83 2 (7f, Donc, Gd, Sep 11)
Meadway 84 4 (5f, Hayd, Sft, Oct 18)
Mecca's Angel (IRE) 84 1 (5f, Souw, SD, Jul 9)
Mekong River (IRE) 100 1 (1m 1f, Leop, Sft, Nov 3)
Meritocracy (IRE) 83 1 (5f 16y, Chep, GF, Jul 12)
Merletta 85 4 (6f, York, GF, Aug 22)
Michaelmas (USA) 87 2 (7f, Leop, Sft, Oct 26)
Midnite Angel (IRE) 89 2 (6f, Newj, Gd, Aug 3)
Miner's Lamp (IRE) 83 1 (1m 14y, Sand, Hvy, Sep 18)
Miss France (IRE) 97 1 (7f, Newm, GF, Sep 27)
Montaly 83 1 (1m 75y, Nott, Sft, Oct 16)
Morning Post 85 1 (6f 110y, Donc, GS, Sep 12)
Mushir 90 1 (6f, York, Gd, Oct 12)
Musical Comedy 84 2 (6f, Hayd, GS, Sep 7)
Mustajeeb 85 1 (7f, Galw, Yld, Jul 29)
My Catch (IRE) 93 5 (5f, Asco, Gd, Jun 18)
My Titania (IRE) 96 1 (7f, Curr, Gd, Sep 29)
Nezar (IRE) 85 3 (6f, York, GF, Aug 22)
Night Of Thunder (IRE) 87 1 (6f, Donc, Sft, Oct 26)
No Leaf Clover (IRE) 89 2 (6f, York, Gd, Oct 12)
No Nay Never (USA) 107 1 (5f, Asco, GF, Jun 20)
Oklahoma City 91 1 (7f, Newm, GF, Oct 5)
One Chance (IRE) 92 3 (5f, Asco, GF, Jun 19)
Orchestra (IRE) 83 2 (1m, Leop, Gd, Aug 15)
Outer Space 83 2 (7f, Asco, GF, Jun 22)
Outstrip 94 3 (7f, Newm, GS, Oct 12)
Pack Leader (IRE) 84 2 (1m, Good, Gd, Aug 23)
Parbold (IRE) 94 3 (6f, York, Sft, Aug 24)
Peniaphobia (IRE) 91 1 (5f 34y, Newb, GF, Jul 20)
Perhaps (IRE) 90 2 (7f, Leop, GF, Jul 18)
Pinzolo 85 1 (1m, Newb, Sft, Sep 20)

Piping Rock 101 1 (7f, Newb, Hvy, Oct 26)
Postponed (IRE) 86 2 (7f, Newm, GF, Oct 5)
Pretend (IRE) 85 1 (7f, Kemw, SD, Nov 6)
Princess Noor (IRE) 85 1 (6f, Asco, GF, Jul 27)
Qawaasem (IRE) 91 2 (7f, Good, Gd, Aug 24)
Queen Catrine (IRE) 88 2 (6f, York, GF, Aug 22)
Red Galileo 86 2 (7f, York, GS, Aug 23)
Red Rocks Point (IRE) 84 1 (1m, Dunw, SD, Sep 27)
Remember 86 1 (7f, York, Gd, Sep 8)
Remember You (IRE) 87 2 (6f, Curr, GF, Sep 1)
Reroute (IRE) 89 5 (5f, Asco, GF, Jun 19)
Rizeena (IRE) 104 1 (5f, Asco, GF, Jun 19)
Rosso Corsa 89 2 (7f, Good, GF, Sep 3)
Royal Mezyan (IRE) 85 2 (5f, York, GF, Jun 14)
Rufford (IRE) 83 2 (6f 8y, Newb, Sft, Sep 21)
Saayerr 98 1 (6f, Good, Gd, Aug 1)
Sacha Park (IRE) 88 6 (5f, Asco, Gd, Jun 18)
Safety Check (IRE) 90 1 (7f, Newj, GS, Aug 24)
Salford Red Devil 83 7 (6f, Good, Gd, Aug 1)
Sandiva (IRE) 90 1 (6f, Naas, GF, Jun 3)
Scruffy Tramp (IRE) 83 6 (5f 216y, Wolw, SD, Dec 7)
See The Sun 83 1 (6f, Thir, GS, Sep 17)
Shifting Power 83 1 (7f, Newj, Gd, Aug 2)
Shining Emerald 86 3 (7f, Leop, Sft, Oct 26)
Simple Love (USA) 83 5 (7f, Leop, GF, Jul 18)
Simple Magic (IRE) 85 1 (5f 216y, Wolw, SD, Aug 12)
Sleeper King (IRE) 89 4 (6f, York, GF, Aug 22)
Sleepy Sioux 83 1 (5f, Hayd, Sft, Oct 18)
Sniper 83 5 (6f, Curr, Gd, Aug 11)
Somewhat (USA) 100 1 (7f, Newb, Gd, Aug 17)
Sound Reflection (USA) 84 1 (7f, Newj, Gd, Aug 3)
Speedfiend 90 4 (6f, Newm, GS, Oct 12)

Steventon Star 97 1 (5f 216y, Wolw, SD, Dec 7)
Strategical (USA) 83 1 (5f 6y, Sand, Gd, Aug 30)
Sudirman (USA) 104 1 (6f, Curr, Gd, Aug 11)
Supplicant 96 2 (5f, Asco, Gd, Jun 18)
Survived 86 6 (5f, Asco, GF, Jun 19)
Sweet Emma Rose (USA) 96 2 (5f, Asco, GF, Jun 19)
Tapestry (IRE) 98 3 (7f, Curr, GF, Sep 1)
Tarfasha (IRE) 87 1 (7f, Galw, Yld, Jul 30)
Terrific (IRE) 89 1 (7f, Curr, Gd, Aug 24)
The Grey Gatsby (IRE) 87 2 (7f, York, GF, Aug 21)
Thunder Strike 91 2 (6f, York, GF, Aug 22)
Tiger Twenty Two 84 3 (1m, Ayr, GS, Sep 21)
Toast Of New York (USA) 91 1 (7f 32y, Wolw, SD, Nov 1)
Toofi (FR) 88 1 (6f, Newm, Gd, Sep 21)
Toormore (IRE) 100 1 (7f, Curr, Gd, Sep 15)
Torrid 84 1 (1m 75y, Nott, Gd, Oct 9)
Trading Profit 83 5 (7f, Newb, Hvy, Oct 26)
Treaty Of Paris (IRE) 88 1 (7f, York, GF, Aug 21)
True Story 84 1 (7f, Newj, GF, Jul 12)
Truth Or Dare 85 3 (1m, Newm, GS, Oct 12)
Ubiquitous Mantle (IRE) 85 1 (1m, Leop, Sft, Oct 26)
Ventura Mist 84 3 (6f, Ayr, GS, Sep 21)
Viva Verglas (IRE) 95 2 (5f, Hayd, Sft, Oct 18)
Voice Of A Leader (IRE) 83 1 (7f 16y, Sand, Gd, Jul 31)
War Command (USA) 104 1 (7f, Newm, GS, Oct 12)
Wedding Ring (IRE) 85 3 (7f, Newj, GF, Aug 10)
Wee Jean 89 4 (5f 216y, Wolw, SD, Dec 7)
Wilshire Boulevard (IRE) 95 2 (6f, York, Sft, Aug 24)
Wind Fire (USA) 99 3 (5f, Asco, GF, Jun 20)
Wonderfully (IRE) 93 1 (7f, Leop, GF, Jul 18)
Zalzilah 86 3 (5f, Asco, Gd, Sep 7)

TOPSPEED: LAST SEASON'S TOP PERFORMERS 3YO+

Above Standard (IRE) 88 6 (5f 89y, York, GF, Aug 21)
Abstraction (IRE) 90 1 (5f, Tipp, GF, Jun 6)
Addictive Dream (IRE) 89 5 (5f 110y, Ches, Gd, Aug 31)
Aeronwyn Bryn (IRE) 90 1 (1m, Thir, GS, Sep 7)
Afsare 96 8 (1m 2f, Asco, GF, Jun 19)
Agent Allison 100 2 (7f, Newb, GS, Apr 20)
Agerzam 90 1 (6f, Linw, SD, Dec 28)
Ahtoug 92 4 (5f, Asco, GF, Jul 28)
Aiken 91 6 (1m 5f 61y, Newb, Gd, Aug 17)
Ajjaadd (USA) 94 1 (5f, Epso, Gd, Apr 24)
Akasaka (IRE) 89 1 (1m, Dunw, SD, Jan 18)
Al Kazeem 115 1 (1m 2f, Asco, GF, Jun 19)
Al Muheer (IRE) 88 3 (1m, York, GF, Jul 13)
Al Waab (IRE) 90 2 (1m 2f 7y, Wind, Sft, Aug 24)
Albasharah (USA) 91 5 (1m 2f, Asco, GF, Jun 21)
Alben Star (IRE) 89 3 (5f 216y, Wolw, SD, Dec 7)
Aljamaaheer (IRE) 108 1 (1m, Asco, Gd, Jul 13)
Almadaa 90 2 (5f, Dunw, SD, Mar 15)
Along Came Casey (IRE) 96 1 (1m 1f 100y, Gowr, Gd, Aug 14)
Aloof (IRE) 89 2 (1m 2f, Curr, GF, Jun 28)
Altharoos (IRE) 92 1 (1m, Thir, GS, Sep 7)
Amarillo (IRE) 98 2 (7f, Newm, GS, Oct 12)
An Saighdiur (IRE) 97 3 (6f, Ayr, GS, Sep 21)
Anaconda (FR) 93 1 (1m, Linw, SD, Nov 16)
Ancient Cross 100 1 (6f, Ayr, GS, Sep 21)
Angel Gabrial (IRE) 95 1 (1m 4f, Asco, GF, May 11)
Angels Will Fall (IRE) 96 1 (5f 140y, Donc, GS, Sep 14)
Annecdote 95 1 (1m, Asco, GF, Jun 19)
Annunciation 96 1 (6f, Donc, Sft, Mar 22)
Another Cocktail 88 2 (1m 2f 18y, Epso, Gd, Apr 24)
Ansgar (IRE) 98 2 (1m, Leop, Gd, Aug 15)
Arctic (IRE) 94 5 (5f, Curr, Gd, Sep 14)
Area Fifty One 104 2 (1m 2f 18y, Epso, GS, May 31)
Artistic Jewel (IRE) 88 1 (6f, Pont, GF, Aug 18)
Ascription (IRE) 94 1 (1m, Donc, GS, Sep 14)
Ashaadd (IRE) 97 1 (7f 16y, Sand, GF, Jun 6)
Ashpan Sam 92 1 (6f, Good, Sft, Oct 13)

Astonishing (IRE) 97 1 (1m 4f, Newm, Gd, Sep 26)
Atlantis Crossing (IRE) 90 3 (7f, Kemw, SD, Jan 30)
Auction (IRE) 94 2 (1m, Asco, GF, Jun 19)
Baccarat (IRE) 89 5 (6f, Ayr, GS, Sep 21)
Ballesteros 96 8 (5f, Donc, SD, Oct 26)
Ballista (IRE) 98 1 (5f 16y, Ches, GF, May 8)
Baltic Knight (IRE) 100 2 (1m, Donc, Gd, Jun 1)
Balty Boys (IRE) 91 2 (7f 122y, Ches, Sft, Sep 14)
Bana Wu 90 3 (1m 2f, Asco, GF, Jun 21)
Barbican 100 4 (1m 4f, Asco, GF, Jul 28)
Barnet Fair 95 5 (5f 89y, York, GF, Aug 21)
Battle Of Marengo (IRE) 109 2 (1m 4f, Asco, GF, Jun 21)
Beach Of Falesa (IRE) 89 1 (1m 4f, Curr, GF, Jun 30)
Beacon Lodge (IRE) 91 1 (7f 100y, Tipp, Yld, Oct 6)
Bear Behind (IRE) 92 6 (5f, Linw, SD, Mar 16)
Beaumont's Party (IRE) 96 2 (1m 4f 17y, Hami, GS, May 17)
Bedloe's Island (IRE) 89 1 (5f, Thir, GF, May 4)
Belle De Crecy (IRE) 101 2 (1m 4f, Asco, Sft, Oct 19)
Benzanno (IRE) 90 1 (1m, Linw, SD, Mar 16)
Bertiewhittle 95 2 (7f, Newc, GS, Jun 29)
Beyond Conceit (IRE) 90 3 (2m 45y, Hayd, GF, Jun 8)
Big Break 89 2 (7f 100y, Tipp, Yld, Oct 6)
Big Johnny D (IRE) 95 1 (7f, Hayd, Sft, Sep 6)
Biographer 106 4 (1m 6f, Newm, GF, May 18)
Bishop Roko 93 1 (1m 4f, Asco, GF, Jul 28)
Blue Surf 99 4 (1m 2f 18y, Epso, GS, May 31)
Body And Soul (IRE) 92 1 (6f, York, GF, Jun 15)
Bogart 14 1 (5f 89y, York, GF, Aug 21)
Boite (IRE) 89 3 (2m, Asco, GF, Jun 21)
Bold Sniper 101 1 (1m 4f, Asco, GF, Jul 13)
Bold Thady Quill (IRE) 91 1 (6f, Cork, Hvy, Mar 30)
Boom And Bust (IRE) 100 2 (7f, Good, Gd, Aug 25)
Boonga Roogeta 90 1 (1m 1f, Newm, GF, May 4)
Boots And Spurs 91 1 (7f 26y, Warw, Gd, Jun 17)
Boston Rocker (IRE) 95 2 (6f, Naas, Sft, May 15)
Brendan Brackan (IRE) 95 2 (1m 100y, Cork, Sft, Oct 19)
Breton Rock (IRE) 104 1 (7f, Asco, Sft, Oct 19)

Bronze Prince 92 5 (1m, Linw, SD, Mar 16)
Brown Panther 89 1 (2m, Good, Gd, Aug 1)
Bubbly Bellini (IRE) 89 8 (6f 63y, Curr, Gd, Jun 29)
Bungle Inthejungle 89 (5f, York, GS, Aug 23)
Burano (IRE) 89 2 (1m 2f, Kemw, SD, Mar 30)
Burn The Boats (IRE) 92 1 (6f 63y, Curr, Gd, Jun 29)
Cafe Society (FR) 92 2 (1m 4f, Linw, SD, Oct 16)
Cai Shen (IRE) 102 3 (1m 2f, Linw, SD, Mar 16)
Caledonia Lady 89 (5f, York, GS, Aug 23)
Camborne 98 1 (1m 3f 5y, Newb, Sft, Sep 21)
Camelot 107 4 (1m 2f, Asco, GF, Jun 19)
Cameron Highland (IRE) 89 1 (1m 3f 135y, Wind, Sft, Aug 24)
Canary Row (IRE) 92 3 (6f 110y, Slig, Yld, Aug 7)
Cap O'Rushes 99 4 (1m 4f, Curr, GF, Jun 29)
Cape Of Approval (IRE) 96 1 (5f, Cork, Sft, Jun 16)
Cape Peron 106 2 (1m, Good, Gd, Aug 2)
Caprella 89 4 (7f, Dunw, SD, Oct 18)
Captain Bertie (IRE) 95 3 (1m, Ripo, Gd, Aug 26)
Captain Dunne (IRE) 93 7 (5f, Epso, Gd, Jun 1)
Captain Joy (IRE) 96 2 (1m, Curr, GF, May 25)
Caravan Rolls On 98 4 (1m 6f, Newm, GF, May 18)
Caspar Netscher 89 4 (7f, Donc, GS, Sep 14)
Castilo Del Diablo (IRE) 91 2 (1m 3f, Kemw, SD, Sep 6)
Cat O'Mountain (USA) 89 1 (1m 3f, Kemw, SD, Sep 6)
Caucus 105 1 (2m 78y, Sand, GF, Jul 6)
Centurius 94 3 (1m 208y, York, Gd, Oct 12)
Chancery (USA) 89 1 (1m 2f 88y, York, GF, Jul 12)
Chapter Seven 104 3 (1m, Newb, GS, Apr 20)
Charles Camoin (IRE) 95 1 (1m 2f, Asco, GF, Jul 28)
Charlotte Rosina 92 3 (6f, Good, Gd, May 31)
Cheviot (USA) 93 1 (5f, Ripo, Gd, Aug 6)
Chiberta King 94 3 (2m 78y, Sand, GF, Jul 6)
Chil The Kite 94 4 (1m, Newb, GF, May 18)
Chilworth Icon 99 3 (6f, Newm, GF, May 18)
Church Music (IRE) 90 1 (5f, Kemw, SD, May 22)
Cirrus Des Aigles (FR) 119 2 (1m 2f, Asco, Sft, Oct 19)
Clancy Avenue (USA) 93 5 (6f 63y, Curr, Gd, Jun 29)
Clear Spring (IRE) 93 1 (6f, Ripo, Gd, Aug 17)
Clockmaker (IRE) 92 1 (7f 30y, Muss, GF, Jun 15)
Clon Brulee (IRE) 89 1 (1m 2f, Redc, GF, May 27)
Code Of Honor 89 2 (1m 1f, Newm, GF, Sep 28)
Colonel Mak 92 1 (6f, Pont, GS, Jul 28)
Common Touch (IRE) 89 4 (7f, Kemw, SD, Nov 21)
Confessional 98 4 (5f, Hayd, Gd, Sep 28)
Continuum 92 6 (1m 4f 5y, Newb, Sft, Sep 20)
Contributer (IRE) 97 4 (1m 4f, Asco, GF, Jun 21)
Count Of Limonade (IRE) 89 1 (1m, Dunw, SD, Apr 10)
Croquembouche (IRE) 90 2 (1m 2f 6y, Pont, Gd, Sep 26)
Cubanita 95 1 (1m 4f 5y, Newb, Hvy, Oct 26)
Custom Cut (IRE) 92 4 (1m, Leop, Gd, Aug 15)
Dalkala (USA) 99 4 (1m 4f, Asco, Sft, Oct 19)
Danadana (IRE) 98 1 (1m 2f 75y, Ches, Gd, May 9)
Dance And Dance (IRE) 89 2 (7f, Newb, Gd, Aug 17)
Dandino 109 2 (1m 4f, Asco, GF, Jun 22)
Dark Crusader (IRE) 98 1 (1m 6f, York, Sft, Aug 24)
Darwin (USA) 95 1 (1m, Naas, GF, Jun 26)
Dashing Star 100 2 (1m 6f, York, Sft, Aug 24)
Dawn Approach (IRE) 127 2 (1m, Good, GS, Jul 31)
De Rigueur 94 1 (2m 45y, Hayd, GF, Jun 8)
Declaration Of War (USA) 122 3 (1m, Good, GS, Jul 31)
Democretes 95 2 (7f, Newj, GF, Aug 10)
Demora 98 1 (5f, Hayd, Gd, Sep 28)
Dick Doughtywylie 90 5 (1m 2f 75y, Ches, Gd, May 9)
Diescentric (USA) 102 1 (7f, Newc, GS, Jun 29)
Dinkum Diamond (IRE) 105 3 (5f, Epso, Gd, Jun 1)
Doc Hay (USA) 89 1 (6f, Ripo, Gd, Sep 28)
Doctor Parkes 97 1 (5f, Donc, Gd, May 17)
Don't Call Me (IRE) 99 6 (7f, Asco, GF, Jul 27)
Dream Tune 92 5 (1m, Newb, GS, Apr 20)
Dubai Dynamo 90 4 (1m, Hayd, Gd, May 23)
Dubai Hills 91 2 (1m, Hayd, Gd, May 23)
Dubawi Sound 93 8 (7f, Asco, GF, Jul 27)
Duke Of Firenze 102 1 (5f, Epso, Gd, Jun 1)

Dundonnell (USA) 98 1 (7f, Newm, GF, May 18)
Dungannon 100 1 (5f, Donc, Sft, Oct 26)
Dutch Masterpiece 94 1 (5f, Curr, Gd, Aug 24)
Dutch Rose (IRE) 97 1 (7f, York, GF, Aug 22)
Educate 98 3 (1m 2f 95y, Hayd, GF, Aug 10)
Ehtedaam (USA) 95 1 (1m 14y, Sand, GF, Jul 17)
Ektihaam (IRE) 94 1 (1m 4f, Asco, GF, May 11)
El Salvador (IRE) 98 3 (1m 6f, Leop, GF, Jun 7)
El Viento (FR) 98 1 (5f 110y, Ches, Gd, Aug 31)
Elik (IRE) 89 2 (1m 6f, Good, Gd, Aug 1)
Elkaayed (USA) 91 5 (1m 2f, Asco, GF, Jun 20)
Elusive Flame 92 1 (6f, Newj, GF, Aug 9)
Elusive Kate (USA) 90 5 (1m, Asco, Sft, Oct 19)
Elusivity (IRE) 93 6 (5f, Newm, GF, May 4)
Emerald Wilderness (IRE) 100 1 (1m, Linw, SD, Feb 2)
Ennistown (IRE) 100 1 (1m 2f 6y, Pont, Gd, Sep 26)
Equitana 91 1 (5f 216y, Wolw, SD, Dec 6)
Ernest Hemingway (IRE) 98 4 (1m 2f, Curr, Gd, Apr 7)
Es Que Love (IRE) 100 5 (1m, York, GF, Aug 22)
Eshtibaak (IRE) 97 2 (1m 2f 75y, Ches, GF, May 9)
Eton Forever (IRE) 90 1 (7f, Hayd, GS, May 11)
Euphrasia (IRE) 89 4 (1m, Naas, Sft, Oct 20)
Even Stevens 93 1 (5f, Catt, Hvy, Oct 19)
Exceptionelle 89 4 (6f, Newm, Gd, Sep 26)
Expert Fighter (USA) 89 2 (1m 5f 194y, Wolw, SD, Oct 26)
Face The Problem (IRE) 101 3 (5f 89y, York, GF, Aug 21)
Fair Value (IRE) 89 2 (5f, Epso, Gd, Jun 1)
Famous Poet (IRE) 93 2 (1m, Asco, Gd, Aug 10)
Farhh 121 1 (1m, Newb, GF, May 18)
Farmleigh House (IRE) 94 1 (6f, Linw, SD, Jan 5)
Farraaj (IRE) 105 1 (1m 2f, Linw, SD, Mar 16)
Fast Shot 89 2 (6f, Ayr, GS, Sep 21)
Fattsota 104 5 (1m 2f 18y, Epso, GS, May 31)
Feel Like Dancing 91 2 (2m, Asco, GF, Jun 21)
Festive Cheer (FR) 100 3 (1m 4f, Curr, GF, Jun 29)
Field Of Dream 90 1 (7f, Newj, GF, Jul 13)
Fiesolana (IRE) 101 1 (7f, Newm, GS, Oct 12)
Fire Ship 104 5 (1m, Good, Gd, Aug 2)
First Mohican 90 1 (1m 2f 88y, York, GS, May 15)
Flying The Flag (IRE) 95 1 (1m 2f, Curr, GF, Jun 28)
Forest Edge (IRE) 92 6 (6f, Linw, SD, Dec 18)
Forgive 94 2 (1m, Asco, Gd, Sep 7)
Forgotten Voice (IRE) 97 1 (1m 2f, Asco, GF, Jun 21)
Francis Of Assisi (IRE) 89 1 (7f, Leop, Sft, Nov 3)
Franciscan 90 2 (1m 3f 107y, Carl, Gd, Jun 26)
Fratellino 98 4 (5f, Linw, SD, Mar 16)
French Navy 97 1 (1m 67y, Wind, Gd, Jun 29)
Frog Hollow 89 1 (1m, York, Gd, Jul 26)
Frontier Fighter 93 1 (1m 4y, Pont, Gd, Apr 22)
Fury 92 8 (7f, Asco, Sft, Oct 19)
Gabbiano 91 1 (5f, Asco, Gd, Jul 26)
Gabrial (IRE) 95 3 (1m 2f 75y, Ches, Gd, May 9)
Gabrial The Great (IRE) 94 4 (1m 2f 95y, Hayd, GF, Aug 10)
Gabrial's Kaka (IRE) 96 2 (1m 208y, York, Gd, Oct 12)
Gabrial's Lad (IRE) 101 1 (7f, Newj, GF, Aug 10)
Gale Force Ten 103 1 (7f, Asco, GF, Jun 19)
Galician 103 4 (1m, Good, Gd, Aug 2)
Galileo Rock (IRE) 104 2 (1m 4f, Curr, GF, Jun 29)
Garswood 94 4 (7f, Asco, GF, Jun 19)
Gaul Wood (IRE) 93 1 (1m 67y, Wind, GF, Jun 30)
Genzy (FR) 92 4 (1m 4f, Asco, GF, Jul 28)
George Guru 92 4 (1m, Linw, SD, Feb 2)
Gifted Girl (IRE) 97 2 (1m 114y, Epso, GS, May 31)
Gladiatrix 90 2 (5f, Asco, Gd, Jul 26)
Glass Office 100 4 (5f, Good, Gd, Aug 2)
Glen Moss (IRE) 93 1 (7f, Newb, Gd, Aug 17)
Glen's Diamond 107 1 (1m 6f, York, Sft, May 17)
Global Village (IRE) 100 4 (1m, Newb, GS, Apr 20)
Glory Awaits (IRE) 92 1 (1m, Newm, GF, May 4)
Goldream 96 2 (5f, York, Gd, May 16)
Goodwood Mirage (IRE) 96 2 (1m 4f 5y, Newb, Sft, Sep 20)
Gordon Lord Byron (IRE) 104 3 (6f, York, GS, May 15)
Gramercy (IRE) 95 3 (7f, Asco, Sft, Oct 19)

Graphic (IRE) 102 1 (1m, York, Gd, Oct 11)
Gregorian (IRE) 102 5 (1m, Good, GS, Jul 31)
Grey Mirage 94 3 (7f 32y, Wolw, SD, Oct 26)
Guest Of Honour (IRE) 103 3 (1m, Asco, GF, Jul 13)
Haaf A Sixpence 95 1 (1m, Newb, GS, Apr 20)
Hallelujah 101 1 (6f 8y, Newb, GF, May 18)
Hamish McGonagall 109 4 (5f, York, GS, Aug 23)
Hammerfest 90 8 (1m 4f, Asco, GF, Jun 22)
Hamza (IRE) 109 1 (6f, Newm, GF, May 5)
Hanseatic 92 1 (1m 2f 95y, Hayd, GF, May 11)
Harrison George (IRE) 99 3 (5f, Donc, Sft, Oct 26)
Harvard N Yale (USA) 89 3 (1m 4f, Asco, GF, May 11)
Hasopop (IRE) 103 1 (6f, Newm, GF, May 18)
Havana Beat (IRE) 89 5 (1m 4f, Asco, GF, Jun 21)
Havana Cooler (IRE) 97 3 (1m 6f, York, Sft, Aug 24)
Hawkeyethenoo (IRE) 108 2 (5f, Donc, Sft, Oct 26)
Hay Dude 93 2 (1m, Hayd, GS, Sep 7)
Haylaman (IRE) 94 2 (1m 2f, Asco, GF, Jul 28)
Head Of Steam (USA) 89 4 (7f, Newj, GF, Aug 10)
Heaven's Guest (IRE) 94 1 (6f, Newj, GF, Jul 12)
Heeraat (IRE) 108 1 (5f 34y, Newb, GS, Apr 19)
Helene Super Star (USA) 94 2 (1m 2f, Curr, GF, Jun 9)
High Jinx (IRE) 91 2 (2m 2f, Donc, GS, Sep 13)
Highland Colori (IRE) 108 1 (6f, Ayr, GS, Sep 21)
Highland Knight (IRE) 96 2 (1m 2f 75y, Ches, Gd, May 9)
Hillstar 111 3 (1m 4f, Asco, GF, Jul 27)
Hint Of A Tint (IRE) 93 5 (1m, Asco, GF, Jun 19)
Hitchens (IRE) 99 1 (6f 18y, Ches, Gd, Aug 4)
Hoarding (USA) 90 1 (1m 2f, Newm, GF, May 18)
Homage (IRE) 90 2 (7f 16y, Sand, GF, Jun 6)
Hoof It 102 4 (6f, Asco, Sft, Oct 19)
Hot Bed (IRE) 99 3 (1m, York, GF, Aug 22)
Hot Snap 96 1 (7f, Newm, Gd, Apr 17)
Hunter's Light (IRE) 106 4 (1m 2f, Asco, Sft, Oct 19)
I'm Your Man (FR) 94 5 (1m 5f 61y, Newb, Gd, Aug 17)
Igugu (AUS) 97 2 (1m, Newm, GF, Sep 27)
Indian Chief (IRE) 89 3 (1m 2f 88y, York, Gd, May 16)
Indignant 98 2 (7f, York, GF, Aug 22)
Inis Meain (USA) 102 2 (1m 2f, Curr, Gd, Apr 7)
Integral 89 1 (1m 14y, Sand, GF, Aug 31)
Intibaah 99 1 (6f, Asco, Sft, Oct 4)
Intransigent 97 2 (7f, Good, Gd, Aug 24)
Intrigo 99 2 (7f, Asco, Sft, Oct 19)
Iptisam 89 2 (5f 216y, Wolw, SD, Dec 20)
Ithoughtitwasover (IRE) 92 3 (1m 4f, York, GF, Jul 12)
Jack Dexter 116 2 (6f, Asco, Sft, Oct 19)
Jack's Revenge (IRE) 94 2 (1m, York, Gd, Oct 11)
Jamaican Bolt (IRE) 89 5 (6f, Donc, Sft, Mar 30)
Jimmy Styles 92 4 (6f, York, Gd, Oct 12)
Jiroft (ITY) 103 5 (5f, Epso, Gd, Jun 1)
Joe Eile (IRE) 97 3 (6f 63y, Curr, Gd, Jun 29)
Joe Packet 90 2 (5f 6y, Sand, GF, Jul 5)
Judge 'N Jury 102 3 (5f, York, Gd, May 16)
Just The Judge (IRE) 98 2 (1m, Newm, GF, May 5)
Justineo 102 3 (5f, Good, Gd, Aug 2)
Jwala 112 1 (5f, York, GS, Aug 23)
Kenhope (FR) 97 2 (1m, Asco, GF, Jun 21)
Kenny Powers 90 2 (7f 32y, Wolw, SD, Mar 9)
Khubala (IRE) 95 3 (6f, York, GF, Jul 27)
King George River (IRE) 91 3 (1m, York, GS, Aug 23)
King Of Eden (IRE) 90 1 (7f, Newc, Gd, Apr 15)
Kingsbarns (IRE) 98 3 (1m, Asco, Sft, Oct 19)
Kingsgate Choice (IRE) 94 3 (5f 34y, Newb, GS, Apr 19)
Kingsgate Native (IRE) 111 2 (5f, Newm, GF, May 4)
Klynch 89 1 (6f, Thir, Sft, May 18)
Kyleakin Lass 96 2 (5f, Good, Gd, May 4)
La Collina (IRE) 91 1 (1m, Leop, Gd, Sep 7)
La Fortunata 98 2 (5f, Epso, GS, Aug 26)
Labienus 91 1 (7f, Asco, GF, Jul 13)
Ladies Are Forever 110 1 (5f, Linw, SD, Mar 16)
Ladys First 94 3 (1m 114y, Epso, GS, May 31)
Ladyship 102 1 (6f, Newm, Gd, Sep 26)
Lahaag 96 5 (1m 4f, Asco, GF, Jun 22)

Lanansaak (IRE) 93 1 (1m, Asco, Gd, Sep 7)
Lancelot Du Lac (ITY) 96 3 (6f, Linw, SD, Dec 18)
Leading Light (IRE) 96 1 (2m, Asco, GF, Jun 21)
Leitir Mor (IRE) 97 3 (1m, Leop, Gd, Aug 15)
Lethal Force (IRE) 120 1 (6f, Newj, GF, Jul 13)
Levitate 98 4 (7f, Asco, Sft, Oct 19)
Libertarian 94 1 (1m 2f 88y, York, Gd, May 16)
Libranno 90 3 (7f, Newm, GS, Oct 12)
Light Up My Life (IRE) 91 6 (1m, Asco, GF, Jun 19)
Lightning Cloud (IRE) 94 1 (7f, Asco, GF, Jun 21)
Lily's Angel (IRE) 90 1 (1m, Kemw, Gd, Apr 13)
Litigant 91 1 (1m 5f 194y, Wolw, SD, Dec 7)
Llaregyb (IRE) 90 1 (1m, Muss, GF, Jun 1)
Lockwood 102 1 (7f, Good, Gd, Aug 25)
London Bridge (USA) 95 3 (1m 4f, Asco, GF, Jul 13)
London Citizen (USA) 93 1 (1m 1f 207y, Beve, GF, Aug 31)
Lost In The Moment (IRE) 98 3 (1m 5f 61y, Newb, Gd, Aug 17)
Louis The Pious 93 2 (6f, Ayr, GS, Sep 21)
Loving Spirit 97 3 (7f, Asco, GF, Jul 27)
Lowther 89 3 (1m, Linw, SD, Apr 30)
Lucky Beggar (IRE) 96 2 (5f 4y, Hami, Sft, May 5)
Lucky Numbers (IRE) 91 1 (6f 18y, Ches, Gd, Jun 8)
Luhaif 96 2 (1m, Linw, SD, Apr 6)
Maarek 96 5 (6f, York, GS, May 15)
Magic City (IRE) 98 1 (7f, Good, Gd, Aug 24)
Magical Macey (USA) 103 1 (5f, Newc, GS, Jun 28)
Magician (IRE) 104 1 (1m, Curr, GF, May 25)
Mahican (IRE) 89 4 (1m 4f, Linw, SD, Oct 16)
Main Sequence (USA) 93 8 (1m 2f, Asco, Sft, Oct 19)
Majestic Myles (IRE) 92 2 (7f, Thir, Gd, Apr 20)
Manalapan (IRE) 89 1 (1m 4f, Gowr, Gd, Aug 14)
Maputo 108 1 (1m 2f, Newj, GF, Jul 11)
March 89 2 (5f 6y, Sand, Gd, Apr 15)
Marcret (ITY) 95 1 (7f 122y, Ches, GS, Jun 28)
Mars (IRE) 93 3 (1m, Asco, Gd, Jun 18)
Masamah (IRE) 99 7 (5f, Hayd, Gd, Sep 28)
Mass Rally (IRE) 102 1 (6f, York, Gd, Oct 12)
Maureen (IRE) 102 1 (7f, Newb, Gd, Apr 20)
Maxentius (IRE) 92 4 (1m, Linw, SD, Apr 6)
Maxios 102 6 (1m 2f, Asco, GF, Jun 19)
Medicean Man 95 5 (5f, Curr, Gd, Jun 29)
Melbourne Memories 95 3 (7f, Newb, GS, Apr 20)
Memory Cloth 89 7 (1m, Newb, GS, Apr 20)
Mezzotint (IRE) 89 2 (7f, Newm, GF, Sep 28)
Mia's Boy 97 1 (1m, Linw, SD, Apr 30)
Miblish 104 5 (1m 2f, Asco, GF, Jun 19)
Mijhaar 108 1 (1m 4f 17y, Hami, GS, May 17)
Mirsaale 91 1 (1m 2f 18y, Epso, Gd, Apr 24)
Misplaced Fortune 91 2 (6f, Newm, Gd, Sep 26)
Miss You Too 92 1 (1m 2f 21y, Yarm, GS, Sep 18)
Missunited (IRE) 97 2 (1m 6f, Leop, Gd, Jun 7)
Mister Music 90 2 (1m, Kemw, SD, Sep 7)
Mizzava (IRE) 89 5 (1m, Asco, GF, Jun 21)
Model Pupil 91 5 (2m 78y, Sand, GF, Jul 6)
Moment In Time (IRE) 89 1 (1m 4f, Donc, GF, May 4)
Monsieur Chevalier (IRE) 91 1 (7f, Linw, SD, Apr 6)
Mont Ras (IRE) 100 1 (1m, York, GF, Aug 22)
Montiridge (IRE) 102 2 (7f, Asco, Gd, Jun 19)
Morache Music 92 1 (6f, Donc, Sft, Oct 25)
Moran Gra (USA) 94 1 (1m, Curr, GF, Sep 1)
Morandi (FR) 101 7 (1m 2f, Asco, Sft, Oct 19)
Morawij 98 1 (5f 6y, Sand, Gd, Jun 15)
Moth (IRE) 93 3 (1m, Newm, GF, May 5)
Mount Athos (IRE) 102 5 (1m 4f, Asco, GF, Jun 22)
Move In Time 96 4 (5f, Curr, Gd, Jun 29)
Moviesta (USA) 108 1 (5f, Good, Gd, Aug 2)
Mshawish (USA) 89 4 (1m, Asco, GF, Jun 19)
Mubaraza (IRE) 96 3 (1m 6f, Newm, GF, May 18)
Mukhadram 114 2 (1m 2f, Asco, GF, Jun 19)
Mull Of Killough (IRE) 105 2 (1m, Asco, GF, Jul 13)
Music Master 89 2 (7f, Newb, GF, Jul 20)
Mutashaded (USA) 101 3 (1m 4f, Asco, GF, Jun 21)
My Freedom (IRE) 103 1 (7f 32y, Wolw, SD, Oct 26)

My Good Brother (IRE) 92 1 (5f, Curr, Gd, Sep 14)
My Propeller (IRE) 94 1 (5f, Ayr, GF, Jun 22)
Naabegha 89 2 (6f 18y, Ches, Gd, Sep 28)
Nargys (IRE) 103 4 (1m, Asco, GF, Jun 19)
Nautilus 93 5 (1m 4f, Linw, SD, Oct 16)
Nazreef 93 2 (7f, Souw, SS, Feb 12)
Nero Emperor (IRE) 94 2 (5f, Curr, Gd, Sep 14)
Nichols Canyon 93 2 (1m 4f 5y, Newb, Hvy, Oct 26)
Nine Realms 94 1 (1m, Asco, Gd, Aug 10)
Ninjago 102 1 (6f, Asco, Gd, May 1)
No Heretic 89 1 (1m 4f, Newm, GF, May 5)
Noble Alan (GER) 94 2 (1m 4f, Asco, GF, May 11)
Noble Mission 103 4 (1m 4f, Asco, GF, Jun 22)
Noble Storm (USA) 99 3 (5f, Hayd, Gd, Sep 28)
Normal Equilibrium 92 1 (5f 16y, Ches, GS, May 10)
Norse Blues 89 1 (1m, Thir, Gd, Aug 3)
Novellist (IRE) 126 1 (1m 4f, Asco, GF, Jul 27)
Nymphea (IRE) 93 6 (1m 4f, Asco, Sft, Oct 19)
Ocean Tempest 90 1 (7f 2y, Ches, Gd, Sep 28)
Ocean War 91 8 (1m 2f, Asco, GF, Jun 21)
Olympic Glory (IRE) 110 1 (1m, Asco, Sft, Oct 19)
Opinion (IRE) 105 1 (1m 4f, Asco, GF, May 10)
Oriental Fox (GER) 102 1 (2m 2f, Newm, Gd, Sep 21)
Osteopathic Remedy (IRE) 98 1 (1m, Ripo, Gd, Aug 26)
Ottoman Empire (FR) 91 4 (1m 2f, Asco, GF, Jun 21)
Paddy The Celeb (IRE) 89 4 (1m 4f, Gowr, Gd, Aug 14)
Paene Magnus (IRE) 90 2 (1m 2f 150y, Dunw, SD, Oct 4)
Pale Mimosa (IRE) 105 1 (1m 6f, Leop, GF, Jun 7)
Parish Hall (IRE) 105 1 (1m 2f, Curr, Gd, Apr 7)
Pasaka Boy 91 1 (1m 2f 18y, Epso, Gd, Jun 1)
Pastoral Player 94 4 (7f, Good, Gd, Aug 25)
Pay Freeze (IRE) 91 3 (7f, Asco, GF, May 10)
Pearl Blue (IRE) 89 4 (5f, Donc, Sft, Oct 26)
Pearl Ice 93 1 (6f, Donc, GS, Sep 12)
Pearl Secret 97 3 (5f, Asco, Gd, Jun 18)
Penitent 93 1 (1m, Newm, Sft, Nov 2)
Pether's Moon (IRE) 90 2 (1m 1f 198y, Sali, GF, May 5)
Phaenomena (IRE) 91 1 (1m 4f, Newm, Gd, Sep 21)
Picabo (IRE) 96 2 (6f, Good, Gd, May 31)
Piscean (USA) 93 1 (5f 216y, Wolw, SD, Feb 1)
Place In My Heart 95 1 (5f 11y, Bath, Gd, Apr 19)
Planteur (IRE) 101 1 (1m 2f, Linw, SD, Feb 23)
Plinth (IRE) 89 3 (1m 4f, Gowr, Gd, Aug 14)
Plutocracy (IRE) 90 1 (1m 4f, Sali, GF, Aug 30)
Polski Max 99 1 (5f 4y, Hami, Sft, May 5)
Poole Harbour (IRE) 95 2 (6f 8y, Newb, GF, May 18)
Prairie Ranger 90 4 (1m 4f, Asco, GF, Jul 13)
Premio Loco (USA) 101 5 (1m 2f, Linw, SD, Mar 16)
Prince Alzain (USA) 98 1 (1m 1f 103y, Wolw, SD, Nov 7)
Prince Bishop (IRE) 92 1 (1m 4f, Newb, SD, Sep 7)
Prince Of Johanne (IRE) 100 1 (1m 14y, Sand, GF, Jul 6)
Prodigality 94 4 (6f, York, GF, Jul 27)
Producer 93 1 (7f, Newj, Gd, Jun 29)
Professor 98 1 (7f, Asco, GF, May 10)
Proud Chieftain 91 3 (1m 1f, Newm, GF, May 4)
Purcell (IRE) 91 1 (6f 18y, Ches, GS, Aug 17)
Pythagorean 89 1 (7f 9y, Leic, GF, May 20)
Queensberry Rules (IRE) 96 3 (1m, Asco, GF, Jun 20)
Racy 100 2 (5f, Hayd, Gd, Sep 28)
Ralston Road (IRE) 91 1 (1m 3f 79y, Ches, Gd, May 25)
Rawaki (IRE) 95 3 (1m 4f, Asco, GF, Jul 28)
Reckless Abandon 106 3 (5f, Hayd, Fm, May 25)
Red Avenger (USA) 97 2 (1m 2f, Newj, GF, Jul 11)
Red Cadeaux 105 2 (1m 5f 61y, Newb, Gd, Aug 17)
Red Jazz (USA) 91 2 (7f, Newj, Gd, Jun 29)
Redvers (IRE) 90 1 (7f, Asco, Gd, Sep 7)
Ree's Rascal (IRE) 89 1 (1m 7y, Newb, GF, Jun 8)
Regulation (IRE) 94 1 (1m, Dunw, SD, Nov 29)
Remote 104 1 (1m, Donc, Gd, Jun 1)
Repeater 92 4 (2m 78y, Sand, GF, Jul 6)
Reply (IRE) 90 1 (7f, Naas, GF, Jun 3)
Resurge (IRE) 100 1 (1m 2f 18y, Epso, GS, May 31)
Rewarded 89 6 (1m 2f 75y, Ches, Gd, May 9)

Rex Imperator 101 2 (7f, Donc, Gd, Jun 1)
Rich Coast 95 1 (1m 1f, List, Hvy, Sep 20)
Riposte 90 1 (1m 4f, Asco, GF, Jun 20)
Riskit Fora Biskit (IRE) 91 2 (5f 10y, Wind, Gd, May 20)
Robert The Painter (IRE) 99 2 (1m, Ripo, Gd, Aug 26)
Robin Hoods Bay 105 1 (1m 2f 95y, Hayd, GF, Aug 10)
Roca Tumu (IRE) 100 1 (1m, Asco, GF, Jun 20)
Rockalong (IRE) 93 3 (1m, York, Gd, Oct 11)
Roman Flight (IRE) 89 3 (1m 4f, York, Gd, May 25)
Rosdhu Queen (IRE) 94 4 (7f, Newb, GS, Apr 20)
Roserrow 93 1 (1m 14y, Sand, GF, Jun 6)
Royal Diamond (IRE) 100 3 (1m 6f, York, Sft, May 17)
Royal Empire (IRE) 102 1 (1m 5f 61y, Newb, Gd, Aug 17)
Royal Skies (IRE) 89 1 (1m 4f, Asco, Gd, Aug 10)
Ruler Of The World (IRE) 117 3 (1m 2f, Asco, Sft, Oct 19)
Ruscello (IRE) 91 3 (1m 3f, Kemw, SD, Sep 6)
Russian Soul (IRE) 103 5 (5f, Curr, GF, Jul 21)
Salutation (IRE) 90 1 (1m 4f 10y, Ripo, GF, Jul 20)
Sandagiyr (FR) 109 3 (1m, Good, Gd, Aug 2)
Santefisio 98 4 (7f, Asco, GF, Jun 21)
Saytara (IRE) 89 5 (1m 4f, Asco, GF, Jul 28)
Scintillula (IRE) 90 1 (1m 1f, Leop, Gd, Jul 25)
Scream Blue Murder (IRE) 95 8 (5f, Curr, GF, Jul 21)
Sea Shanty (USA) 89 1 (1m 14y, Sand, GF, May 23)
Seal Of Approval 108 1 (1m 4f, Asco, Sft, Oct 19)
Secret Gesture 94 2 (1m 4f 10y, Epso, GS, May 31)
Secret Number 92 4 (1m 2f, Asco, Gd, Jun 20)
Secret Witness 99 6 (5f, York, Gd, May 16)
Secretinthepark 94 1 (6f, Newm, GF, May 4)
Seek Again (USA) 104 1 (1m 208y, York, Gd, Oct 12)
Seeking Magic 94 1 (6f, Good, Gd, Aug 3)
Sennockian Star 96 2 (1m 2f 95y, Hayd, GF, Aug 10)
Set The Trend 99 1 (7f, Hayd, GF, Jul 20)
Seussical (IRE) 90 1 (1m 2f 88y, York, Gd, Oct 12)
Shamaal Nibras (USA) 96 2 (1m 14y, Sand, GS, May 30)
Shamexpress (NZ) 99 7 (6f, Newj, GF, Jul 13)
Shea Shea (SAF) 113 2 (5f, York, GS, Aug 23)
Sheikhzayedroad 92 2 (1m 2f, Asco, GF, Jun 21)
Shikarpour (IRE) 95 2 (1m 2f, Asco, GF, Jun 20)
Short Squeeze (IRE) 90 1 (1m, York, GS, Aug 23)
Shrewd 92 3 (1m 4f 10y, Ripo, GF, Jul 20)
Shropshire (IRE) 93 4 (6f, Donc, Sft, Mar 30)
Side Glance 100 7 (1m 2f, Asco, GF, Jun 19)
Silken Express (IRE) 89 1 (5f, Souw, SD, May 8)
Silvery Moon (IRE) 91 1 (7f 200y, Carl, Gd, Jun 26)
Sir Bedivere (IRE) 89 3 (1m 4f 5y, Newb, Sft, Sep 20)
Sir Ector (USA) 102 1 (1m 6f, Leop, Sft, Nov 3)
Sir Graham Wade (IRE) 98 6 (1m 4f, Asco, GF, Jun 22)
Sir John Hawkwood (IRE) 104 1 (1m 2f 75y, Ches, GF, May 9)
Sir Patrick Moore (FR) 89 2 (7f, Newb, Gd, Apr 20)
Sirius Prospect (USA) 104 1 (7f, York, GF, Jul 27)
Sirvino 92 1 (1m 4f, York, Gd, May 25)
Sky Lantern (IRE) 109 1 (1m, Asco, GF, Jun 21)
Slade Power (IRE) 117 1 (6f, Asco, Sft, Oct 19)
Smart Daisy K 89 3 (6f 18y, Ches, GS, Aug 17)
Smarty Socks (IRE) 100 2 (1m, York, GF, Jul 13)
Smoothtalkinrascal (IRE) 104 2 (5f, Epso, Gd, Jun 1)
Snow Queen (IRE) 91 5 (1m, Newm, GF, May 5)
Snowboarder (USA) 90 3 (1m, Good, Gd, Aug 2)
Society Rock (IRE) 114 2 (6f, Newj, GF, Jul 13)
Soft Falling Rain (SAF) 99 1 (1m, Newm, GF, Sep 27)
Solar Deity (IRE) 95 2 (7f 32y, Wolw, SD, Oct 26)
Sole Power 115 1 (5f, Newm, GF, May 4)
Songbird (IRE) 90 2 (1m 4f 5y, Newb, Gd, Aug 4)
Songcraft (IRE) 98 6 (1m 4f, Asco, GF, Jun 22)
Sovereign Debt (IRE) 109 2 (1m, Newb, GF, May 18)
Spa's Dancer (IRE) 100 1 (1m 14y, Sand, GS, May 30)
Spifer (IRE) 92 3 (1m 2f 6y, Pont, Gd, Sep 26)
Spinatrix 94 7 (6f, Donc, Sft, Oct 25)
Spirit Quartz (IRE) 101 5 (5f, Newm, GF, May 4)
Sruthan (IRE) 94 1 (7f 100y, Tipp, Yld, Oct 6)
St Nicholas Abbey (IRE) 92 1 (1m 4f 10y, Epso, Gd, Jun 1)
Star Lahib (IRE) 94 1 (1m 4f, Asco, Gd, Aug 10)

Stencive 104 2 (1m 4f, Asco, GF, Jun 22)
Steps (IRE) 100 2 (5f 140y, Donc, GS, Sep 14)
Steps To Freedom (IRE) 101 3 (1m 2f, Curr, Gd, Apr 7)
Summerinthecity (IRE) 92 2 (6f, York, GF, Jul 27)
Sun Central (IRE) 100 2 (2m 45y, Hayd, GF, Jun 8)
Swan Song 96 1 (5f, Epso, GS, Aug 26)
Sweetnessandlight 92 4 (7f, York, GF, Aug 22)
Swiftly Done (IRE) 90 1 (1m, Redc, Sft, Sep 10)
Swing Easy 91 1 (1m 1f 198y, Sali, GF, May 5)
Swiss Spirit 107 2 (5f, Hayd, Fm, May 25)
Taajub (IRE) 92 (5f, Epso, Gd, Jun 1)
Tac De Boistron (FR) 99 1 (1m 4f 66y, Ches, Sft, Sep 14)
Tahaamah 93 5 (1m 4f, Asco, GF, May 11)
Take Cover 95 1 (5f, York, Gd, Oct 11)
Talent 102 1 (1m 4f 10y, Epso, GS, May 31)
Talented Kid 92 1 (1m 67y, Wind, GF, Aug 19)
Tales Of Grimm (USA) 91 2 (1m 1f, Newm, GS, Oct 12)
Tamayuz Star (IRE) 98 2 (7f, Good, GS, May 25)
Tangerine Trees 106 3 (5f, Newm, GF, May 4)
Tarikhi (USA) 95 3 (1m 2f, Newj, GF, Jul 11)
Tarooq (USA) 99 1 (6f, Linw, SD, Dec 18)
Tawhid 100 3 (7f, Asco, GF, Jun 19)
Tax Free (IRE) 90 1 (5f, Newj, Gd, Jun 28)
Telescope (IRE) 109 1 (1m 1f 218y, Leic, GF, Jul 18)
Teophilip (IRE) 90 1 (7f, Linw, SD, Mar 16)
Tepmokea (IRE) 96 3 (1m 2f, Linw, SD, Feb 23)
Tha'ir (IRE) 93 2 (1m 2f, Newm, GF, May 18)
The Fugue 105 1 (1m 4f, York, GF, Aug 22)
The Gold Cheongsam (IRE) 89 1 (7f, Newb, GF, Jul 20)
The Lark 92 3 (1m 4f 10y, Epso, GS, May 31)
The Rectifier (USA) 98 1 (1m, York, GF, Jul 13)
Thistle Bird 99 1 (1m 114y, Epso, GS, May 31)
Thomas Chippendale (IRE) 111 1 (1m 4f, Asco, GF, Jun 22)
Thouwra (IRE) 93 1 (1m 114y, Epso, Gd, Sep 29)
Thunderball 97 1 (6f, Donc, Sft, Mar 30)
Tickled Pink (IRE) 101 6 (5f, York, GS, Aug 23)
Tiddliwinks 94 9 (5f, York, GS, Aug 23)
Tiger Cliff (IRE) 98 1 (1m 6f, Newm, GF, May 18)
Tigers Tale (IRE) 89 2 (1m 14y, Sand, GF, Jun 6)
Timeless Call (IRE) 98 2 (5f, Linw, SD, Mar 16)
Times Up 93 1 (2m 2f, Donc, GS, Sep 13)
Tinshu (IRE) 97 4 (1m 2f, Linw, SD, Mar 16)
Tobann (IRE) 93 5 (1m, Curr, GF, Sep 1)
Top Notch Tonto (IRE) 100 2 (1m, Asco, Sft, Oct 19)

Top Trip 106 2 (1m 6f, York, Sft, May 17)
Toronado (IRE) 129 1 (1m, Good, GS, Jul 31)
Trade Storm 107 4 (1m, Good, GS, Jul 31)
Trading Leather (IRE) 113 2 (1m 4f, Asco, GF, Jul 27)
Trail Blaze (IRE) 94 2 (7f, Asco, GF, Jul 27)
Travel Brother 98 1 (1m, Linw, SD, Apr 6)
Tres Coronas (IRE) 91 3 (1m 2f 18y, Epso, GS, May 31)
Troopingthecolour 91 1 (1m 3f, Kemw, SD, Oct 2)
Tropical Beat 91 2 (1m 6f, Muss, Gd, Aug 9)
Tropics (USA) 105 1 (6f, York, GF, Jul 27)
Two For Two (IRE) 95 5 (1m, York, Gd, Oct 11)
Universal (IRE) 107 5 (1m 4f, Asco, GF, Jul 27)
Unsinkable (IRE) 93 3 (1m, Linw, SD, Apr 6)
Urban Dance (IRE) 89 1 (1m 2f, Newj, Gd, Aug 3)
Ustura (USA) 94 3 (1m 4f, Asco, GF, Jun 22)
Valbchek (IRE) 91 5 (6f, Linw, SD, Nov 16)
Validus 92 9 (1m, York, GF, Aug 22)
Vasily 96 2 (1m 2f, Asco, Gd, Jul 26)
Venus De Milo (IRE) 97 2 (1m 4f, York, GF, Aug 22)
Victrix Ludorum (IRE) 93 4 (6f, Newm, GF, May 18)
Viztoria (IRE) 101 3 (6f, Asco, Sft, Oct 19)
Voodoo Prince 89 4 (1m 3f, Kemw, SD, Sep 6)
Wadi Al Hattawi (IRE) 90 3 (1m 4f, Donc, Gd, Aug 3)
Wannabe Better (IRE) 97 1 (1m, Naas, Sft, Oct 20)
Warlu Way 91 1 (1m 3f 107y, Carl, Gd, Jun 26)
Webbow (IRE) 89 7 (1m, Linw, SD, Feb 2)
Wentworth (IRE) 106 1 (1m, Good, Gd, Aug 2)
Whaileyy (IRE) 95 2 (6f, Linw, SD, Jan 5)
Whozthecat (IRE) 97 1 (5f, Curr, GF, Jul 21)
Wild Coco (GER) 96 1 (1m 6f, Good, Gd, Aug 1)
Willing Foe (USA) 94 1 (1m 5f 61y, Newb, GF, May 18)
Willow Beck 91 3 (1m 4f, Newm, Gd, Sep 21)
Windhoek 106 2 (1m 1f 207y, Beve, GF, Aug 31)
Winning Express (IRE) 92 4 (1m, Newm, GF, May 5)
Winterlude (IRE) 104 1 (1m 4f, Linw, SD, Oct 16)
Woodland Aria 95 3 (1m, Asco, GF, Jun 19)
Woolfall Sovereign (IRE) 92 1 (5f 20y, Wolw, SD, Jan 1)
Yellow Rosebud (IRE) 102 1 (7f, Galw, Hvy, Aug 1)
York Glory (USA) 97 5 (5f, Linw, SD, Mar 16)
You Da One (IRE) 89 1 (7f, Good, GS, May 25)
Yulong Baoju (IRE) 95 3 (5f, Curr, GF, Jul 21)
Zanetto 99 1 (6f 8y, Newb, GF, May 17)
Zero Money (IRE) 89 1 (6f, Ling, GF, Sep 3)
Zurigha (IRE) 98 1 (1m, Newm, GF, Sep 27)

INDEX OF HORSES

INDEX OF HORSES